Battleground New Jersey

Rivergate Regionals

Rivergate Regionals is a collection of books published by Rutgers University Press focusing on New Jersey and the surrounding area. Since its founding in 1936, Rutgers University Press has been devoted to serving the people of New Jersey and this collection solidifies that tradition. The books in the Rivergate Regionals Collection explore history, politics, nature and the environment, recreation, sports, health and medicine, and the arts. By incorporating the collection within the larger Rutgers University Press editorial program, the Rivergate Regionals Collection enhances our commitment to publishing the best books about our great state and the surrounding region.

Battleground New Jersey

Vanderbilt, Hague, and Their Fight for Justice

Nelson Johnson

RUTGERS UNIVERSITY PRESS
NEW BRUNSWICK, NEW JERSEY, AND LONDON

Library of Congress Cataloging-in-Publication Data
Johnson, Nelson, 1948–
  Battleground New Jersey : Vanderbilt, Hague and their fight for justice / Nelson
Johnson.
     p. cm.
  Includes bibliographical references and index.
  ISBN 978-0-8135-6972-7 (hardcover : alk. paper) — ISBN 978-0-8135-6974-1
(e-book)
  1. Vanderbilt, Arthur T., 1888–1957 2. Hague, Frank, 1876–1956. 3. Judges—United
States—Biography. 4. New Jersey—Politics and government—1865–1950. I. Title.
  KF373.V3J64 2015
  347.749'035092—dc23
  [B]
  2014004946

A British Cataloging-in-Publication record for this book is available from the British
Library.

The author received no compensation for work performed on this book since assuming
judicial office in the state of New Jersey. All royalties on sale of this book will be paid to
charities designated by the publisher.

Visit our website: http://rutgerspress.rutgers.edu

Manufactured in the United States of America

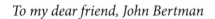

To my dear friend, John Bertman

No lawyer ever had a better mentor.

"Good and great are seldom in the same man."

—*Winston Churchill*

CONTENTS

ACKNOWLEDGMENTS

Writing history is an adventure. At the end of my work I marvel at the surprises I've encountered and the new friends I've made. While researching the lives, and then telling the story of the people who populate my books, they visit my thoughts daily. When my work is over, I miss them, but know they will always be with me. That is especially true with this book. Arthur Vanderbilt and Frank Hague were giants; their deeds make me feel like a runt. The same is true of Alfred Driscoll. None of them have received their due from history. I hope my book encourages others to look further into their lives and times. There's much to be learned.

One of the best gifts my mother gave me was my love for libraries. I feel at home the instant I enter a library. In researching *Battleground New Jersey* four libraries and their staffs were indispensable to my efforts. They are the Newark Public Library; the Jersey City Free Public Library; the Olin Library at Wesleyan University; and the New Jersey State Library and Archives. My initial research began at the Newark Public Library where I was aided in my efforts by the head librarian, George Hawley, and his assistants, James Lewis and Dierdre Schmidel. They helped me find early writings on Arthur Vanderbilt's career and ancient volumes on the New Jersey Judiciary. The staff persons at the Jersey City Free Public Library who guided me through the many thousands of writings on Frank Hague's career were the director of the New Jersey Room, Cynthia Harris, and her assistants, Daniel Klein and John Beekman. But for their wise advice, I would still be lost in the forest of learned treaties, scholarly profiles, and news articles on Hague's life written by hundreds of authors. The magnificent Olin Library is where I found the treasure trove of Arthur Vanderbilt's personal files, so essential to my work and understanding the Warrior Lawyer. Librarians Jennifer Hadley and Suzy Taraba appreciated the long distance I had to travel and always had the materials I requested waiting for me. Lastly, the staff at the New Jersey State Library in Trenton helped me find original documents critical to my research.

Finally, there are six people who were essential in making *Battleground New Jersey* a reality. Finding a friend in Arthur T. Vanderbilt II was the pleasantest surprise of my adventure. He is one of the finest gentlemen I know. His biography of his grandfather, *Order in the Courts*, is a gem and was my bible throughout my research. On all three of my books, the first people to read my work were the Hon. Steven P. Perskie (JSC, Ret.) and my go-to person of many years, Sheryl McGrotty. Steve is a rigorous editor; Sheryl is a tireless proofreader. I am indebted to both of them for the many hours they have donated to my writings. My friend Dennis Burroughs came through at crunch time, selecting the photos on Frank Hague. I can't imagine writing a book without Dennis's guidance on just the right images to compliment the narrative. My publisher, Marlie Wasserman, is a joy to work with. She must have known how much I enjoy challenges; why else would she have blown up my initial effort comprising twelve chapters and 250-plus pages and told me to start over? Marlie has a way of focusing my work as a writer unlike anyone else I've ever met. I am grateful to her and the entire staff at Rutgers University Press.

Finally, my wife, Johanna, is my port in the storm; she always knows what I need. I frequently remind her what a low-maintenance husband I am, especially when I spend vacation days in a library or squirreled away in my office writing. I'm grateful for her indulgence of my obsessions.

Battleground New Jersey

Power Doesn't Corrupt: It Reveals

Newark lawyer Arthur Vanderbilt was furious. He knew that Jersey City Mayor Frank Hague would do anything to control the New Jersey governorship, but this?

With twenty of twenty-one counties reporting, Essex County Republican Lester Clee was leading by more than 84,000 votes. Finally, long after everywhere else had reported, the vote out of Hudson County had Democrat Harry Moore besting Clee by nearly 130,000 votes. The numbers were bogus; the math said it all. If 90 percent of all eligible voters were registered and 90 percent of them had voted, Jersey City could have produced *at most* 119,000 votes—instead, they totaled 145,000. It was fraud beyond the Republicans' worst fears. Clee had been blindsided in a street fight, and he demanded a recount; given who did the counting, Moore's margin held up.

Litigation ensued; a nightmare followed. Every step of the way, as the Republicans fought to expose what a sham the vote count had been, they were met by a Hague judge or Hudson County Election Board official erecting one obstacle after another. Proof of election fraud was overwhelming: dead people had voted, patients in a mental hospital had voted, even a rabbi who had moved to Massachusetts three years earlier had voted—his affidavit confirmed he hadn't. Yet the court ruled the evidence wasn't enough to grant Clee a hearing to present testimony. As November became December, and then January, Lester Clee saw his victory slipping away.

In desperation, the Republican legislature appointed an investigative committee; it reaped only frustration. All the while, Mayor Hague was wintering in Florida. Finally, after months of stalling and a mere seven days before

Inauguration Day, long-time Hague pal Chief Justice Tom Brogan formally dismissed Clee's appeal, finding no basis for fraud and leaving no path for relief. The proxy war of Moore v. Clee was over. Hague won; Vanderbilt seethed. Worse still, the law meant nothing.[1]

Controlling the governor's chair was essential to Arthur Vanderbilt's plans to overhaul New Jersey's government. For years, he had bent the ear of anyone willing to listen on the need to dismantle the state's antiquated court system. Newark's Warrior Lawyer needed a governor of his own, and 1937 was supposed to be his year. Vanderbilt had anointed a Presbyterian minister, Lester Clee, to be his front man on rewriting New Jersey's Constitution. But Hague hated Vanderbilt and his kind and would stop at nothing to hold onto power.

Arthur Vanderbilt wasn't a patrician, but he had the bearing of one, and despite his surname (distant kin of the railroad tycoon), his beginnings were humble. An accomplished litigator and political reformer, distinguished law school professor, and former president of the American Bar Association, by age fifty-six Vanderbilt was one of the best-known and most respected lawyers in America. He was considered for appointment to the U.S. Supreme Court.

Beginning his career at a sprint and never looking back, Vanderbilt had a rare talent for getting close to the right people and for generating legal fees that were the envy of his peers. By age thirty, when most attorneys his age were churning out deeds, leases, and wills at five dollars each, he routinely earned fees in the tens of thousands of dollars. Within a decade of graduating from law school he commanded a far-flung law practice in Newark, hiring teams of lawyers working under his direction. One long-time ally, Alan Lowenstein, observed, "I doubt that he had many close friends. He was a team player, but only if he could serve as captain. . . . He was a driven man, standing above his peers, admired by many and hated by some."[2]

While Vanderbilt had attained national stature in the legal community, he was obsessed with bringing New Jersey's court system into the twentieth century; that was the legacy he craved. Arthur Vanderbilt dwarfs most of today's lawyer-politicians. Nonetheless, scrutiny of his career yields conflicting reactions: admiration and skepticism. Were his hands as clean as portrayed by his biographers? Could the captain compromise for the sake of the team?

Vanderbilt's nemesis, Frank Hague, wanted no part of reform. Hague had earned a Ph.D. in human nature on the streets of Jersey City and viewed the Newark lawyer and his ilk as a bunch of blueblood cranks. Hague too understood the critical role of the courts in New Jersey and wasn't about to let go of the strings to the puppets he had appointed to the bench. For nearly thirty years Frank Hague was the single most powerful person in New Jersey, influencing who held the key positions in city, county, state, and federal offices, especially the judiciary. The Celtic Chieftain sneered at Vanderbilt's obsession. Because of his mastery of the ballot box, no statewide election was considered over until the results from Hudson County were known.

In Hague's own inimitable way, he had achieved national stature: he epitomized the rawest form of bullyboy political corruption in America. He was a favorite target of muckraking, reform-minded journalists, the frequent focus of stories in newspapers and magazines across the nation, and even the subject of a scholarly book by an Ivy League professor, still studied today. There's no one else like him in American history. Yet Frank Hague's life summons starkly different reckonings: disdain and fascination. How could he dominate his world as long as he did? Was he the monster historians have painted him?

By the end of the 1930s, history's currents had brought New Jersey to a critical moment, and it was no accident that the fight had come down to Vanderbilt versus Hague. They were the faces of the two cities that had the most to say in New Jersey politics. American history offers no parallel where two dissimilar cities, so close to the other, had such influence in the development of their states. San Francisco and Los Angeles, Dallas and Houston, Philadelphia and Pittsburgh come to mind, but those are hundreds of miles apart. Newark and Jersey City are separated by Newark Bay and the Jersey Meadowlands, less than six miles. Nonetheless, in their prime these cities might as well have two different countries.

Newark was a city of grandeur, taking its role in New Jersey life seriously, setting the standard for everything from finance, insurance, and technology to architecture, law, and the media. Jersey City was a gritty town with a chip on its shoulder. Teeming with uneducated working poor, willing to follow a strong leader, it made its presence felt on Election Day. Appreciating the role of these cities in New Jersey's history and how each influenced the principal players in our story is vital to understanding the struggle to overhaul a corrupt court system that had been outdated for more than a century.

Yet the gulf between their cities and the inability of Vanderbilt and Hague to compromise was part of a larger dynamic. Wherever America is going,

New Jersey usually gets there first. Prior to the final decades of the nineteenth century, the Garden State's mind-set was essentially white Anglo-Saxon Protestant in its outlook on life and the role of government. Industrialization had fractured a staid, agricultural society, igniting WASP fears of being overrun by foreigners whose first allegiance was to the pope of the Roman Catholic Church, or, equally troubling, to their rabbi. Out of confrontations over white Protestants' fixed notions of how society ought to be structured versus the desires of newcomers hoping to grab a piece of the American dream, two very different political value systems emerged.

One system—exemplified by Vanderbilt and the Essex County Republicans—was grounded in centuries-old WASP political traditions that citizens had a duty to be engaged in public affairs and that government was best organized in accordance with the fundamental principles of the English common law and the U.S. Constitution. For WASP Republicans, government wasn't about curing social ills but rather moderating society's extremes by limiting people's conduct and protecting their rights through the rule of law. Foreigners needed to "fit in" by pulling themselves up by their bootstraps.

Focusing on the urgent needs of strangers in a strange land, another system emerged from the immigrants' inexperience—exemplified by Hague and the Hudson County Democrats. The peasants of Europe had survived for centuries by submitting to a hierarchy that protected them. Once in America, they had needs greater than simply keeping their employers happy: they hoped to make a place for themselves in this new world. As a result, many of the newly arrived immigrants placed far more reliance upon the ward heelers who came to their doors offering help in exchange for their votes than on allegiance to any high-sounding phrases out of American history.

Finally, religion was central to the confrontation: the WASPs detested the non-Protestant immigrants, sometimes branding them as "papists" and "kikes."

These two political value systems and each side's refusal to engage the other on a personal level led to conflicts occupying much of the twentieth century. This clash in cultures played out in voting booths not just in New Jersey but across America. Staggered by having one election after another stolen away, Arthur Vanderbilt despised Frank Hague for blocking his path to reforming New Jersey's government.

Although they never met, the two dominant figures at this juncture shared a common sentiment: their disdain for each other. Were they living today, they'd be annoyed to find themselves side by side in this book. Hague, the ruffian outfitted in expensive hand-tailored suits that had the sheen of a tuxedo, with a diamond tie tack, versus Vanderbilt, the law professor attired in understated classic three-piece suits, with a Phi Beta Kappa key. Hague, loud and profane, spewing four-letter words with an Irish brogue, jabbing people in the chest for emphasis, versus Vanderbilt, an elegant orator with the common touch and a sense of humor, even when arguing before the U.S. Supreme Court.

Both were renowned far beyond New Jersey; they were two of America's great political bosses. Vanderbilt had enough self-esteem to match his several careers—he forged his stature by mastering the law, writing scholarly essays as dean of New York University's law school, traveling nationwide preaching court reform, and deftly organizing the new suburban voters before other politicians recognized their importance. Hague may be the most successful sixth-grade dropout ever—he amassed his power by exploiting peoples' foibles, crushing his rivals, accumulating a fortune through extortion, subverting the law, and taking care of business in his own backyard. Both lived by Machiavelli's tenets.

Notwithstanding the enormous gap in their education, heritage, and style, they shared common traits. Neither had casual moments with anyone but trusted allies; neither had time for opinions that didn't suit their agenda; neither drank alcohol or had dalliances with women. Both exuded an intensity that either attracted people or repelled them; both craved power to bend the world to their vision; and both were ruthless—Vanderbilt when he had to be and Hague because he knew no other way.

Despite being the punch line for countless jokes and its modern-day tag as a "blue" state, New Jersey has long been a battleground for competing visions of America where change comes through conflict. Rival interests dig trenches—some blatant, others subtler—that are the stuff of nightmares for reformers. Vanderbilt was tormented by the fact that most of the state's judges and lawyers viewed him as an oddity. They were content with the archaic system that had come down from the eighteenth century, reaping fees by shepherding clients through the cockamamie mumbo jumbo that New Jersey's courts wallowed in. No matter that the cozy relationships among bench, bar, and politicians made a travesty of justice; all was well with the ruling class.

Delays, confusion, and uncertainty brought about by two separate court systems, overlapping jurisdictions, ancient rules, and puppet judges created a Dickensian aura of absurdity that sent litigants from the state's courthouses dreading the thought of returning. The hodgepodge of courts, which had evolved over the centuries at the whim of politicians, was at best hit or miss when it came to ensuring the rule of law. But the public's frustration was for naught—the courts didn't exist for the general public; rather, they existed to protect the powerful from change and to serve the people who made their incomes from the system. Vanderbilt bristled at such a mind-set and ached to set things right.

Brimming with self-importance, Arthur Vanderbilt believed he was the hinge on which New Jersey could swing in a new direction. While his deeds as an attorney, scholar, and reformer rank him at the top of his profession in American history, Vanderbilt's role as a power broker is often overlooked. Like Hague, his clout in his home county made him a kingmaker for candidates of his party seeking statewide office. Yet politics was a means to an end. Vanderbilt had witnessed Hague and others of his sort wangle their way through the courts, making a mockery of the law, and realized that this ruthlessness had to be countered in kind.

Newark's Warrior Lawyer was on a crusade. He believed that democracy could flourish only if people have faith in the rule of law. For him, the guarantee of a fair trial was an indispensable cornerstone of personal freedom. Everyone must be equal in the eyes of the law; otherwise no one's rights are secure. And while free and honest elections are essential, politicians come and go. When people have legal problems—large or small—the courts, more personal than politics, must be a sanctuary, a place where all citizens know they will be treated fairly.

Vanderbilt regarded the law as sacred; his mission was to level the floors in New Jersey's courtrooms by creating a professional and autonomous judiciary. Yet his obsession drove him to abandon his lofty ideals for a devilish undertaking that he managed to conceal during his lifetime.

Rummaging through New Jersey's past and studying Arthur Vanderbilt's battle with Frank Hague sheds light on more than this tiny portion of our republic. We see that while America is forever becoming something new, moving government to address changes in society is a struggle. For genuine reform to occur it must be pursued relentlessly, and sometimes that pursuit consumes the crusader. Finally, the rule of law is not a given; each generation must be vigilant. There will always be bullies eager to trample the rights of others and political insiders yearning to manipulate the law to their own ends. Vanderbilt grasped these truths tightly and persisted when others relented.

To understand how New Jersey arrived at this intersection in time and what Arthur Vanderbilt was up against we need to glimpse the workings of the court system that he found so alarming. A look back reveals that filing a lawsuit in the Garden State could be the start of a bizarre endurance test. A telling example is the ordeal of Sadie Urback.

CHAPTER 1

Sadie's Saga

Sadie Urback hadn't planned on being a widow so soon. Her husband Jack's job—driving a laundry truck—wasn't dangerous. When he suffered a fatal brain aneurism in November 1937 at age thirty-nine, Sadie was bereft. Despite the shock, she knew her husband had been paying premiums on a life insurance policy. Jack was conscientious about his health and went to doctors whenever he was ill and sometimes, as a precaution, when he was feeling well. Several years earlier he had seen his doctor for fainting spells. Newark, like the rest of the nation, was suffering through the Great Depression, and the diagnosis was that Jack's blackouts were caused by "hysteria due to stress" from financial problems. In general, Jack Urback's health was found to be "perfectly normal." Sadie recalled that prior to issuing the policy, the insurance company had its own doctor do a physical exam: he found that "the insured is a first class risk."[1]

Yet Jack's insurer, Metropolitan Life, didn't respond in a first-class way upon learning of his death. Rather than paying the death benefits, the mighty insurance company put Sadie through the paces, ping-ponging her between courts for years on end.

Sadie's saga begins with Metropolitan rejecting her claim based on its determination that Jack had committed fraud in answering the questions on his application little more than a year earlier. In addition to his fainting spells, Metropolitan was concerned that Jack had had his tonsils removed in 1934 and failed to disclose that when he completed the life insurance application. Without ever explaining what a tonsillectomy had to do with a brain aneurism, Metropolitan denied Sadie's request for payment. Her only hope was the courts.

Her lawyer sued promptly for breach of contract in the Essex County Circuit Court, seeking payment of her death benefits, demanding a jury trial. Metropolitan countered with a lawsuit of its own in a different court, the Court of Chancery. The insurer claimed that Jack had defrauded them and sought a court order cancelling the policy, voiding it entirely. Initially, Chancery ruled it could take no action until "a hearing is had and all the evidence presented."[2]

Sadie's claim went to a jury the following year and the jurors found in her favor. On appeal, the Court of Errors and Appeals (the E & A), New Jersey's highest court, ruled that the trial judge had erred in permitting the jury to decide whether Jack's answers to Metropolitan's questions when the policy was issued were "material" to the risk. On remand for a new trial, the trial judge ruled that the questions and answers were material and that "the evidence was conclusive of fraud,"[3] entering a verdict in favor of Metropolitan.

Sadie persisted. On her second appeal to the E & A, the high court ruled again that the trial judge got it wrong. While the judge had to rule on "materiality," only a jury could rule on "fraudulent intent." A new trial was ordered for a second time for different reasons. At the same time, Metropolitan continued pressing its case in the Chancery Court. The insurer had already gone to the E & A on Chancery's initial refusal to cancel Jack's policy, a decision favoring Sadie. Having the benefit of both the first jury trial and the three decisions of the E & A, the Chancery Court entered a verdict denying Metropolitan's demand to cancel the policy, finding no facts to support the claim of fraudulent intent by Jack.

Yet another appeal by Metropolitan was taken to the E & A, with the high court ruling that it agreed with the Chancery Court. There were no facts to support fraud. In May 1946, eight and one-half years after Jack's death, Sadie finally got her money.

Why such an ordeal? Metropolitan knew something that anyone who has ever been a party to a lawsuit quickly learns: litigation fills the crevices of your mind. For the inexperienced layperson, getting involved in lengthy court proceedings is like having a stranger come to visit and then refuse to leave. You go to sleep at night and he's in your bedroom. You wake up and he's in the kitchen. Whenever you aren't thinking of a loved one, or performing a task for work or at play with something you truly enjoy, the stranger dominates your thoughts. When you are a party to a lawsuit it becomes the default position of your brain. You think of nothing else, and the stranger doesn't leave until the litigation is over.

Metropolitan was banking on wearing Sadie down. It had not only lots of lawyers to do its bidding but also a rickety, corrupt conglomeration of courts that legal scholars and historians alike cited as the most archaic judicial system in America. For her generation, Sadie Urback's predicament wasn't all that unusual. New Jersey's court system was an old tree with many decaying branches. It was so incoherent that only the well-heeled, armed with lawyers learned in arcane rules and practices, were confident navigating its eccentric procedures. For anyone else, beware.

Why such a mess? Finding the answer requires a look at the tree's roots.

New Jersey's courts were a throwback to a long-forgotten era. In 1702, responding to conflict between aristocrats and commoners, who felt the courts favored the aristocrats, Queen Anne of England decided to appoint her cousin, Edward Hyde, Lord Cornbury, as royal governor of New York and New Jersey. He took the job because he needed an income. Although he is widely remembered as one the worst governors in the history of the British Empire, Lord Cornbury left his mark on New Jersey for the dual court system resembling that of England —common law and equity—that he put in place.[4]

That system created the basic framework that would control New Jersey's legal system for more than two centuries. By the time Arthur Vanderbilt was practicing law, "Jersey justice" was the label attached to the legal shenanigans ensnaring people like Sadie Urback. Following the English system, the colonial courts included a Supreme Court, and the Courts of the Queen's Bench, Common Pleas, and Exchequer. The other courts of the colony were the Justices Court, the County Courts of Sessions and Common Pleas, the Vice Admiralty Court, the Prerogative Writ Court, and, finally, the Chancery Court.

Despite the fact that the Supreme Court was supposedly the highest court, there was another one above it, the Court of Appeals (later Errors and Appeals), consisting of the governor and the legislative council, all structured to resemble their English counterparts. Having final say over everything—including the acts of the elected colonial assembly—was the royal governor himself. That was pretty much the status of things until the time of the American Revolution.

Conveniently ignored in both New Jersey and American history is the fact that Benjamin Franklin's son was royal governor of New Jersey at the time the Revolution erupted. Benjamin Franklin was one of a tiny circle of patriots worthy of the label "founding father," and during his life was the best-known and most influential person in the American colonies. Largely because of his writings, most Americans felt they knew Franklin personally. Illustrating this is his "Thirteen Virtues," which appeared in *Poor Richard's Almanack* and were read widely throughout the colonies. Franklin's son William remains lost in his father's shadow, absent from American history, and with good reason.[5] Partly through his own guile and mostly because of his father's prestige among London's elite, William Franklin, in 1762, at age thirty-four, was appointed royal governor. With the coming of war his reign was overwhelmed by turmoil. William Franklin's service as the last colonial governor of New Jersey was something his father tried to forget.

Little discussed in high school history classes is the concept that for several of the thirteen colonies—including New Jersey—the American Revolution was essentially a civil war between loyalists to the crown and patriots who had had enough of England's meddling in their lives. Through it all, William behaved poorly. He relished being royal governor and knew his open-ended term would come to an end if the American colonies left the British Empire. Despite his father's urgings, William couldn't warm up to people he considered lawless rabble. Beginning in early 1776, William set upon a course that made him a disgrace to his father and enraged New Jersey's patriots.

On January 2, 1776, the Continental Congress adopted a resolution urging "speedy and effective measures to frustrate the . . . wicked practices" of anyone attempting to undermine "the principles of the friends of American liberty."[6] Governor Franklin viewed the Continental Congress's resolution as an act of rebellion and prepared a report to London including "hostile remarks about the revolutionists."[7] The report was intercepted by the rebel forces, and within days—six to be precise—Benjamin Franklin's son was under house arrest. Then things got worse.

On June 14, 1776, William was asked to sign a "parole" and remain on his farm in Burlington County as a neutral. No one else's son would have seen such deference. Following a bitter confrontation before a committee of the Continental Congress—William refused to answer their questions—the full Congress voted to "deport" William Franklin to Connecticut. He was now a prisoner of war. Then things got much worse.

While he was banished to Connecticut, William's wife, Elizabeth, begged her father-in-law to intercede. She had remained in the governor's mansion and was deeply troubled by the separation from her husband. Elizabeth Franklin wasn't a strong person to begin with and the arrest of her husband left her "completely distraught."[8] She sent letters pleading for help. Benjamin Franklin was unmoved. A little more than a year later, in July 1777, she died, some say from nervous exhaustion, never to see her husband again, leaving William a broken and bitter man.

As time wore on, Governor Franklin became a bargaining chip. Because of the esteem in which his father was held, in 1780, four years after his arrest, he was exchanged for the rebel governor of Delaware who was being held by the British. The deposed governor, a bereaved widower, and spurned son, was obsessed with revenge. Upon his release, rather than going quietly into retirement, William Franklin created a semimilitary organization, the Board of Associated Loyalists, and convinced the British to join him in invading New Jersey to restore it to royal allegiance. The invasion failed miserably. William Franklin and the British were repelled in June 1780. At war's end he sailed to England, where he lived out his life in disgrace, never to speak with his father again.

Important to understanding the mind-set confronting Arthur Vanderbilt as he began his reform efforts a century and a half later is the impact William's actions had on the New Jersey Constitution. On July 2, 1776, the same day that New Jersey's provincial congress (the legislative body in opposition to the royal colonial assembly) ratified the Declaration of Independence, it also approved a new state constitution. It was written by a ten-man committee that had been formed eight days earlier, on June 24. Working in the shadow of imminent war, the committee hastily crafted a document transferring all the powers of the royal governor to the legislature.

Conceiving anew how government should function wasn't discussed. As noted by the legal historian John Bebout, "The provisions of New Jersey's first constitution made it clear that . . . the new government was to be as nearly as possible a replica of the familiar one of colony days."[9] Despite the thirteen years between the approval of New Jersey's 1776 constitution and the adoption of the new U.S. Constitution in 1789, no thought was given to taking a second look at the state's founding charter. And it's not as if learned advice wasn't available. The state's charter was so poorly drawn that it got the attention of no less an authority than James Madison. Specifically citing New Jersey's constitution as an inferior one in *The Federalist Papers,* he warned, "The accumulation of all powers, legislative, executive, and judiciary, in the same hands, whether of one, a few, or many, and whether hereditary, self-appointed, or elective, may justly be pronounced the very definition of tyranny."[10]

No matter. New Jersey's patriots were pleased with their efforts. The British were gone and the new constitution was just fine. The royal way of doing business was over. There would be no all-powerful governor like William Franklin overriding acts of the legislature or appointing judges favoring the aristocrats. Now "the people" were supreme. Now, *all* power would be exercised by the legislature made up of the legislative council or "upper house" (later, the state senate) and the assembly. The two houses, "sitting in joint meeting," made all decisions of government, including appointing their cronies as judges. As for governor, the joint meeting would elect "some fit person within the colony" for a one-year term. The distribution of power of the legislature versus the governor was akin to that of a St. Bernard versus a Boston terrier. As for the courts, they weren't even mentioned in the constitution and were an appendage to the legislature: "the very definition of tyranny."

Despite calls for revision of the constitution in 1790, 1797, 1819, 1827, and 1840, none gained traction with the public. Finally, in 1844, fifty-eight delegates were elected to meet in convention to frame a new constitution.[11] The convention met for several weeks that spring and a new state charter was approved by the voters on August 13, 1844. Even with those changes much of the 1776 document remained intact.

Nonetheless, there was some tinkering with the judiciary. The E & A was established, composed of the chancellor (head of the Chancery Court), seven justices of the Supreme Court (a court of general jurisdiction—both original and appellate), and six lay judges, to ensure that the politicians and old guard WASP powerbrokers were represented. Getting the power to name who became a judge was still a tussle. A compromise was worked out permitting the governor, with the senate's consent, to appoint the chancellor of equity, the justices of the Supreme Court, and the judges of the E & A. The legislature retained total control over appointments to the county-run Common Pleas Court, assuring "home rule" by partisan politicians. As in the past, competency in the law wasn't critical for serving. As for appointments within the executive branch, they were shared between the governor and the legislature. The governor's appointees frequently had terms of office longer than his own; he had no removal power and his veto power over any legislation could be overridden by a simple majority of both houses.

One special position coming out the 1844 constitution was "justice of the peace." Influenced by the popularity of President Andrew Jackson in the second quarter of the nineteenth century—the Jacksonian Revolution—the 1844 constitution provided for the popular election of justices of the peace. Not an ounce of thought went into qualifications for the office. The "justices" held court everywhere from the back rooms of retail shops and taverns to the kitchens in their homes, or, weather permitting, their lawns. Making matters worse, as one historian of New Jersey's courts noted, "The compensation of these *justices* depended on the number of their convictions, a situation that darkened the reputations of their office. The advent of the automobile in the twentieth century further increased the opportunities for plunder when the fixing of tickets became an accepted practice"[12] among justices of the peace throughout the state.

Following the American Civil War, with New Jersey experiencing swift and huge spurts of industrialization, the growing commercial community joined forces with enlightened politicians to demand a more modern government. They were weary of a government living in the past. Under the leadership of widely respected lawyer-politician Governor Joel Parker, another constitutional commission was appointed, meeting in the summer and fall of 1873; significant amendments—twenty-eight in total—were proposed. The principal thrust of the commission's work was the insertion of language needed to drag the legislature into the nineteenth century. New Jersey's elected officials had a penchant for private legislation.

Although the power to grant divorces, and with it control of people's lives, had been barred in 1844 by a provision stating, "No divorce shall be granted by the Legislature," more amendments were needed to block private laws and to steer the legislators toward general issues affecting the public at large. One new provision (Art. IV, Sec. V, par. 11) spelled it out in detail, reciting more than a dozen types of legislation declared off-limits to the legislature: everything from creating roads, appointing municipal officials, and empanelling grand juries, to granting corporate charters, setting salaries of individual public officers, and changing venue in civil or criminal cases. The amendments made clear that the legislature could no longer run state government like a private club.

Some historians view the twenty-eight amendments ratified by the voters in 1875 as tantamount to a new constitution.[13] Yet what didn't change was the structure of the judiciary. While the legislature and the governor continued to share the appointment of the judges of the higher courts, home rule reigned supreme, and the legislature, sitting in joint meeting, still controlled appointment of the county-level judges. Most of the county courts were as much a part of the political system as of the judicial system. Justices of the peace were often so closely associated with political organizations that if, for instance, a lawyer was a supporter of a local senator or assemblyman he was likely to get a favorable decision from a justice who owed his election to a local political organization, regardless of the merits of the case. Some justices of the peace were full-time politicians, appointing their clerks—with no authority in the law—as acting judges.

At the top of the judicial tree was the most archaic branch, the notorious E & A. Arthur Vanderbilt once described this court of last resort with fourteen members as "a little bigger than a jury and a little smaller than a mob."[14] The six lay judges—none trained in the law—remained members of the E & A, included to ensure that the old guard had a voice on the court. Adding to the quirkiness of the E & A is that its members all had other duties. The chancellor supervised the hundreds of employees of the Court of Chancery and acted as the surrogate general in the Prerogative Court, as well as sitting on the Court of Pardons. The Supreme Court justices heard appeals and oversaw the Court of Common Pleas, the Orphans Court, and the Court of Oyer & Terminer; they also empaneled grand juries and on occasion presided at jury trials. As for the six lay members, they heard appeals to the E & A and sat on the Court of Pardons in addition to engaging in their private businesses. Nothing prevented any of the members of the E & A from being involved in their county political organization.

Key to understanding where control of the courts lay is the unchanged language of the article on the judiciary in the 1844 constitution. "The judicial power shall be vested in a court of errors and appeals in the last resort in all causes, *as heretofore* [that is, 1776]; . . . and such inferior courts as now exist, and *as may hereafter be ordained . . . by the legislature*" (emphasis added). The legislature's mastery over the courts remained, and as the years went by, the legislators ordained new judicial positions at random, having nothing to do with the administration of justice and everything to do with their political agendas.

With the changes sweeping over the state in the final decade of the nineteenth century and the first three decades of the twentieth, there was a growing disconnect between society and the courts. The 1844 judiciary had been established when New Jersey was primarily a farming community, a time when the state's population was 373,306, with the largest city having 17,298 residents. By 1930, New Jersey's population exceeded 4,000,000, with Newark alone approaching 500,000 and Jersey City more than 300,000. Many of those residents were foreign-born, lured to the state to work in factories and to do the dirty work longtime residents had no interest in.

And Newark and Jersey City weren't alone. By the dawn of the twentieth century, businesses in Paterson, Elizabeth, Hoboken, Millburn, Bloomfield, Rahway, Trenton, and Camden employed hundreds of thousands of factory workers, making everything from leather products, jewelry, millinery goods, liquor, and beer to paper, pottery, concrete, and iron and steel components used in construction, plus ships for exporting America's manufactured goods to the world.

Within the span of less than two generations a loosely joined network of tiny farming communities overseen by a simple government now had to contend with a complicated industrial economy that was driving the state in a new direction. As a state historian observed, "The annual cost of running the state government had risen from $100,000 to $100,000,000. Between 1900 and 1930, the population of the State increased 168%, the tax ratables 593%, the number of actions begun in the State Supreme Court, 935%. It was a wonder that the Judicial machinery had not yet suffered a complete collapse, that it was able to function at all."[15] By 1930, New Jersey's court system had evolved into a "hydra-headed monster of confusion,"[16] and as the volume of lawsuits grew, more courts were created by the legislature.

New Jersey's politicians believed more was better—especially when it came to doling out judgeships to their allies—so new courts were created to take care of their friends. In addition to the E & A, the Supreme Court, the Court of Chancery, the Prerogative Court, the Court of Common Pleas, the Circuit Court, the Orphans Court, the Surrogate's Court, the Court of Oyer & Terminer, two more state courts, the Court of Quarter Sessions and the Court of Special Session, were added. Other county courts created by the legislature were the Juvenile and Domestic Relations Court, the Civil District Court, the Criminal Judicial District Court, the Small Cause Court, and the County Traffic Court.

There were more to come. Advocates of home rule demanded more municipal courts: the police courts, the magistrate courts, the mayors' courts, the justice of the peace courts, and the family courts. Any meaningful distinction between some of the courts was at best ambiguous; in many instances their jurisdictions overlapped. Compounding this craziness was the fact that the procedures of each court were spelled out by separate statutes, many ignored for decades. Additionally, some of the courts adopted rules of their own, as did different divisions of the courts sitting in the twenty-one counties of the state. It was common for litigants to learn after filing a lawsuit that it was necessary to go to several courts before their case could be resolved. Of the total number of written opinions in the law court and chancery court each year, as many as one-third entailed questions of jurisdiction.

Few people questioned that the Chancery Court was the most troublesome root of the decaying tree that the state's court system had become. It was the ability to petition the Chancery Court and to start separate legal proceedings—even while there was a lawsuit pending in the common law courts—that enabled Metropolitan Insurance Company to drag Sadie Urback through the courts for eight and a half years.

Despite the constitutional revisions in 1844 and 1875, the separation of the common law and the law of equity persisted. This dual court system had its origin in medieval England. The common law we know today dates back to the twelfth and thirteenth centuries and derives from the reign of Henry II, who appointed judges to resolve disputes among his subjects. The meaning of the term "common law" was twofold: the English Court of Common Pleas addressed issues in which the king had no interest, that is, quarrels among *commoners*, and the intent was to create a collective body of law based upon local customs, that is, a unified system of law *common* throughout all of England.

Notwithstanding the English people's devotion to the rule of law, the king as sovereign was ultimately responsible for the just treatment of his subjects, and if a decision by a Common Pleas judge produced a harsh result, litigants could appeal to the crown. Over time, it was the chief secretary to the king, the lord chancellor, who heard the appeals. By the fourteenth century, a formal system to handle these appeals was created, namely, the Court of Equity. The problem was that none of the early chancellors had any legal training.

Things changed in 1529 when a lawyer, Sir Thomas More, was appointed chancellor. In the several years he served (prior to his beheading by Henry VIII), Thomas More set standards that required records to be kept of all equitable proceedings. This led to the formal development of equitable doctrines and procedures giving equity litigants more predictability than had previously existed. Every chancellor who followed More was a lawyer.

As the law of equity developed, it grew to be a parallel body of jurisprudence intended to remedy the defects in the common and statutory law, granting relief whenever the enforcement of a court order or law resulted in an injustice. Because of its ties to the king, Equity had final say. It was a system rife with the opportunity for gamesmanship. Wily litigants could file pleadings in both divisions or begin new litigation in Equity following an unsatisfactory ruling in a law court, prolonging the battle or possibly obtaining a different result, especially if their lawyer was connected politically to the person responsible for appointing the Chancery Court judge. This dual system was transplanted to New Jersey by Lord Cornbury, and the refusal to merge these two legal systems—something other states had already done—created serious problems.

Although the dual system may have worked in medieval England, by the twentieth century in New Jersey the two separate legal systems were a recipe for mischief, undermining respect for the rule of law and severely damaging public confidence in the judiciary. England itself had merged the two courts in 1873, but in New Jersey inertia proved a potent force. People less persistent than Sadie Urback were ground to bits.

During the years following adoption of the 1844 constitution, and the amendments in 1875, the legislature expanded the appointment powers of chancellor of the Equity Court. Prior to 1844 the Chancery Court consisted of one chancellor who heard occasional requests for equitable relief from a harsh law court ruling. By 1930, the chancellor's powers increased to where he exercised the powers of an imperial potentate: dispensing patronage on a grand scale, appointing vice chancellors, advisory masters, and special masters—all paying well and all highly prized political plums. Now, the single chancellor had ten vice chancellors, twelve standing advisory masters, and several hundred special masters, plus nonlawyer "receivers" in various types of commercial litigation, all exercising judicial powers. The primary qualification for appointment was the candidate's political connections. In time, Equity became known as the "rich man's court" where, with the right legal counsel, powerful moneyed interests were assured favorable results.

After 1875, the last chance for any meaningful reform of New Jersey's court system came and went with Woodrow Wilson's abbreviated term as governor.[17] Wilson was a crusader and one of the leaders of the Progressive Era, hoping to transform American society in response to the upheavals wrought by industrialization and immigration. Following a distinguished career in academia as president of Princeton University, Wilson was elected governor of New Jersey in 1910 on a pledge to bring his progressive agenda to the statehouse in Trenton. He was no sooner in office then he was off and running for president in 1912; nevertheless, Wilson had a major impact on how things were done in state government.

Within months after his inauguration in March 1911, Wilson won legislative approval for reforms intended to modernize New Jersey's government. Combining the scholar's language of idealism with votes secured in exchange for patronage positions for urban politicians, Wilson pushed through legislation creating a workmen's compensation law to protect people injured in the workplace, enabling legislation permitting nonpartisan "commission" form of local government, a primary election procedure, local option for referendum, initiative, and recall, and expanded authority of the Public Service Commission to set fair utility rates.

There's little record of fundamental judicial reform being high on Wilson's agenda. Nonetheless, as president-elect, prior to going off to the White House, he proposed the convening of a state constitutional convention. The proposal was defeated in the state senate. The only legislation of significance dealing with the court system was the Practice Act of 1912. Spearheaded by Frank Sommer, a progressive Republican lawyer from Newark, it was important legislation that discarded the antiquated "common law pleading" method, which relied upon archaic legal principals and jargon dating back hundreds of years. At the end of the day, the structure of the judiciary remained untouched, and for many of those having political power or making their living in the court system that was just fine. They didn't want any change that might disrupt the sweet arrangement among lawyers, politicians, and judges—many of whom were politicians themselves. The idea of a truly independent judiciary was outside their experience and something they'd rather live without.

Yet there was a rookie lawyer mentored by Frank Sommer who would push for judicial reform with a determination that Sommer never mustered. Arthur Vanderbilt was the protégé every senior lawyer hopes for—the pupil taking up the unfinished work of the teacher. The more this young lawyer learned his way around New Jersey's courts, the more convinced he was that things had to change.

"Relentless" only begins to describe the bundle of energy and hunger for success that was young Arthur Vanderbilt. He kept a schedule that would have challenged the stamina of several people. Appreciating his roots in the community where he came of age, the education he received, and his devotion to the law are vital to understanding Newark's Warrior Lawyer.

CHAPTER 2

Roseville's Prodigy

Catching the 7:40 A.M. train out of Newark to lower Manhattan, then scrambling to catch the uptown subway, Arthur Vanderbilt arrived at Columbia Law School two hours after leaving home. The remainder of the day was devoted to attending class and studying in the library. On the return trip he read case law and started reviewing his lesson plans for the classes he taught nightly at Newark's Central Evening High School. When night classes ended at 9:00 P.M., nearly fourteen hours after he had left for Columbia, Arthur went home to prepare for tomorrow's schoolwork—day and evening both. Lights weren't out until the wee hours of the morning.

Not long after his graduation from law school, Vanderbilt exchanged one part-time teaching position for another. He moved on from uplifting the lives of young factory workers to guiding aspiring lawyers as a professor at New York University Law School, a position he held for more than thirty years. To lawyers of his generation, it seemed as though Arthur Vanderbilt's tank never emptied. His inspiration was his mother, his drive from a yearning not only to excel but to outshine his peers. Neither was inherited from his father, Lewis Vanderbilt.

Lewis Vanderbilt's family roots in New Jersey predated the American Revolution by several generations. His family had been working the land in Hunterdon County, New Jersey, for as far back as anyone could remember.[1] But Lewis wanted nothing to do with raising crops or animals. He had spent enough time doing farm chores to know that wasn't for him. He was off to the city.

Following the American Civil war the next several decades saw the city of Newark evolve into one of the most dynamic and sophisticated urban centers in America. The village that grew to be a leading city was founded in 1666 by Puritans who had left Connecticut with the hope of creating a theocracy. As noted by an early Newark historian, Frank Urquhart, their aim was to establish "the purest form of government possible on earth."[2] Among the small band of adventuresome Puritans were two tanners. Thanks to their talent, hard work, and business savvy the craft took hold in the community and, as the years went by, leather goods—everything from harnesses for horses to shoes for soldiers' feet—played a major role in Newark's economy. Newark became known to the rest of the country as the leader in manufacturing leather products, and by the middle of the nineteenth century, it was said by many northern businessmen that "the South walks on Newark shoe leather."[3] Know-how in leather making translated into other fields of manufacturing. Over time Newark's reputation as home to highly skilled craftsmen lured inventors and tinkerers—most prominent among them being Thomas Edison—looking for workers with the nimble hands and minds needed to turn prototypes of their ideas into mass-produced products.

There were probably more "back of the house" facilities in Newark than any other industrial city in the northeastern United States. New products were often conceived in a studio, workshop, or research lab in New York City, then manufactured in Newark. The city's workers labored in steel mills, on assembly lines, and in millineries, making everything from street lamps, pipe, and carriages to watches, hats, and luggage. Adding to the city's dynamism in an era when heavy machines were in growing demand was the fact that Newark's foundries were renowned not only for expertly producing specially designed metal parts but also for perfecting electroplating, a process extending the lifespan of the machines and tools needed in America's factories.

Although Newark would never rival New York City, it was a comely replica in miniature form and every bit as diverse and sophisticated. In its prime, Newark held its own with the nation's other leading cities. With its industrial might came the accumulation of capital requiring a sophisticated coterie of bankers and financiers to channel investments in expanding both the industrial base and the community—and all those assets needed to be insured. Newark's insurance companies were so successful that by 1895, the city ranked fourth nationally in insurance assets, topped only by Hartford, Philadelphia, and New York. Its banks' assets were in the top ten nationally as well.

Yet Newark became a city that was about much more than trade and commerce. Its leading families took special pride in their city, seeing it as more than a place to make money. They were committed to nurturing a great city with the same passion the Puritans had when carving their village out of the wilderness, and the Newark elite developed a social infrastructure with a strong and proud identity to uplift the city's residents. As expressed by historian John Cunningham, by the end of the nineteenth century, "Visitors to Newark were impressed by the skyscrapers, the new fine buildings, the fine library and the strenuous efforts to build enough schools to cope with the rising population."[4] They also saw well-lighted streets, stately homes, beautiful parks, a clean and efficient public transportation system, and splendid statues of notable figures important in both national and local history.

By the time Lewis Vanderbilt arrived in Newark in 1881, its economic, political, and cultural reach made it the most influential city in New Jersey. Having one of the most vibrant, idea-based industrial economies of any city in the nation, Newark was a magnet for ambitious young men eager to make their way in the new world of manufacturing. It was a city abounding in opportunities. Yet Lewis Vanderbilt wasn't looking to be part of an innovative economy, nor was he hungry for financial success; he was content with the meager paycheck of a telegraph operator. The most difficult thing he'd have to learn was Morse code. He would never be his son's hero; Lewis is absent from the many writings about Vanderbilt's life, those of others as well as his own.

Arthur T. Vanderbilt—he had no middle name, and added the "T" for gravitas[5]—was born in Newark on July 7, 1888. Arthur spent his youth in the Roseville neighborhood, in a tiny two-story frame house on North Ninth Street, located between the bustling train station of the Delaware, Lackawanna and Western Railroad (D. L. & W. R.) and the nurturing Roseville Methodist Episcopal Church.

Like most American cities in the late nineteenth and early twentieth centuries, Newark was a growing collection of neighborhoods—miniature cities within a city tied together by public transportation. Roseville was one of those communities. Until the outbreak of the Civil War, Roseville was farmland, but its proximity to New York City during the conflict made it ideal for a Union Army training center. After the war, residential development began in earnest following the construction of a streetcar line from Newark's city center. More growth was spurred by the erection of the D. L. & W. R. passenger station, where Lewis Vanderbilt worked for Western Union.

For several generations Roseville's population swelled with people looking to escape the crowded tenements of Newark's core manufacturing areas, and it became a suburban-style community within the bounds of the city. One of the neighborhood's cornerstones was the Roseville Methodist Episcopal Church, and one of the church's mainstays was Arthur's mother, Alice Leach Vanderbilt, a high-energy, self-educated woman who served as a trustee of the church for many years.[6] Of English descent, Alice was a loyal Methodist and an ardent believer in the church's teachings. To her, deeds mattered more than words. As another devout Methodist often said to her son, "I'd rather see a sermon than hear one."[7]

Methodists were progressive long before that term gained widespread use and varied meanings. The original Methodist movement began as a "Holy Club" of students at Oxford University in the mid-1720s. Led by John and Charles Wesley, this small group of Anglicans developed their own "methods" of worship and service, seeking to follow the teachings of Jesus Christ by ministering to the needs of poor people in London. They began by establishing missions in private homes from which to distribute food and clothing to those in need.

Upon beginning their efforts the Wesley brothers were overwhelmed. Although they hadn't started out to found a new church, the enthusiastic response they received from the people, combined with rejection by the Anglican Church, eventually resulted in a separate Protestant denomination. A principle tenet of Methodists was the belief that helping one another was the reason for mankind's existence. Over time, the Wesleyan movement made its way across the Atlantic, and by 1784, at a conference of the movement's American leaders, the Methodist Episcopal Church was formed. The Leach family was Methodist and Lewis conformed to his wife's church preference.

Alice was twenty-five at the time of Arthur's birth, and Lewis was twenty-seven. Alice was determined that both her sons—Leslie was born four years later—would receive a proper education and work at meaningful careers. Young Arthur was a lackadaisical grade-school pupil, "until I hit the fourth grade where they had a brand new teacher who really wanted to teach and knew how and I skipped half a year. I had the same teacher again in the sixth grade and again skipped a half year. By this time I was started."[8]

Attending Newark High School, Arthur graduated at the top of his class at age sixteen, serving as school newspaper editor in his senior year. His classmates were dazzled by his easy brilliance and charming ways, electing him class president all four years. At graduation the class yearbook predicted great things, "No actor, pastor or well *fusser* he. But—lawyer, senator, U.S. Pres.—*May-be!*"⁹ Even so, college wasn't a given for the telegraph operator's son: "In my last year of school I rather doubted whether it was worthwhile for a chap in my circumstance to go to college."¹⁰

Yet there was never any doubt in his mother's mind that he would be attending college. Despite the fact that cash for school was scarce, the plan was for Arthur to spend a year earning money working on the survey crew of the D. L. & W. R. Lewis probably played a role in getting his son the job, and by living at home Arthur was able to save his salary; that, together with Alice's sister, Aunt Sarah, lending him money, he was able to pay the first year's expenses.

When autumn 1906 arrived Arthur was off to Middletown, Connecticut, to attend Wesleyan University. Named for John Wesley, Wesleyan was among the earliest of the original Methodist colleges in the United States; the precepts of the Methodist movement were integral to its curriculum. Yet, interestingly, from its inception Wesleyan offered a liberal arts program emphasizing social sciences, education, and preparing young Methodist men for the professions rather than theological training. In contrast, nearly all the other early Methodist colleges, for example, Duke, Vanderbilt, and Boston Universities, began as theological academies for the study of "sanctified learning," with one profession in mind, the clergy.

What set Wesleyan apart from other such schools—and nourished the spirit of Arthur Vanderbilt—was its focus on uplifting the condition of people in this world rather than worrying about the next one. The school's philosophy of learning was expressed well by Wesleyan's first president, Wilbur Fisk. "The great object which we propose to ourselves in the work of education is to supply, as far as we may, men who will be willing and competent to effect the political, intellectual, and spiritual regeneration of the world."¹¹ Throughout its history, Wesleyan has been a leader in educational progress, erecting one of the earliest comprehensive science buildings devoted solely to undergraduate science instruction of any American university. Likewise it has maintained a larger and more sophisticated library collection than many institutions of comparable size.

Wesleyan was not a school for pious clergymen, curious dilettantes, or social elites. Its purpose was to educate agitators to go out and change the world. Alice Vanderbilt was sending her son to a college where his brilliance would gain purpose; where his energy could be harnessed for regenerating America's legal system.

There's no way of calculating which—the school or the student—made a greater mark on the other during Arthur Vanderbilt's four years at Wesleyan University. The activities he was involved in, the campus efforts he led, and the lives he touched were so numerous that they defy the confines of this narrative. His footprints at the school remain to this day. Vanderbilt's relationship with Wesleyan was such that the entirety of his forty-plus years of personal and professional files are archived there.

Autumn of 1906 was when "life really began"[12] for eighteen-year-old "Art Van" as he became known around campus. Standing five feet ten inches tall and weighing 175 pounds, he was of medium build and fair complexion, with thick dark hair parted in the center. Always well dressed, he was the picture of the earnest pupil. At that time the Wesleyan student body numbered no more than three hundred, and it wasn't long before everyone on campus knew the student from Newark, New Jersey.

He had already set his sights on a career in the law, and college was where the people in Art Van's orbit first appreciated his ability to juggle his time, energy, and talent. In four years he completed the course requirements for both B.A. and M.A. degrees in history and government, the first student to ever do so. In addition to his studies, he earned his tuition money by working as the steward of his fraternity house. He also was a reporter and editor of the *Argus*, the semi-weekly campus newspaper at Wesleyan. Somehow his schedule allowed him to earn spending money keeping the books of the Forrest City Laundry, a business in Middletown. Yet that wasn't enough; he was a member of the debating council, earned a varsity letter for four years as a manager for the football team, and was elected president of his class all four years, as well as student body president in his senior year.

Exposed to a broad range of thinkers and writers at Wesleyan, Art Van was taken by the teachings of two people in particular: one living and the other long dead. Professor Raymond Dodge was a pioneer in the field of dynamic psychology, impressing upon his students the value of thought and action. Years later, Vanderbilt would say that he had learned from Dodge that "the mark of an educated man . . . is the ability to act on the basis of all available evidence at the moment when action is indicated."[13] He learned the difference between acting decisively and being impulsive, between solving a

problem rationally and efficiently rather than procrastinating and overana-
lyzing. He also became a devotee of *Poor Richard*.

Nearly two centuries after first presenting his "Thirteen Virtues" to
the American colonists, Benjamin Franklin was still attracting followers.
Absorbing a regimen that entailed self-critical analysis on issues ranging
from temperance, resoluteness, and industry to sincerity, humility, and justice, many of America's early leaders were ardent followers of his precepts.
Along with each virtue Franklin included a principle to follow, defining a
person of good character. Franklin's virtues were appealing to Alice Vanderbilt's son and served as valuable guideposts in the early years of a person
destined to spend his life juggling demanding pursuits and leading diverse
people. Upon Art Van's graduation from Wesleyan, William Shanklin, president of the university, said, "Arthur T. Vanderbilt was the most unusual and
gifted undergraduate I have known in all my college experience."[14]

Within days of his graduation from Wesleyan, Vanderbilt was clerking
with the law firm of Sommer, Colby & Whiting in Newark. Fortune smiled on
Arthur Vanderbilt: he and Frank Sommer bonded immediately. Strengthening the tie between the two of them were Sommer's roots in Roseville. At the
beginning of the career of every successful attorney, or any professional, is a
caring mentor, someone who wants to see a young person excel and is willing
to devote the time, energy, and patience required to develop his or her talent.
And what motivates these mentors? The love of their calling and the understanding that wisdom must be shared if their profession is to have a future.

Frank Sommer had come to the law in a way that was common for his
generation. Born into a poor family in Roseville shortly after the Civil War,
he left school at age twelve and went to work in a real estate office. From
being involved in realty transactions he became interested in the law. Sommer began reading law books and going to the Essex County Courthouse to
observe judges and lawyers in action. While still in his teens he was called
as a witness at a trial involving his employer. His testimony was so articulate
and precise that he was offered a position as an office boy with the Newark
law firm handling the lawsuit.[15]

While working with the law firm, Sommer began reading serious legal trea-
tises, going to court, serving his clerkship, and eventually becoming a member
of the firm. The tall, thin, bespectacled, yet refined-looking young man looked
like a lawyer, and after he severed his ties with the sale of real estate, the law
became his life. At the time, no formal bar exam was required to become an

attorney, and Frank Sommer was arguing cases in court by the time he was in his early twenties. Despite his lack of a formal education Sommer was a lawyer's lawyer, keenly aware of the law's expanding role in twentieth-century America. By 1893, while still in his twenties, he was hired as a professor at NYU's law school, eventually becoming dean and serving for twenty-seven years. To this day, an annual award is made in his name to the student exhibiting outstanding scholarship, character, and professional activities.[16]

Sommer realized that knowledge of the law together with skillful advocacy enables a single person to expand the law's envelope of rights and responsibilities. When that person possesses extraordinary knowledge and skill he/she becomes akin to a force of nature in the affairs of society. Sommer recognized that his protégé was exceptional. He saw a young man with a superior education whose aspirations were the same as his: to be a lawyer as a public person, capable of influencing public policy.

Practicing and teaching law weren't enough for Frank Sommer; he was involved in government during most of his career, often as an advocate for reform. His initial entry into politics came with the formation of the "New Idea" movement, an insurgent group of progressives within the Essex County Republican Party. The group got its start following a tragic railroad accident at a street-level crossing in 1903, which resulted in the death of nine schoolmates of fifteen-year-old Arthur Vanderbilt. Grief and outrage overwhelmed the Roseville community.

Frank Sommer was determined that changes had to be made to railway crossings and spearheaded a drive for legislation forcing the railroads to make needed safety upgrades to their crossings at street level. The mighty railroads were indignant at being told how to run their operations and fought against the legislation up to the U.S. Supreme Court. Sommer defended the law through every level of the railroads' appeals, emerging victorious. But Frank Sommer was also a political animal and an admirer of President Theodore Roosevelt. He had decided it was time to steer Essex County into supporting the progressive programs of the president. The group's goals were direct primaries to reduce the power of political bosses; establishment of civil service for municipal employees to minimize political patronage; making the railroads and utilities pay their fair share of taxes; and the creation of juvenile courts and detention centers, separating children from adult criminals.

Although only a high school student, young Arthur was first drawn to Sommer's meetings because of the loss of his schoolmates; he needed a way to channel his emotions. As Sommer moved on from railroad safety to broader issues such as uniform zoning and building codes, workplace safety standards and municipal playgrounds, Vanderbilt became intrigued by the New Idea movement. There aren't many fifteen-year-olds eager to attend political rallies—then or now—but young Arthur Vanderbilt was drawn to Frank Sommer's dynamism and knowledge of the law.

Vanderbilt followed Sommer's career and admired him greatly, and with good reason. During his career in the law and government Frank Sommer was elected Essex County sheriff on a reform ticket in 1906, served as president of the Newark School Board, chairman of the New Jersey Board of Bar Examiners, special counsel to the chancellor of the Chancery Court on disbarment matters, New Jersey railroad commissioner, and, especially noteworthy, he worked with Governor Woodrow Wilson's administration drafting legislation for landmark reforms.[17]

Easily forgotten into today's toxic environment of two national political parties constantly bickering with each other is a time when politicians found a way to work together after an election. Buried even deeper in the American psyche is the fact that at the dawn of the twentieth century it was the progressive wing of the Republican Party that led the fight against powerful economic interests to prevent exploitation of the working class and to expand opportunities in education, access to health care, and women's rights. The children and grandchildren of the antislavery agitators who formed the core of the abolitionist movement saw the pressing needs of the immigrants coming to America and reached out to them.

Working shoulder to shoulder with urban Democrats, progressive Republicans battled to ensure that "life, liberty, and the pursuit of happiness" remained accessible to the newly arrived immigrants working in the nation's factories. Democratic governor Woodrow Wilson recruited Republican lawyer Frank Sommer to help write reform legislation addressing everything from the costs of public utilities, worker's compensation, and commercial arbitration to local land use controls, civil service, and modern election laws. Frank Sommer was young Arthur Vanderbilt's role model.

Entering the world of lawyers in the summer of 1910 by doing routine research, filing court papers, sitting in on the deposition of witnesses, and tagging along with Sommer to watch him in court, Arthur absorbed the experience for all it was worth. Sommer took a keen interest in his protégé. As one of Vanderbilt's biographers relates, "He introduced Arthur to legal classics like Pollock and Maitland's *History of the English Law* and took him to the Court of Chancery and the Court of Errors and Appeals at the old State House in Trenton, where 'many of the greatest cases in this State in corporate matters were being heard.'"[18]

As any young person might be, Arthur was impressed with the eloquence of some of the advocates; nonetheless, Sommer cautioned him that excelling as an attorney was far more about mastering the law and marshaling the facts than it was about oratorical skills. Sommer's uncommon talents as both an advocate and a counselor, combined with his unfailing civility toward his adversaries, impressed upon young Arthur that the role of lawyers is critical to maintaining a civilized society through the rule of law.

That fall, Arthur began his first year at Columbia University Law School. While he probably could have studied law anywhere he wanted, finances dictated that he live with his family in Newark, commuting daily to New York City. It was a daunting schedule.

Leaving home shortly after 7:00 A.M., he walked from his parents' home to the train station and boarded a train, via the new Hudson River train tunnel, to lower Manhattan where he boarded a second train taking him uptown to Columbia. When classes were over he reversed his trip, heading for work in Newark. "Work" was teaching four half-hour classes to students who had been forced to leave school to work in factories; night classes were a Newark tradition dating back to the town's early industrialists of the nineteenth century who believed in educating their workforce. Arthur's teaching salary was four dollars a night, which he squirreled away, making plans to marry his fiancée, Florence "Floss" Althen. The two were longtime sweethearts from high school days, when Floss was class secretary and Arthur class president,[19] and although living apart, they were together whenever his studies permitted. Working into the early morning hours, he prepared his lesson plans for his students and studied his law assignments before going to bed.

In his spare time, twenty-two-year-old Arthur—heeding Frank Sommer's advice—scrutinized leading New Jersey court decisions. Columbia taught a national law curriculum; Vanderbilt knew he would be practicing in New Jersey and was determined to keep up with state court rulings. He also found time to work on his master's thesis, "The Origin and Establishment of the Supreme Court of the United States," needed to complete the degree requirements at Wesleyan. In the spring of 1912, Arthur returned to Middletown, taking part in commencement and receiving his master's degree in history and government.

During his final year at Columbia, Arthur witnessed Frank Sommer modernizing an important aspect of the New Jersey legal system. At the request of Governor Wilson, Frank Sommer overhauled the format for filing lawsuits. The requirement of "common law pleading" was introduced to colonial New Jersey's judicial system by Lord Cornbury. Dating to the fifteenth century, it mandated various claims and types of relief to be stated very precisely; in some instances common law pleading commanded the use of all manner of archaic jargon and obscure phrases, often in Latin. Over time the English courts had abandoned the practice, as had nearly every state in America, but it persisted in New Jersey.

By the twentieth century, common law pleading had become an extraordinarily antiquated set of procedural rules and writs having little to do with the rule of law. There were so many arcane subtleties encrusted onto the rules for pleading by various court decisions and statutory amendments of the legislature that the requirements for pleading a particular cause of action were baffling. Only the most knowledgeable lawyers had mastered them. Placing form above substance, making how an issue was phrased more important than the merits of the issue itself, the court's rules on pleadings made a mockery of any notion of fair and efficient administration of justice. And there were serious consequences: a less than careful lawyer who failed to state the precise relief sought could find his client's claim tossed out of court in an instant because he failed to use ancient phrases having no meaning to anyone but the judges and lawyers who delighted in their use. Many New Jersey residents found themselves agreeing with Charles Dickens's character Mr. Bumble in *Oliver Twist*: "The law is a ass."

Frank Sommer's innate curiosity and "encyclopedic mind" had enabled him to navigate the impenetrable nonsense of the court rules and their ancient jargon despite his belief that they didn't serve justice.[20] On occasion he poked fun at the system by playing games with his pleadings: concocting silly terms and fake writs and foisting them on judges unlearned in the law whom he knew would never catch on. One example was his "Writ of Pluckitendo."[21]

Bewildered by having his case dismissed without explanation, a fellow attorney sought Sommer's advice on how to get his client's claim back on track. Without hesitation, Sommer told the novice that his problem could be solved with a Writ of Pluckitendo. The confused lawyer admitted that he had never heard of any such writ and asked Sommer if he would prepare one, a chore that Sommer undertook gleefully, producing a document of high-sounding Latin phrases, going on at length. The purpose of this fanciful writ was to "pluck" the litigation from the county district court and to transfer it to the court of common pleas.

Perplexed but dutifully following instructions, the lawyer presented the elaborately worded writ to the common pleas judge, who balked at first but relented when he learned that Frank Sommer had drafted the document. It was then off to the county clerk, who didn't recognize it as anything he had ever seen before but figured the judge who signed it had to know what he was doing, so he affixed the court's seal. When the writ reached his desk, the district court judge was irate; nonetheless, he abided by the terms of the official-looking order and tore out the pages of the district court's records of the proceedings, forwarding them to the common pleas judge. All was well, yet when Sommer next appeared before the common pleas judge he was told that should the story ever be learned by anyone but the two of them during the judge's lifetime that he would declare Sommer in contempt of court.

But Sommer was about more than poking fun at the system: he led the charge for modernizing New Jersey's courts, drafting language to amend the state constitution. In 1903 and 1909, Sommer and a coterie of reform-minded lawyers had spearheaded efforts for statewide ballot questions proposing to overhaul the judicial article in New Jersey's constitution. With no support from the organized bar, each time the voters said no.

In 1912, despite these defeats—or because of them—there was still enough momentum left in the New Jersey progressive movement to adopt the Practice Act of 1912 prior to Woodrow Wilson's departure for the White House. The needed legislation was drafted by Frank Sommer working with Judge Alfred Skinner and Charles Hartshorne, all of Essex County. Although a long way from transforming the state's judicial system, it made important improvements. Now if a lawsuit was filed in the wrong court it was transferred instead of dismissed; types of relief previously the exclusive domain of either the chancery or law courts could be heard by either; and much of the power to adopt the court rules was transferred from the legislature to the E & A.

Following adoption of the Practice Act, Arthur Vanderbilt saw up close how committed to the past some lawyers were. Within days after the act was adopted, Sommer's protégé witnessed old guard practitioners arriving unannounced at Sommer's law office threatening to leave the legal profession. They were bitter at the change of rules, which they had been able to exploit throughout their careers, and they were fearful that their livelihoods were in jeopardy. "[T]he new Practice Act brought tears to the eyes of some of the older lawyers"[22] who came complaining to Frank Sommer, distraught about the changes.

As one well-informed biographer has cogently noted, Arthur Vanderbilt's ringside seat to the uproar surrounding the Practice Act of 1912 made an indelible impression. As a result of "beginning his legal career in one of the few jurisdictions where the law was still hopelessly enmeshed in the formalities of common law pleading [and] having a preceptor who poked fun at this maze of technicalities by calling it *intricate nonsense*, and learning that the law need not be rigid and immutable,"[23] seeds were being planted for what would be his life's work.

Although excelling as an attorney was his primary goal, young Arthur readily saw that here was a serious opportunity for furthering the Progressive agenda, expanding beyond social issues and getting to one of the most fundamental rights of citizens in a free society: the right to a fair trial, something that was never a given in New Jersey. Every lawyer knows that on occasion the law and justice are not one with each other, but that should always be the goal. Yet, with "Jersey justice" political connections often trumped the rule of law. The fairness, competence, and political ties of the judge hearing the case and the impartiality of the jurors were always question marks for a lawyer going to trial. Following the path of Frank Sommer as an innovator in the law was the route Vanderbilt would take. These were heady times for the twenty-four-year-old son of a Western Union telegraph operator. Years later, speaking of Sommer, Vanderbilt would say, "He has influenced my life more than any man I have ever known."[24] Yet they both had to know that Arthur would go his separate way.

Arthur had a vision of his role in the law that would have been impeded by being a member of a firm. For him, the law was more than a learned profession or a business; it was a calling. His devotion to his career had a singleness of purpose evident from the very beginning. He was fixated on success and pursuing excellence in all he did; compromise didn't come naturally. As Nathan Jacobs would recall years later, Vanderbilt had a "ruthless fixity of purpose."[25] While he could be affable, as demonstrated by his election as class president in both high school and college, there was a less sunny side to his personality, which emerged when he didn't get his way. Roseville's prodigy needed the freedom of being answerable to no one. The role he saw for himself as a progressive Republican was very much part of the tumultuous times he was living in and the changes he was witnessing in Newark.

In addition to social, education, housing, and health issues, there was a wing of the Progressive movement focused on America's legal system. Two lawyers who influenced young Arthur Vanderbilt and were role models to many young attorneys of the day were Louis Brandeis (1856–1941) and Roscoe Pound (1870–1964).

As both a practicing attorney and a jurist, Louis Brandeis moved the law in new directions. He was once characterized by the *Economist* as "the Robin Hood of the law" for his work fighting powerful corporations and defending laws that protected workers. Brandeis's role in modern American jurisprudence is so large that no single case represents his thinking. Several worth noting are *Muller v. Oregon* (1908),[26] in which he argued successfully for workplace safety regulations bitterly opposed by big business; his dissent in *Olmstead v. United States* (1928),[27] articulating the right to privacy, or the "right to be let alone" by government; and *Erie v. Tompkins* (1938),[28] requiring federal courts to apply state common law in diversity of citizenship actions, thwarting the efforts of multistate corporations to avoid local laws. The appointment of Brandeis to the U.S. Supreme Court in 1916 may have been Woodrow Wilson's single most important contribution to the Progressive movement.

Roscoe Pound was a graduate of Harvard Law School and later its dean. In 1906 he delivered an address to the American Bar Association that made him a threat to the status quo. The speech, "Causes of Popular Dissatisfaction with the Administration of Justice," was a broadside attack on the American judicial system, reciting its flaws in stunning detail and warning that the rule of law was in danger. Pound promptly became a national leader on the subject of judicial reform, inspiring an entire generation of lawyers to pursue excellence in service of the public. Arthur Vanderbilt was one of those lawyers.

Following graduation from law school and the required clerkship, with Frank Sommer as his preceptor, Arthur headed out on his own. Although he was nominally, and briefly, in a partnership with Chester Fairlie, a Newark lawyer and Wesleyan alumnus several years his senior, Vanderbilt was always committed to an individual practice.

During the brief period of 1914–1915 when Fairlie & Vanderbilt practiced law together, three significant events occurred in Arthur's life. First, thanks to Frank Sommer, Arthur was hired by NYU's law school to teach two evening classes a week, something he would do for the next thirty-four years. Second, with what Arthur described as the "munificent stipend of $1,400" per year,[29] he and his fiancée, Floss Althen, could finally afford to marry. She was the love of his life and his refuge throughout many battles. Only the elegant and charming Floss could coax him away from his frenetic schedule. Third, he was retained to represent the Depositors Protective Committee of a failed bank, the Roseville Trust Company, which generated fees other young lawyers could only dream of.

Every lawyer approached to take on the tedious task of running down deadbeats to collect on the failed bank's past-due loans and mortgages worried that the debts were either totally uncollectible or that the people owing the money would resist paying a debt to a bank that no longer existed, making the proposed contingent-fee arrangement unprofitable. The head of the depositors committee of Roseville Trust was friendly with Chester Fairlie and asked if he could refer a young lawyer willing to take on the assignment. Despite having no experience in commercial collections, Vanderbilt accepted the offer and treated the committee as if it were his only client, which it pretty much was.

According to biographer E. C. Gerhart, "Chester Fairlie's new partner threw himself into the job like a whirlwind. Vanderbilt hurried home from [teaching at NYU] law school and worked late at night pounding on his typewriter all the legal papers incident to foreclosing a mortgage, suing on notes, and all the legal drudgery necessary to dun debtors."[30] Within a few months Arthur realized that if he was diligent in the preparation of his court filings and vigilant in zeroing in on those debtors who had the means to pay, his new collection practice wasn't so bad after all.

Knowing that the head of the depositors committee could be tough to deal with, and realizing that the agreed upon fee of 5 percent of the debts recovered was on its way to becoming a sizable number, Arthur decided not to bill his client until the task was complete. He was fearful his client might renege. The green lawyer conferred with Frank Sommer, who agreed that restraint on his billing statements was in order. Sommer had also been keeping tabs on Vanderbilt's performance in the courtroom on many of the contested-debt collection suits. Apparently, the new lawyer was a tad too aggressive and was annoying judges and members of the bar alike. Many years later, Arthur reminisced that Sommer had counseled him, "You have to learn how to holler without raising your voice."[31]

After more than a year of pursuing debtors Arthur was ready to submit his bill. He had collected approximately $700,000 and was entitled to fees of more than $35,000 (equivalent to more than $500,000 today). To his relief, the committee paid the entire amount without trying to renegotiate his fees. The members of the depositors committee were pleased, and they told other businesspeople in Newark.

Successful law careers are grounded in referrals, and Vanderbilt's handling of the bank debts led to many more claims involving commercial debts. Adding to his referrals, the people in Newark's banking world overlapped with those in the city's insurance community. In a short time he was representing key players in both sectors of the city's thriving commercial economy. There would be time for family, friends, and public service, but for now all his waking hours were consumed by his law practice.

Still in his twenties, Arthur Vanderbilt was taking big steps toward becoming part of a small circle of Newark lawyers known for handling sophisticated problems involving large sums of money. Although there would be fees earned from deeds, leases, and wills, plus occasional traffic violations, they would not be the mainstay of his practice.

Vanderbilt committed all his energy and talent to being a go-to lawyer for clients with complex matters. As he received files involving specialized work from high-profile clients, he developed the traits possessed by highly skilled litigators. Most laypeople do not appreciate the frequent need of an attorney preparing for trial to become an expert in various fields. Once grounded in the subject matter, a lawyer must not only retain the facts of the case and each witness's version of what occurred but also anticipate how his/her adversary will approach the same facts and witnesses. Finally, the lawyer must blend a brief statement of the facts with a cogent analysis of the law into a concise, unadorned, straightforward delivery, whether spoken or written, whether the decision maker is a judge or a jury. Vanderbilt was routinely earning fees in the tens of thousands of dollars (think hundreds of thousands in today's dollars) while his contemporaries were handling minor transactions, fender benders, and drunk-driving cases and realizing fees a tiny fraction of his.

Before he was thirty, Vanderbilt was on his way to being an elite member of his profession, respected for his skill as an advocate and consistently commanding large retainers. In time his prowess in both the law and politics eclipsed that of his mentor, Frank Sommer. As he matured and his law practice grew, his involvement in politics meant even greater sums would flow to his law firm.

CHAPTER 3

The Lawyer as Public Person

World War I was raging and many of Newark's factories were working over-time manufacturing materials for the war effort. It was late afternoon, and Vanderbilt was returning from arguing a case out of town when he was met at the train station by a client, the head of a large tool company. The business-man was frantic. A lawyer was his only hope. The day before, his key foreman had been arrested by Newark's finest for driving his car on the downtown sidewalks for the sheer joy of frightening pedestrians, terrifying people leav-ing church; amazingly, no one was injured. There were scores of witnesses to swear he had been drinking—driving drunk on a Sunday morning.

Trial before a local justice of the peace, a retired schoolteacher who pic-tured himself as a distinguished jurist, was set for that evening. He "held court" in his kitchen, a fairly common venue for traffic violations in New Jersey. The charge called for a minimum jail sentence of thirty days, a calam-ity to the tool company's operations. To accommodate an overflow crowd, a table was set up in the justice's garden and the trial was to be alfresco. Vanderbilt had his work cut out for him.

Multiple witnesses eagerly testified, recounting the defendant's madcap joy-ride. As later recounted by Vanderbilt, "Fortunately, none of them seemed to bear him any ill will."[1] Most agreed that the foreman was ordinarily an upstand-ing citizen. Vanderbilt challenged none of the witnesses, following their lead that the event was out of character for his client. When all the witnesses had testified, the justice of the peace asked if counsel had anything to add.

Without skipping a beat, Vanderbilt enthralled the crowd with a folksy homily about the vital role of America's factories, the sensitivity of the foreman's duties, and all the brave young men in uniform—including the foreman's three sons—"the flower of youth doing their duty all over the globe."[2] When he was finished, many of the women were teary-eyed and some of the men were blowing their nose. The justice of the peace, owing his election to his ward leader, couldn't help but notice the effect on the people in attendance.

Sprinkled into Vanderbilt's remarks was the word "intoxication" as stated in the violated statute, as opposed to being "drunk" as testified to by the witnesses. Following a brief recess the justice of the peace emerged from his kitchen, statute book in hand, reading aloud the section the foreman was charged with offending. Laying great stress on the fact that all the witnesses had testified that the foreman was "drunk" but no one had said he was "intoxicated," the retired schoolteacher announced that "he had no choice but to acquit the defendant."[3]

Part showman, part politician, part cagey advocate, and totally a lawyer in tune with his surroundings, Arthur Vanderbilt never lost sight of his audience and, more important, who the decision maker was and what it took to woo him. He wasn't the first attorney to exploit the juncture between the law and politics to obtain legal fees, but he was one of the most skillful of his generation at profiting from extracurricular activities. And what a grand stage Newark was for making the most of those two worlds.

In the era during which Arthur Vanderbilt was rising to the top of his profession, Newark was more than the most prominent city in New Jersey: it ranked as one of the most sophisticated cities in North America. Ranked fifteenth in population (Frank Hague's Jersey City wasn't far behind at twenty-second) and eleventh in industrial output among America's cities, it wasn't just Newark's economic prowess that made it great: in New Jersey it was a city of many educational/social/cultural firsts.

Whether it was schools, libraries, and museums or public transportation, a regional newspaper, and a baseball team, no city in the state—and few in America—rivaled its grandeur. For people born after 1960, coupling Newark and "grandeur" is puzzling. Yet a visit today reveals the skeleton of what once was a great city. What made it a great city was the fact that Newark's leaders took themselves and their town seriously and strived for excellence. Newark was also home to New Jersey's first statewide newspaper, the *Newark Evening News,* which over time became a vocal supporter of many of Arthur Vanderbilt's efforts.

Understanding the implications of Benjamin Franklin's oft-quoted phrase, "New Jersey is a barrel tapped at both ends," in 1873 a handful of enlightened journalists and businessmen pledged to publish "a bright, independent newspaper, untrammeled by politics and unhampered by corporate influence," the *Newark Evening News*. For its day, when many newspapers were partisan rags, the *Newark Evening News* reported—with exceptional integrity—on events throughout the entire state. It circulated in all twenty-one counties; it was widely read and respected, and it influenced the outcome of many issues during its ninety-nine-year history.

Newark's leaders and its prominent families, along with the newspapers, strove to build a city that would stand shoulder to shoulder with the great cities of America—and they succeeded. While Newark's old guard wasn't any happier with the tide of immigrants flowing into their town than were the WASPs of other cities in America, they managed to deal with the situation a whole lot better, ultimately sharing power on the establishment's terms.

Maybe it was the ethos of the early Puritans, or more likely the mature realization that everyone needed to share in the prosperity of their city, that prompted Newark's leaders to recognize the importance of these newcomers' labor. Rather than simply exploiting their labor, the city put in place the building blocks needed to integrate newly arrived workers into the community, setting standards for an inclusive society long before most cities in America. Stacked one upon another, those building blocks created a sparkling community equal to any city in the Northeast, with the exception of the much larger cities of New York, Philadelphia, and Boston. Newark's leaders never doubted that their city ranked first in New Jersey and that they had a responsibility for leading the state, albeit sometimes with a self-importance that people from other regions in the state found overbearing.

By the time of World War I, Essex County—primarily because of Newark, its county seat—was a trendsetter among U.S. counties. Essex was considered one of the six major counties in America. Its per capita income, real property valuations, expenditures by government, retail sales, wholesale revenues, and the county's combined total of manufactured goods placed it in the first tier of counties in America. Despite encompassing little more than 127 square miles, the county's population of more than 600,000 exceeded that of fourteen states. Dwarfing the population of every county in New Jersey with the exception of Hudson, Essex was respected, admired, and/or feared by the leaders of every facet of the state's life. As someone in the hunt for political clout, Vanderbilt was fortunate to have roots in a county with such stature.

Though there's little in his life story revealing a desire to be a candidate, his thirst for recognition and hunger for power were real. Vanderbilt wanted to be more than merely the hand behind the throne. He wanted to have his own base of power and the ability to influence events without ever having to run the risk of being rejected by the voters. Not long after graduating from law school, he told a colleague, "I'm itching to get into politics."[4] He focused his energy on acquiring power in Essex County.

Vanderbilt's first opportunity to play a leadership role arose from the mismanagement of a county-operated hospital for mentally ill patients. Despite the publication of repeated dire warnings regarding conditions at Overbrook Hospital by the *Newark Evening News* dating back to 1914, the Essex County Board of Freeholders persisted in ignoring the serious need for repairs. Several boilers used in generating heat and electricity were in significant need of replacement. In December 1917, the heating and electric systems broke down.

Condensing a convoluted, sad, and very ugly story to its essence: forty-three patients died of exposure that December and the public was incensed. An investigation followed, revealing corruption, fraud, and incompetence.[5] A grand jury returned an indictment for criminal negligence against the members of the freeholder board, but thanks to a system that looked after its own, all were ultimately acquitted on technicalities.

Being aroused by the self-dealing and ineptitude of the freeholders was one thing; getting organized to do something about it took a lot more. The election following the hospital deaths saw the victory of the three Democratic candidates—a first in Essex County in more than a decade—and they pushed for an investigation, which revealed looting of the public coffers by the Republican freeholders. Again, nobody went to jail, but it was embarrassing to honest Republicans like Vanderbilt. He and other progressive Republicans were determined to take their party back from those who they viewed as thieves.

In the early years of the twentieth century, especially among the WASPs of Essex County, there was a widespread public mind-set, which people today have difficulty relating to. For many old guard Republicans there was a natural linkage of law enforcement, honest government, and the "problem of booze." With the approval of Vanderbilt and others of his generation, Prohibition was coming to America. The adoption of the Eighteenth Amendment to the U.S. Constitution was making its way through the nation's state legislatures; it was poised to become the law of the land in 1920, enforced by the Volstead Act.

Temperance as a social movement had been around for several generations; many Protestant church groups condemned the evils of alcohol, among them Methodists, Baptists, Disciples, and Congregationalists. There's no doubt Alice Vanderbilt shared those sympathies. Prohibition—an outright ban of the sale of alcoholic beverages—didn't become a goal, however, until the Anti-Saloon League began pushing for it in the 1890s. With the hindsight of history we can see that the league was the first modern lobbyist movement obsessed with forcing its views on social policy upon the rest of the nation. Its efforts stand as a monument to the unintended consequences of single-issue politics. Nonetheless, given his background and the era in which he came of age, it was only natural that Vanderbilt, the teetotaling Methodist from Roseville, would join forces with them.

In February 1919, James Shields, the state superintendent of the Anti-Saloon League, with offices in Newark, called a meeting, inviting fellow Republicans concerned about the political rot afflicting their party. Vanderbilt was on the invitation list. On the night of February 20, at a gathering of progressives "thoroughly disgusted with their Republican organization,"[6] the Essex County Republican League was born and thirty-year-old Arthur Vanderbilt was elected its first president. Vanderbilt and his allies hoped to pick up where Frank Sommer's New Idea insurgency had left off. Looking for support from the Anti-Saloon League, their candidates would run under the slogan "Republican League: Clean County Government."

Their target voting base were the educated, middle-class voters of Essex County—Republican and independent alike—many of whom resided in Newark's growing suburbs. Some of these "suburbs" were within the confines of the city; others were in adjoining communities linked with the commercial and industrial sectors of Newark by train, streetcar, and bus. By and large, the residents of these growing urban neighborhoods didn't have strong ties to either political party. As noted by T. H. Reed, reporting on the Progressive Era in Essex County, Vanderbilt and the Republican League were to benefit from "the naturally independent character of the commuter vote. Essex County possesses an unusually large number of successful men and women who have gravitated to the New York area from every part of the United States. They possess qualities of leadership and initiative to an

THE LAWYER AS PUBLIC PERSON

unusual degree, and never under any circumstances would they submit to the dictation of a [political] boss."[7]

At the outset, the League was very loosely organized, so much so that Vanderbilt's one-time partner, Chester Fairlie, described it as follows: "The fact is that for some years the League was a mere fiction, a trade name, as it were, under which Arthur did political business in Essex County. Arthur issued the statements and gave out the stories, and the local newspapers accepted the 'League' as if it were an important organization in fact."[8] Years later Vanderbilt conceded as much by joking, "It was to be claimed that we held our meetings in a telephone booth. That was not literally true. But it was in fact, a day of small beginnings."[9] Lacking serious money or an organization, Vanderbilt relied heavily on progressive newspapers to endorse his candidates, the two most prominent being the *Newark Evening News* and the *Newark Sunday Call.* The League found support from both papers.

Holding press conferences, issuing news releases, and writing letters to the editor, the Republican League's plucky young leader began making use of the verbal brass knuckles he couldn't unleash in a courtroom, ruthlessly attacking the old guard Republicans. Although that was entertaining, Vanderbilt's most important role as leader of the League was recruiting candidates. He would never be a candidate or a street fighter himself, but he was learning the moves of a savvy pol, and because of his brilliance, wit, and directness, others followed his lead. Looking to the next election in 1919, his goal was not only to prevent the Democrats from repeating their success from the previous year but also to elect a new breed of progressive Republicans.

Vanderbilt recruited Henry Hines, Edwin Bell, and Wilbur Driver, all respected members of the community who embraced his progressive ideals. Hines had served three terms in the state assembly as a Sommer's New Idea Republican and had a solid base of voters throughout the county. The old guard Republicans had seen enough of Hines, and his presence on the primary ballot excited the opposition. The primary election of September 1919 was hard fought, with the regular Republicans outspending the League by a margin of more than $60,000 to $4,442.50, yet Hines and Bell won the nominations and went on to be successful in the November general election. The lone regular Republican candidate won as well. People drawn to Essex County politics were looking to January and what issues the two League freeholders would pursue.

Experienced politicians know that local government reorganization meetings can be tricky business, filled with surprises and sometimes drama. Plans can go awry without warning. With six Republican freeholders on the nine-member board, four of whom were from the regular Republican camp, the selection of freeholder chairman by the old guard appeared assured—yet it wasn't.

There's more than one version of what occurred on New Year's Day 1920, but suffice it to say that both Hines and Bell reportedly told people they didn't know who they would vote for at the reorganization meeting. Nonetheless, what was obvious is that *three plus two equals five*. Whether through chicanery and moxie on the part of Vanderbilt and his two new League freeholders or the agenda of the minority-party Democrats, the three Democratic freeholders voted with Hines and Bell in naming Hines the new chairman. The regular Republicans never saw it coming; they were reeling. As freeholder chairman, Hines had the power to appoint committees that not only oversaw county government operations but could launch investigations and, in turn, make headlines.

Edwin Bell, who had considerable experience in the construction business, was named chairman of the building committee. Within weeks of taking office, Bell introduced a resolution demanding a halt to any further work on a sewage plant being built to service the county hospital. His next move was to appoint none other than Arthur Vanderbilt as special investigation counsel. The old guard knew they were in trouble. Moving quickly at taking testimony, reviewing contract documents, and inspecting site work, Bell's committee was ready to make recommendations for action in little more than ninety days. On April 30 Bell's committee report was presented to the full board. As Vanderbilt biographer Gerhart notes, "It is a very cogent document, bearing unmistakable marks of Vanderbilt's skill in marshaling evidence."[10] Vanderbilt's handiwork revealed that the agreement with a favored contractor had been improperly drawn by the county counsel, that the work had not proceeded according to the approved specifications, and that the county engineer had approved work that had never been performed.

County counsel happened to be State Senator Charles Pilgrim, and he was outraged by the actions of the upstart lawyer. The following week Pilgrim issued a statement charging that "the investigators have exceeded their authority in drawing conclusions" on the workings of county government, asserting that the report was colored by "political partisanship."[11] Vanderbilt shot back a fierce retort citing the fact that in addition to being county counsel, Pilgrim was also on a yearly retainer with Averill-Mathews, the contractor that had been so derelict in its duties.

Pilgrim's attorney-client relationship with Averill-Mathews had been left out of Vanderbilt's report, but now the gloves were off. Vanderbilt was merciless in his counterattack. Sarcastically poking fun at Pilgrim's hypocrisy, he called the challenge to the committee's report "the rarest of humor." Dismissive of Pilgrim's attack, he was confident that "the public will be much more interested in learning what he has to say on the merits of the case than in his abuse of the committee or its counsel."[12] How right he was. The upshot was dismissal of the engineer and a lawsuit against the contractor resulting in the recovery of $90,000 of misspent public funds (more than $1 million today). For icing in the cake, Pilgrim's terms as both state senator and county counsel were his last. His career as a public person was over.

Vanderbilt and the Republican League were off and running. There would be more investigations and more fraud, waste, and political back scratching uncovered: a saving of over $300,000 on paving contracts (more than $3 million today) that had been rigged for insiders by requiring the use of "patented asphalt." The League freeholders also exposed to the public a "farmer's cottage" for the caretaker of county-owned land. It was a sprawling custom home featuring ten rooms, an oak-paneled library, cathedral glass windows, and French doors, built for the pleasure of the regular Republicans, some observers viewing it as a political clubhouse at the taxpayers' expense.

Roseville's prodigy was getting an education and learning the difference between the law and politics. "When you try a case or argue and appeal, you are through with it. But in a political organization, you write down success or failure, advance or retreat at the end of every day."[13] He also learned that for genuinely committed players, politics is a time sponge. As he confided to Chester Fairlie early in his political career, "He was devoting more time to politics than to all the others combined, at times spending twelve hours a day, day after day, on politics, but always behind the scenes like a puppeteer, never running for elective office and never stumping in the campaign."[14]

These efforts were producing results. With the positive publicity flowing from Bell's, Hines's, and Vanderbilt's efforts, the League had no difficulty recruiting candidates for the primary in September of 1920. All three candidates won the nomination and were swept into office on the strength of Warren G. Harding's landslide victory that November.

When the freeholder board reorganized in January 1921, five of its nine members had come from the Republican League. For his efforts, Vanderbilt was named county counsel, a lucrative position he would hold for the next twenty-six years. He promptly positioned himself in a manner that had to raise eyebrows. Immediately upon being named county counsel, Vanderbilt abolished the offices of assistant county counsel and assistant county attorney, largely because he believed they "would be sure to get in the way."[15] He and he alone would be the go-to guy on legal questions in county government. Over time, he and he alone would call the shots in the most populous county in New Jersey.

Enhancing Vanderbilt's sway over the decision-making process was the structure of county government. As historian T. H. Reed notes, "In a somewhat decentralized form of local government like that of Essex County, in which there is no distinct executive head, the office of legal adviser becomes one of great influence. It may be regrettable, but it is a fact that the legal authority upon which the County must proceed in many matters is hidden away in ancient statutes and moldy court decisions from which only a good lawyer can extract it. No important action can be taken except upon the advice of the County's legal adviser."[16]

Vanderbilt held the keys to the kingdom. By eliminating assistants to rival him with differing opinions, he had made himself indispensable to the people who were running things in Essex County. Nonetheless, being both head of the Republican League and county counsel weren't the same as being "boss." That would come later.

Building on his successes in Essex County politics, Vanderbilt's entrance into statewide campaigns came in the gubernatorial election of 1922; it proved to be a highly profitable experience. Although the office of governor had little of the power attached to the office today, it was still a prize worth fighting for, especially the authority to appoint people to the upper court judgeships and state agencies and commissions. The election of 1922 saw the Democrats of Hudson and Middlesex Counties align to select a candidate, County Judge George Silzer of New Brunswick. The Republicans, with an aggressive effort by the Essex Republican League, selected William Runyon, a Teddy Roosevelt Progressive admired by both Sommer and Vanderbilt.

William N. Runyon was a favorite of the Essex Republican League, and Vanderbilt was a favorite of Runyon. Three years earlier the League and Vanderbilt had backed Runyon, but he was defeated in the Republican primary by Newton Bugbee, a successful businessman from Mercer County who lost the general election to Frank Hague's pick, Edward Edwards, a banker from Hudson County. Three years later, Bill Runyon wanted another shot at running for governor. He had proven himself an effective progressive during his years in public office. Runyon had served with distinction as a progressive member of the Plainfield City Council, in the state assembly, and as state senator from Union County.

On his second run for governor, Runyon tapped Vanderbilt to be his campaign manager for the general election and waged an aggressive campaign in all twenty-one counties. It was a long-shot investment of his time, but Vanderbilt was willing to take on the challenge. What Runyon hadn't bargained for was his race becoming an afterthought to the race for U.S. senator between outgoing Governor Edwards and incumbent Senator Joseph Frelinghuysen, a supporter of the Volstead Act and a favorite of the Anti-Saloon League. The Democrats succeeded in turning it into a referendum on Prohibition. Hammering away at the crime and corruption of local officials spawned by Prohibition, Edwards promised that once in Washington he would push for legislation permitting the sale of wine and beer under federal supervision. And if the Eighteenth Amendment prohibited that too, then he'd fight for the repeal of Prohibition. Frelinghuysen held steadfast to the national Republican Party's position and went down to defeat, some say dragging Runyon with him.

Yet the election was more about the rise of Frank Hague than about Prohibition. That year, and every three years thereafter for what amounted to a lifetime in politics, the vote margins in Hudson County were fatal to any hope of electing a progressive Republican as governor. Despite having a commanding lead after tallying the votes in the other twenty counties, Runyon was clobbered by the votes in Hudson County and lost to Silzer. But that's not the end of Vanderbilt's relationship with Runyon.

Politicians take care of their own. People who have served together in public office or worked tirelessly as part of a unit in a political campaign develop an affinity similar to members of an athletic team. The bond survives the last election.

Within days following the gubernatorial election, Senator Frelinghuysen— blaming himself for Runyon's loss—telephoned Vanderbilt in an effort to heal Runyon's wounds. "I can't change the verdict of the polls, but I do have some influence with the Harding administration in Washington. Do you think

Runyon would like to be named federal judge for New Jersey?"[17] The campaign manager was confident his candidate would accept, and within a month after William Runyon's defeat, President Warren G. Harding appointed him to a federal judgeship.

Not long after being named to the bench, Judge Runyon was assigned to handle litigation involving a giant corporation that was being forced into reorganization by its creditors. Lawsuits had been filed by several banking groups who were growing anxious about the financial troubles of the Virginia-Carolina Chemical Company and its principal subsidary, Southern Cotton Oil Company. With combined assets of nearly $135 million (think many billions today), the firms' troubles were sending ripples through the nation's financial sector. One aggressive creditor, Steel Cities Chemical Company, had started the litigation by filing suit in New Jersey Federal District Court and others joined in.

Simplifying a complex problem, World War I had ended too soon for the Virginia-Carolina Chemical Company. The company had acquired large inventories at war-inflated prices, and when the war came to an end their profit margins shriveled, leaving the company with many unsold goods and angry creditors. Manufacturing and selling everything from chemical, paints, and cottonseed oil to drugs, lard, and soap, this corporate behemoth had hundreds of creditors, all in panic mode. It was a towering challenge for any lawyer—and one capable of generating enormous fees. Many bankers and creditors assumed that the attorney appointed receiver would be from a large Newark or New York City law firm. What they hadn't considered was the bond between politicians.

Little more than four months after the election, Runyon's campaign manager, Arthur Vanderbilt, was appointed receiver of the Virginia-Carolina Chemical Company. The appointment of a thirty-four-year-old solo practitioner caught many people by surprise. Greatly exceeding the opportunity presented by the Roseville Bank collections, it was the largest industrial receivership in American history up to that time. This was the collection case of a lifetime and a challenge filled with legal chores that would have consumed several attorneys. The brash young lawyer from Roseville threw himself into the task, appreciating not only the effort required and the potential fees, but also that the established Newark law firms would be scrutinizing his every move.

The Virginia-Carolina Chemical Company was a far-flung financial empire with operations throughout the Midwest, as well as in Mexico and

Germany. Following World War I, its sales plummeted, and bankers and suppliers were banging down the door. Desperate, and with prodding from the court, the board of directors empowered its president and Vanderbilt to reorganize the company to avoid a forced sale of its assets. Raising money through issuing preferred shares of stock, which are much like a secured loan, selectively selling and spinning off less profitable holdings, and pursuing debts owed by customers who were withholding payment while hoping for the company's failure, Vanderbilt was able to salvage the core assets.

Little more than two years after Vanderbilt's appointment as corporate receiver, the reorganization of Virginia-Carolina was complete and control of the company returned to its board of directors, with a fund of working capital of nearly $19 million. Vanderbilt would eventually receive fees totaling $175,000 (about $2.5 million today), making him the envy of every Newark lawyer of his generation. It isn't often that legal fees in private matters become news, but these fees did, resulting in a scolding editorial by the *Newark Evening News*, which was generally supportive of Vanderbilt.[18]

Fees from the Virginia-Carolina Chemical Company receivership were a life-changing event. Arthur Vanderbilt was now acknowledged as one of the premier attorneys in New Jersey. As he noted years later, "Up to that time I had been a rising young lawyer, but from that time on I was something else; I was a so-and-so who was trying to steal the business of the older firms. I had broken in on the monopoly."[19]

In time, the money earned from this one receivership together with other fees generated through politics would make many things possible in Vanderbilt's life. There would be a sprawling manor house sitting on two acres of rolling shaded grounds in Short Hills, a large Georgian Colonial retreat on Casco Bay in Maine, plus family trips to expensive resorts. Legal fees earned as a result of his sharp elbows in the political realm would make him a prince in the legal community—admired by some, hated by others. More important, such fees created opportunities for Roseville's prodigy to be more than a warrior; now he had the luxury to be a crusader for the progressive agenda. First stop on his crusade: Paterson, New Jersey.

CHAPTER 4

A Force in Four Worlds

John Butterworth and Roger Baldwin may have had names reminiscent of Colonial era Puritans, but they weren't pious pilgrims. Butterworth was a union activist, a relentless, tough, in-your-face agitator, ready to wage war for the rights of workers. He was the leader of the Associated Silk Workers Union and viewed the owners of Paterson's silk mills as the enemy. Baldwin had served time in federal prison for his very public resistance to the military draft during World War I and was a founder of the American Civil Liberties Union (ACLU). Labeled a Communist by many for his public support of Russia, which he termed "a great laboratory of social experimentation of incalculable value to the development of the world,"[1] Baldwin was a notorious rabble-rouser. But the factory owners of New Jersey's Silk City wanted no part of "social experimentation."

Paterson, one of several manufacturing centers originally conceived by Alexander Hamilton, had grown into an industrial powerhouse. It produced garments sold around the world and the nation, but Paterson was a far cry from a worker's paradise; exploitation of employees was the norm. Emboldened by their financial success and a perverse concept of American freedom as the liberty to get away with anything, the city's predatory mill owners corrupted the newspapers, the legislature, and the courts to ensure their dominance.

Still, the workers refused to suffer in silence, and Paterson became a cauldron of labor unrest. The mill owners would have the last say, though. As New Jersey historian Thomas Fleming notes, "By discouraging naturalization and threatening to fire people, Paterson's bosses even managed to prevent most of the workers from voting." For decades, there had been one failed strike after another—put down by the courts and police—making the relationship between mill workers and factory owners "a virtual state of war." As aptly characterized by Fleming, at the turn of the century, "Paterson was the headquarters of American anarchism."[2]

In the fall of 1924, labor war was being waged again. John Butterworth was the leader of eight thousand workers of Paterson's silk mills in their battle against a four-loom production system being planned by manufacturers. It essentially called for fewer workers, more production, harder work, less pay; hundreds of jobs were at stake. The strike had been going on since August 1, and by late September Butterworth was growing weary. His plans for staging mass street demonstrations—seeking the attention not only of employers but also the nation—had been stymied by a series of court-ordered injunctions banning picketing and forbidding strikers from assembling publicly in crowds. With strikers lacking the ability to gather on the streets as pickets, many people forgot there was a strike. By October, fifteen separate injunctions had stifled any chance of gaining the public's sympathy for the workers' plight.

Making matters worse, in the last week of September the city's chief of police informed Butterworth that daily meetings at the union's hall must cease. The chief was enraged by reports that some of the strikers had been publicly criticizing the judges and police for shutting down their picket lines. At his wit's end, Butterworth turned to Roger Baldwin and the ACLU for help.

Baldwin's strategy was to organize a free speech demonstration. The hope was that the demonstrators would be arrested, forcing the New Jersey courts to grapple with their rights under the U.S. Constitution. Led by two young women carrying the American flag, thirty people marching in pairs proceeded from the union's headquarters to City Hall Plaza—a distance of a block and a half. As reported in the court proceedings, "They were followed by an increasing number of onlookers," eventually totaling fifteen hundred to two thousand. "There were hurrahs and acclamations from among the crowd about the plaza, on the approach of the flag and the procession."[3] Some forty policemen were at the plaza to greet them, intent on dispersing the crowd.

With everyone in place, Butterworth began to read the Bill of Rights, which guarantees the freedoms of speech and assembly. He was arrested before he could finish. Efforts to scatter the crowd were met with resistance and several people were injured, but none were police officers. Butterworth and Baldwin, along with several strikers, were indicted for unlawful assembly. The indictment charged Butterworth and Baldwin with planning "unlawfully, routously [sic], riotously, and tumultuously . . . to disturb the public peace and to commit assault and battery upon the police officers . . . and to . . . destroy and wreck the city hall,"[4] all under a state statute dating back to 1796 that prohibited unlawful assembly.

With the court relying upon "printed posters openly distributed" that "laid out a program in defiance of the constituted authorities . . . intended in a spectacular fashion, to emphasize a disapproval of the action of the police," all the defendants were convicted at a bench trial before Judge Delaney in Passaic County. An appeal to the state Supreme Court brought by an ACLU lawyer, the (in)famous Samuel Untermyer—thought to be every bit the "Bolshevik" Baldwin was—had failed. In sustaining the trial court's verdict, Justice Charles Black found, "The situation created by the defendants presented an analogy to a fire with obvious danger of a conflagration if not checked, and this tendency the principal defendants well knew."[5]

Appeal to the state's highest court, the E & A, was a given, but *who* would bring it was not. As a member of the ACLU committee of lawyers, Felix Frankfurter wanted to take a more practical approach; he demanded that Untermyer be removed from the case because he was "indulging in the dramatic love of a fight"[6] with no hope of success.

Frankfurter believed that the ACLU, coming off its loss in the Scopes "monkey" trial, needed a victory. The appeal "touched off a bitter fight" within the ACLU, and when it was over, Arthur Vanderbilt's offer of his services on a pro bono basis was accepted by Baldwin's organization.[7] The teetotaling Methodist Republican from Roseville was eager to jump into the fray, championing the cause of the likes of Butterworth and Baldwin; for good measure, he was joined by the dean of NYU's law school, Frank Sommer, and retired Judge Harry Osborn on the brief. The three of them loved winning even more than fighting the good fight.

Vanderbilt gave the task all his energy. Mastery of the facts surrounding the meeting where the arrests were made was the key. He needed to convince the court that, even accepting the sworn testimony of Paterson's police officers as true, it didn't support their overblown fears of violence. He began with humor.

Relating the details of the union's procession to City Hall Plaza, Vanderbilt said it was led by "two beautiful girls carrying American flags."[8] He was interrupted by one of the justices asking, "Mr. Vanderbilt, I have read the record, and I see no evidence to support your statement that these girls were beautiful." Vanderbilt replied with faux indignation, "Surely your honor will take judicial notice of the fact that any girl carrying the American flag is *ipso facto* beautiful."[9] The justice replied, "Quite so, quite so." In ruling unanimously to reverse Judge Delaney, the high court said the appeal " necessarily depends upon the object and character of the meeting, and whether or not the overt acts . . . are of such a nature as to inspire a well-grounded fear of . . . danger to life and property." In answering its own question the court concluded, "We find an utter absence of any such proof."[10]

Victory for the ACLU and the silk workers made national news, and Vanderbilt's reputation was expanding far beyond the Garden State. Can it be said that his pursuit of the ACLU as a client on such a high-profile case was a headline-seeking stunt? Yes, but notice who he was joined by: a law school dean and a distinguished retired judge. It was about more than grandstanding for the three of them; they were committed to protecting citizens' rights of protest, regardless of how unpopular those citizens' views were. What's more, Vanderbilt gave the appeal, and the cause of free speech, his full attention. History demonstrates that the American people praise the First Amendment in the abstract, but become angry, sometimes violently so, when they don't like what's being said. As his career evolved, Butterworth and Baldwin's appeal was only one of several instances where Vanderbilt took on a conspicuous cause knowing it would annoy defenders of the status quo. A publicity hound or not, "Art Van" was living the Wesleyan creed and upholding the ideals of his mentor, Frank Sommer.

Vanderbilt's representation of the ACLU was the second in a string of twenty-five appeals he argued before the E & A from 1928 to 1932. He won them all. The appeals involved everything from shareholders seeking to prevent a corporate merger to the rights of a second mortgagee to insurance proceeds, the validity of a gift challenged by heirs of an estate, a dispute between a landlord and tenant, termination of a municipal employee, and a husband seeking divorce based upon the wife's adultery. It's the uncommon advocate willing to take on such a range of issues.

Not surprisingly, half of the appeals were referred by other lawyers; that was because of Vanderbilt's reputation for preparation and dedication to his client's interests. His success in the courts brought clients from all over the country. Among corporations from across the nation, particularly insurance companies doing business in the New York metropolitan region, Arthur

Vanderbilt was gaining a reputation for excellence in America's legal community.[11] By the time he was forty, many lawyers considered him the New Jersey's preeminent appellate advocate.

As Vanderbilt's reputation increased, his workload—and income—grew considerably, requiring a flock of attorneys to assist him. The substantial fees he was generating, together with the allure of working with such an outsized law practice and on occasion dealing with novel issues and notorious clients, enabled him to hire some of the best young talent in the greater New York region. And he had to look no further than his classes at NYU, where twice a week he interacted with young minds eager to learn from him.

As noted by one longtime colleague, "Vanderbilt had a remarkable faculty for attracting and associating with him and holding a group of competent and hardworking young lawyers, which he was able to keep replenishing and complementing from the cream of his law school students. That arrangement afforded him all that might be gained from a partnership without entailing any limitation over his complete freedom."[12] Not long after the ACLU appeal, he hired a Harvard Law School graduate, Nathan Jacobs, who proved crucial to Vanderbilt's lifelong ambitions. Some observers speculate that it was Jacobs's professor at Harvard, Felix Frankfurter, who may have steered Jacobs to Vanderbilt.

Still, Vanderbilt's singleness of purpose ensured there would never be partners in his law practice. By 1920, despite the fact that he employed as many as seventeen younger lawyers as associates and an equal number as law clerks to assist him, the name on the door of his law firm's offices in the National and Essex Building remained: Arthur T. Vanderbilt: Counsellor at Law.[13] And as any sole proprietor knows—regardless of the business—when you're the owner, troubles float upstream.

Administering the office and managing staff, payroll, and billings—the lifeblood of a law firm—were only part of his responsibilities. Disappointed clients always demand to speak with the person whose name is on the checks they write. What's more, whether it's a legal brief in need of rethinking, an opinion letter to be revised, or a client to be soothed, an associate won't suffice, the person whose name is on the door must step up.

Young associate lawyers might share in the challenge, excitement, and fees but not in the renown; that was Vanderbilt's alone. Despite his admiration for Benjamin Franklin's "Thirteen Virtues," Arthur Vanderbilt never fully embraced the virtue of humility; as we shall see, patience with allies and compromise with adversaries were other virtues he never fully grasped.

At the end of 1935, he had his staff prepare a list of clients he had represented during the preceding five years.[14] It's a stunning document. Now tucked away in the archives of Wesleyan University, the list runs on for nearly fifty pink, crinkly carbon-paper pages. The single-spaced list is organized into multiple categories ranging from insurance companies, banks, and savings and loans to professional associations, municipal governments, and manufacturing enterprises. Vanderbilt had an astonishingly wide-ranging law practice that handled everything from debt collection, will contests, contract disputes, and foreclosures to securities fraud, commercial real estate litigation, corporate liquidations, and defense of insurance claims. Insurance law was where Vanderbilt shone.

Insurance executives are curious, restless, and often pugnacious clients, ever willing to probe the limits of their exposure, or, more precisely, their obligation to pay claims made against their policies. Vanderbilt was their kind of guy, and representation of insurance companies quickly became the mainstay of his law practice. His insurance client list covers nearly every letter in the alphabet (none for D, L, or Z) and totals more than 175 firms.[15] By way of illustration, his clients included regional insurance companies based in the northeastern cities of Providence, Pittsburgh, Buffalo, and Boston; the midwestern cities of Columbus, Indianapolis, Milwaukee, and Detroit; the western cities of St. Louis, Seattle, Los Angeles, and Phoenix; and the southern cities of New Orleans, Nashville, Richmond, and Baltimore.

Vanderbilt's office likewise represented national insurance carriers with offices in New York, Chicago, Hartford, Philadelphia, and his hometown of Newark. And if that weren't enough to cause the leading law firms in Newark to covet his client base, there were insurance accounts from London, Liverpool, Edinburgh, Holland, Tokyo, and Paris, as well as Montreal and Toronto. The ability of a solo practitioner (that is, a law firm in which there is a single owner), albeit with many associates, to attract national and international clientele in the insurance field engendered more than envy among his colleagues.

One telling moment of apparent jealousy and resentment toward Vanderbilt came in 1937, the same year he was elected president of the nation's bar association. In that year, Robert H. McCarter, a former N.J. attorney general whose law firm was based in Newark, published reflections on his career, *Memories of a Half Century at the New Jersey Bar*.[16] The book profiles nearly forty judges and lawyers, with nary a word on Vanderbilt. His name can't even be found in the index, despite the fact that he was Newark's number-one insurance attorney, or maybe because he was Newark's number-one insurance attorney, as well as being president of the American Bar Association (ABA). It's unlikely that Vanderbilt noticed McCarter's slight; he was too busy lawyering.

Insurance clients meant appeal work, and Vanderbilt loved oral arguments. Between 1927 and 1937, Vanderbilt argued more cases in the state and federal courts than any other New Jersey lawyer with the single exception of Newark attorney Merritt Lane. Some observers believe Merritt Lane was Arthur Vanderbilt's equal as an appellate advocate, and going by their records, it's likely he was. The two stand alone as the leading attorneys of their generation in New Jersey. Interestingly, Lane shares a solitary sentence with another lawyer in McCarter's book. Like Vanderbilt, Lane maintained a solo practice assisted by competent young associates, and he fared well against the leading law firms of the state on any legal issue.

Unlike Vanderbilt, the law consumed Lane's waking hours, and he eventually became a chancery judge; in contrast, Vanderbilt's professional life had several other facets, and he excelled in all of them. In addition to maintaining a far-flung law practice, he continued to find time for the second career that had predated his meteoric rise as a lawyer, one more like play than work to him, namely teaching at NYU Law School. Initially his hiring by NYU had made it possible for him to marry Florence, but he continued as a member of the faculty long past the time when a professor's salary meant anything to him financially. NYU's law school offered him the opportunity not only to mold young minds and pick over prospective associates for his law practice but also to be part of something larger than himself.

New York University has long played a special role in the history of legal education in America. Although Harvard boasts of having established America's "first" law school in 1817, its law school had a long and slow development. Ten years after its founding, "in 1827, the struggling young law school was down to only one faculty member and one student."[17] Things never really got going until more than fifty years after its founding when Dean Christopher Columbus Langdell arrived in 1870. The "first modern law school, with a comprehensive curriculum, a faculty of experts in different fields, and a three-year program" had been established thirty-five years earlier at NYU by acclaimed attorney Benjamin F. Butler, former U.S. attorney general for President Andrew Jackson. It was only natural that New York City would be home to the first modern law school. Its thriving commercial sector needed legal talent to counsel business people, handle litigation, and coordinate the transactions of a booming economy, and the NYU School of Law was there to play a key role in the city's advances.

Vanderbilt not only hoped to follow in the footsteps of his hero, Frank Sommer; he also realized that one of the best ways to learn is through teaching, which requires not just preparation for class and the questions of students but provides the opportunity to reflect on issues and relate them to your daily experiences. Echoing the perspective of many serious educators, he once said, "You can never be sure you know a subject until you can teach it, and in those early days I learned to teach a good many subjects. It was there that my own legal education really commenced."[18]

For thirty-four years Vanderbilt traveled two evenings a week to New York City to teach. With his reputation growing yearly, the students came to value the way he brought the breadth of his experience into the classroom. "To the discussion of cases and law, he added the experiences and understanding gained from his own work, often illustrating a point with a case then pending or just decided."[19] His practical insights as a litigator who could take a set of facts and discuss them, from the filing of the lawsuit to trial and appeal, placed him in favorable contrast to many others on the faculty.

To the superstar lawyer, with a stable of prestigious clients and money in his pocket, many of his fellow professors appeared shallow, staid, and overly bookish. As noted by Vanderbilt's grandson in his biography, *Order in the Courts*, "Vanderbilt had little respect for those professors who were continually quoting cases in conversation and dubbed them *the versus lawyers*—A vs. B, C vs. D *ad nauseam*."[20] During one semester or another, Vanderbilt taught almost every subject in the law school curriculum, conducting classes on everything from contracts, corporations, equity, and insurance to civil procedure, taxation, trusts, wills, and, a particular favorite of his administrative law.

Others might have viewed trekking repeatedly from Newark to Manhattan as drudgery, but for Vanderbilt it was a respite. Twice a week he was free from the tensions of his law practice. He could educate, entertain, and regale his students with experiences in the courtroom and politics. As he later reminisced, "Moreover, on those infrequent but unhappy occasions when I found the juries here in New Jersey stupid or the judges a bit opaque, it was great relief to be able to cross the River and cast my pearls before bright young minds that could appreciate them."[21]

Another audience that appreciated Vanderbilt's progressive approach to the law was the national organized bar and those political leaders who understood the need for an independent judiciary capable of addressing the needs of a dynamic America. Here, Vanderbilt was at a distinct advantage, being both legal scholar and a politician moving between the two worlds effortlessly. He had instant credibility with both circles. What matters is that somehow, despite trial and appellate work and serving as a law professor, he had time left to undertake a third career: leadership of his profession at both state and national levels.

From his early association with Frank Sommer he was identified with the need for law reform. In 1930, the New Jersey State Bar Association created a committee, called the Judicial Council, to recommend measures for the improvement of judicial administration in New Jersey. The state bar association president appointed Vanderbilt to the committee, and he was immediately chosen as chairman, serving in that position for two five-year terms. Nonetheless, as one legal historian notes, in New Jersey, councils and commissions to study constitutional reform were generally "a dilatory device: problems would be studied and restudied until the winds of change hopefully subsided."[22] Eventually, Vanderbilt understood that.

Throughout the 1930s, Vanderbilt was "working the chairs," advancing each year in the leadership of both the American Bar Association and the New Jersey State Bar Association. It was at his instigation and through his leadership that the ABA had created its Insurance Section, which promptly became the single largest section of like-minded lawyers in the nation. The Insurance Section gave him a base of supporters—and referrals—who respected his prowess as a litigator, which in part explains those pink carbon pages in Wesleyan's archives. He was scheduled to be elected state bar president in 1937 but declined it to seek the presidency of the ABA.

During his one-year term as ABA president—when commercial aviation was still in its infancy—Arthur Vanderbilt flew more than seventy-two thousand miles. He attended meetings and made speeches urging the simplification and modernization of the U.S. court systems. His wife, Floss, accompanied him on every one of those trips. Their relationship was the one constant in Arthur's frantic existence; at the end of the day, he had to be with Floss, and equally important, she had to be at his side when he awoke in the morning.

During the first six years of their marriage, they had five children—Jean, Betty, and Lois, together with twin sons Bob and Bill; William was named for Judge William Runyon. Within months of receiving the legal fees earned from the reorganization of the Virginia-Carolina Chemical Company, Arthur and Floss bought an elegant new home for their growing family. They had outgrown their house in East Orange, and with Arthur's law practice prospering and his prominence in county and state politics increasing, they needed home to match his growing stature. They decided on an elegant mansion: an eighteen-room English Tudor sitting on two acres of rolling tree-shaded grounds in Short Hills, in suburban Essex County. Within a short time, Floss had designed and supervised the home's landscaping, creating such a beautiful property that it was featured in national magazine photo spreads.[23]

When he wasn't at a bar function or teaching at NYU, Arthur's evenings were spent at home. Being home didn't always equate to relaxation, however. Frequently, after dinner with his family and his secretary, Arthur would retire to his large second-floor study, where he would dictate legal work to his secretary for two or three hours, after which the Vanderbilts' caretaker drove her home. Other evenings he might meet with associates of his law firm to discuss pending cases, or with people from Clean Government to strategize politics. For Arthur, a quiet evening was reading, researching, and writing in his study while sipping his personal concoction of root beer and buttermilk, wearing his black Wesleyan varsity sweater.[24] One area of research he was continually drawn to was the career of the eighteenth-century British jurist Lord Mansfield, and his hope was to write a biography of his hero. On Arthur and Floss's several trips to England, they purchased dozens of books on seventeenth- and eighteenth-century English history to bring home.[25]

Books were everywhere throughout the Vanderbilt home. They lined the front hall, the living room, and the upstairs study; there were bookcases in all the bedrooms and in the solarium, with even more books in the storage rooms on the third floor, into the recreation room, and to the room above the garage. There were books on everything from history, philosophy, and political science to biographies, essays, novels, poetry, and art. If Vanderbilt had a hobby, it was collecting books. He believed that a broad range of literature was helpful for attorneys to maintain a clear-headed perspective on society and were a useful source of conversation for the many new acquaintances and friends he made in his travels.[26]

During his term with the ABA, Vanderbilt developed friendships and supporters in every important city of the United States, making him a national figure, with many people viewing him as someone worthy of appointment to the U.S. Supreme Court. Following the end of his term as ABA president, Vanderbilt was elected president of the American Judicature Society, which gave him a platform from which to continue speaking on the need for judicial reform.

His service as president of the ABA gained him the attention of U.S. Attorney General Homer Cummings. In 1938, Cummings appointed Vanderbilt chairman of a committee of lawyers to confer with a panel of senior federal judges appointed by Chief Justice Hughes of the U.S. Supreme Court; the committee recommended the creation of an Administrative Office of the United States Courts, a subject close to Vanderbilt's heart. Not long after the committee issued its report, Congress adopted its proposal. Contemporary legal scholars such as Judge John Parker termed the U.S. Administrative Office of the Courts "the most important piece of legislation affecting the judiciary since the Judiciary Act of 1789."[27] The only thing sweeter to Vanderbilt would have been to achieve that type of reform in New Jersey.

Soon after the Cummings appointment, in 1939, a new U.S. attorney general, Frank Murphy, asked Vanderbilt to serve on the Advisory Committee on Administrative Procedures chaired by Dean Acheson. The committee's charge was to establish procedures for the sprawling federal agencies that had been created under the New Deal. These agencies were exercising extraordinary new powers, and not necessarily in a uniform or predictable manner. Many of President Franklin Roosevelt's agencies served as rule maker, investigator, prosecutor, and judge, each crafting its own rules and procedures. It was a recipe for confusion. Administrative law was an area of expertise for Vanderbilt, who had been teaching the course at NYU School of Law for years. His work with the Advisory Committee took years to get Congress's attention, but the committee's recommendations were finally adopted in 1946.

Not long after Vanderbilt's work on administrative law was finished, U.S. Chief Justice Hughes again appointed him chairman of an advisory committee to draft Rules of Criminal Procedure for adoption by the U.S. Supreme Court. After several years of work and many drafts, the committee's report was submitted to the Supreme Court. On March 21, 1946, Congress promulgated the rules proposed by Vanderbilt's committee. Judge Parker observed, "They were quickly recognized as models of simplicity and flexibility."[28] Less than a week after the Federal Rules of Criminal Procedure became effective, Secretary of War Robert P. Patterson selected Vanderbilt to chair the War Department's Committee on Military Justice; the army's courts-martial system was in serious need of reform. The recommendations of Vanderbilt's committee served as the basis for legislation that eventually became the Uniform Code of Military Justice in 1950.

When considering Vanderbilt's direct roles in such diverse fields of law it is easy to understand the stories attached to his name as a possible candidate for appointment to the U.S. Supreme Court. He was a leading national lawyer and political leader of the Republican Party in New Jersey, and there was intense speculation that had his candidate, Thomas Dewey, been elected president in 1944 or 1948, Vanderbilt would have been named to the U.S. Supreme Court.

All the time that Vanderbilt was practicing law, teaching at NYU, and working on national reforms to the law, he never lost sight of his home state, continuing to serve on New Jersey's Judicial Council. Year after year, the council made draft proposals, and through the efforts of people of like mind, legislation—in substantial part written by Vanderbilt—was introduced calling for constitutional reform. Several times legislation supported by reformers was passed in the assembly, only to die a silent death in the state senate. Once a reform measure was approved by the senate, only to be defeated in the assembly.

Vanderbilt's frustration was heightened by the knowledge that Jersey City mayor Frank Hague played the crucial role in each defeat in mustering the needed votes to quash the reform proposals. Vanderbilt knew that the roadblock to reform was in Jersey City. Yet he hadn't a clue how to get around Hague.

Bridging the gap separating the worlds of Arthur Vanderbilt and Frank Hague required more than traveling the six miles between Newark and Jersey City. The clash between the mind-sets of these titans and their cities was a microcosm of the conflicts occurring in urban America. The immigrant invasion that accompanied the industrialization of New Jersey had disrupted what had been a fairly homogenous society dominated by WASP values.

With the advent of large-scale production of goods in factories, between 1870 and 1920 America's cities became a magnet for immigrants from Europe.

The languages, religions, and customs of the immigrants, combined with their unprecedented numbers, created tensions no one saw coming. The conflicts between the yearnings of the immigrants and the conservative ideals of the WASPs spawned two very different systems of political ethics.

Essex County's Republicans—progressives and old guard alike—stood for long-held WASP political notions that government was best organized in accordance with the Anglo-Saxon traditions of the law and the principles of the U.S. Constitution. Hudson County's Democrats represented the reply to the WASP political ethic. The working classes of Europe had survived for centuries by being subservient to hierarchy. Feudalism doesn't encourage free thinkers; the newly arrived immigrants put more faith in the ward heelers who registered them to vote and helped them find their way in a new land than in abstract principals of American justice. As the noted historian Richard Hofstadter observes, "It was chiefly upon this system of values that the political life of the immigrant, the boss, and the urban machine was based."[29]

Refusal of the WASPs to work toward finding common ground with the newcomers played out in election battles throughout much of the twentieth century in both New Jersey and the rest of the United States. And when we view Arthur Vanderbilt's role in these battles an irony bubbles up. This was the person who taught factory workers in night school; many of his students were immigrants and probably Roman Catholics, few of whom shared his view of the world. Despite his family's American roots going back two centuries, and his Methodist upbringing, Wesleyan education, and progressive attitudes toward the law, Vanderbilt couldn't bring himself to reach out one to one and travel six miles to meet with Frank Hague. The Ivy League lawyer capable of strategizing the thorniest legal or political problem didn't have the capacity to empathize with a sixth-grade dropout. There's no hint that Vanderbilt ever tried to see the world as Hague did in Hudson County, a county where hypocritical, power-greedy, prejudiced WASPs had rewritten the laws in their effort to subjugate the Irish Catholics. Vanderbilt even boasted that he and the mayor had never met: "I learned early in politics that it was important not to know certain people as it was to know certain others."[30]

Instead of making use of his enormous talents in an effort to try to understand Hague and possibly placate him, Vanderbilt scorned him and engaged in name calling, referring to him as the "two-bit Hitler on the Hudson." Yet Vanderbilt's refusal to seek some sort of accommodation with the single most powerful person in New Jersey meant the perpetual delay of his hoped-for reform of New Jersey's court system.

Immersed in the reality of this conflict of political cultures, Arthur Vanderbilt was slowly coming to a realization. He could not walk away from his "fourth career." His hopes for reforming New Jersey's antiquated constitution and creating a professional and autonomous judiciary could only be realized by becoming even more deeply involved in politics. He had no choice but to remain active in the political turmoil of Essex County, the state's largest. If he was to have a base of power from which to pursue his goals, he couldn't abandon the Essex County Republican League. What's more, he had to gain complete control of his base.

From the time he was thirty Vanderbilt had been waging an insurgency in Essex County Republican politics: selecting progressive candidates to oppose the regular Republicans, raising the money, and creating the campaign message. Although he had filled a majority of the freeholder board seats with his League candidates, the regular Republicans weren't going away. Between 1922 and 1935, the face of the old guard with whom Vanderbilt clashed was County Republican boss Jesse Salmon. He was as old guard as they came.

Stocky, well-dressed, sporting expensive Panama hats and chomping on Cuban cigars, Salmon reveled in his role as party chairman and resented the prissy piss-ant law school professor trying to make a name for himself in politics at Salmon's expense. Like many political bosses of urban America, Jesse Salmon viewed the Eighteenth Amendment and Prohibition on the sale of alcoholic beverages as a gift from "those beautiful, ignorant bastards"[31] in Washington.

It was widely believed that Salmon was involved in bootlegging operations and that he demanded a tariff on every truckload of whiskey transported through Essex County. He used these illegal profits to support his Republican organization.[32] Members of the Anti-Saloon League in Essex County were allied with the Republican League and in the fall of 1923 they filed a petition with county government demanding an investigation of the regular Republicans campaign finances.

Salmon followed the wisdom of then-president Calvin Coolidge: "I have never been hurt by anything I didn't say." And he wasn't talking. Not long after the ruckus over the source of his money had begun, Salmon left town for a couple of months. When he returned his standard reply on campaign finances whenever the issue was raised was to shrug off the entire issue as "the quintessence of political asininity."[33] But that didn't stop Arthur Vanderbilt from jabbing away at Salmon and all his campaign money from unidentified sources. Year after year, Vanderbilt's progressive movement battled with Salmon and the regular Republicans for control of the Essex County Freeholder Board. Throughout most of the 1920s—despite the fact that every primary election was hotly contested—the Republican League's philosophy of managing government professionally prevailed, and that meant there were fewer patronage jobs for Salmon to dole out. But the Great Depression changed things.

In 1931, in the depths of the Great Depression, a large portion of Essex County's employees resented the salary cuts that had been forced by the need for austerity. They abandoned Vanderbilt's League Republicans and switching their allegiance to Salmon's organization, which was flush with cash. The result was victory for Salmon's candidates in the Republican primary, but it didn't benefit him as all three of his freeholder candidates lost to Democrats for the first time since 1918. The following year, 1932, the League's candidates for county freeholder and Republican county committee, hoping to unseat Salmon as party chairman, were clobbered. The same year, 1932, Salmon went for Vanderbilt's throat, moving to unseat him as county counsel, but was unsuccessful.

In 1933, the League couldn't muster a slate, raising fears that the progressive movement in Essex County was withering. Looking back on the experience in comments to a friend, Vanderbilt remarked, "I for one was so discouraged by the seeming apathy of the public as to whether they had decent government or not . . . so depressed by the chronic cynicism . . . that I was almost convinced that it would be folly to attempt another fight against entrenched political corruption in our party."[34] Darkening his mood further, and distracting him from politics, were serious financial problems stemming from an earlier set of business ventures.

Widely acknowledged as one of the leading advocates of Newark's insurance companies, the forty-year-old Vanderbilt had wanted to set up a company of his own. The period from conception to reality wasn't a year. Working with a group of local insurance experts, in 1928 he founded the Public Fire Insurance Company of Newark. The Roaring Twenties were heady times for many people, and Vanderbilt and his fellow investors—some of the most prosperous and best-connected businessmen in the state—could see no end to the riches awaiting them.

In no time, Public Fire Insurance was licensed in thirty-six states, and the number of agents, cash reserves, and stock value were all soaring: Vanderbilt had even created a second insurance business, the Public Indemnity Company. But, alas, the golden boy of Newark's legal community was about to get his comeuppance. "Black Tuesday," October 29, 1929, began the unraveling of many successful businesses.

Although the two companies initially continued to prosper, they each fell victim to increased competition for a shrinking number of business clients. Within five years both companies were forced to shut their doors, leaving Vanderbilt with massive personal debt. In 1933, in order to avoid personal bankruptcy, he was forced to borrow $600,000 (more than $6 million in today's money), from the National State Bank of Newark, which he agreed to repay over a ten-year period.[35]

His financial chaos under control, Arthur Vanderbilt applied all his energy to the things he knew best, law and politics. His client base as strong and diverse as ever, and with referrals from other lawyers unabated, his law practice still required a large number of associates. He found that lawyering could be just as profitable in bad times as in good. He continued handling high-profile, lucrative trials and appeals. Turning his attention to politics—following the bitter humiliation in 1932 and the no-show in 1933—Vanderbilt and his progressive allies let the greater Newark community know they had merely taken a breather and were in the fight to stay.

With help from Boss Salmon putting his foot in his mouth by publicly admitting in December 1933 that he was financing his operation with money from bootleggers, the Clean Government slate, no longer the Republican League, swept to victory in the 1934 primary election. A candidate recruited by Vanderbilt to lead his slate was a Presbyterian minister, Lester Clee, the dynamic pastor of Newark's Second Presbyterian Church. Some believe Clee's large congregation, along with support from the Anti-Saloon League, were decisive to the victory.

Yet Salmon wasn't going away quietly. In November he and his cronies supported the Democratic slate. Denouncing Vanderbilt as the "lily white statesman," as "the political renegade," and as "the million dollar prize receiver," he charged Vanderbilt with being up to his eyeballs in conflicts of interest and as someone with a "lust for power."[36] It was a nasty, hard-fought campaign but the entire Clean Government slate of candidates sailed to victory.

Salmon's last hurrah came the following May in the 1935 Republican primary. Vanderbilt's group nominated candidates, not only for freeholder but for every position on the ballot, including the Republican County Committee posts, the local district representatives who select the party's chairman. This required an extraordinary hands-on effort, with numerous foot soldiers—one that it's hard to imagine Vanderbilt pursuing when he started out in county politics fifteen years earlier. This was the lawyer who sat in his office writing press releases and letters to the editors of favorable newspapers, not a street fighter willing to wage a door-to-door campaign, yet that's what total control of the county committee required and he made it happen.

When the full slate of Clean Government people won, Jesse Salmon announced his retirement from politics. Vanderbilt's handpicked candidate, Stanley Nauright, was named to replace Salmon. At the time of Salmon's death in 1938, it was learned that he had left an estate of about $400,000, of which $300,000 was in cash (more than $6 million today). Jesse Salmon had rewarded himself well.[37]

Vanderbilt had achieved unchallenged control of the Essex County Republican organization and county government. He was accorded the respect and admiration shown a benevolent dictator, or, more precisely, an enlightened monarch. Magnifying his image further was a book published in 1938 recounting the reform era in Essex County written by Thomas H. Reed, a political science professor from the University of California at Berkeley.

Reed was an authentic progressive in the tradition of Woodrow Wilson. His focus was the reform of municipal government, and he sought to separate politics from public administration, treating the management of local government as a scientific discipline. His book, *Twenty Years of Government in Essex County*, was his eleventh, and it burnished Vanderbilt's aura as the fair-haired do-gooder, slugging it out with the corrupt Boss Salmon, working tirelessly to bring honesty, ethics, and efficient government to the people of Essex County.

Gushing with praise for the Republican leader, Reed began "The Advent of Reform," chapter 4 of his book, by stating:

> While the Republican Old Guard had been blithely enjoying the fruits of
> its power . . . a new force had arisen in Essex County politics—the Essex
> County Republican League. . . . Its first president and most active spirit

was a thirty-year-old Newark lawyer who sported a Phi Beta Kappa key, degrees from Wesleyan (A.B.) and Columbia (LL.B.) and crossed over to New York twice a week to teach law at New York University. There is, of course, nothing unique in a young lawyer taking a flier in local politics on the reform side. Arthur T. Vanderbilt's entrance into politics as a reformer, however, was significant because it was the beginning of nearly twenty years of consistent and successful effort. It is heartening to observe that neither culture, brains, nor honesty proved in his case an insuperable handicap to political success.[38]

Curiously, Reed thought so much of Vanderbilt that he permitted him to review and edit his manuscript prior to publication. That's hardly the detachment one might expect from a professor at a major university. Yet Vanderbilt's personal records stored at Wesleyan reveal that he collaborated in the writing of the story of the reform movement of which he was the leader. There are some who think he encouraged the writing of this history by providing the author with a financial incentive. While that can never be confirmed, the history of progressivism in Essex County wasn't the only time Vanderbilt worked closely with a college professor in the writing of a treatise on local government. Only that other book would be a ruthless political assassination posing as a serious biography.

For now, what matters to our story is that Arthur Vanderbilt was New Jersey's leading Republican. Little more than twenty years after graduating from Columbia Law School, Roseville's prodigy had become a powerhouse in politics and the law. In both Essex County and New Jersey he was a force to be reckoned with. Nonetheless, seven decades of hindsight reveal that Arthur Vanderbilt was fortunate to have begun his career in Newark. Had fate located him in Jersey City—a place sorely in need of reform—and had he tried to wage an insurrection in Hudson County, Frank Hague would have squashed him like a bug. Compared to Hague's fiefdom, politics in Essex County was quaint.

CHAPTER 5

Up from the Horseshoe

Hague. Hague, who grew up in poverty so severe that children in his neighborhood became petty thieves to help their families survive, yet who while serving as mayor amassed a fortune through grand theft, the true scale of which will never be known. Hague, who learned early how to use his fists and made them part of his political arsenal, never flinching at punching a man in the face when things weren't going his way. Hague, who hated WASPs intensely and allied himself with only one—someone who was little more than his puppet. Hague, who used his power to curry the favor of the hierarchy of the Roman Catholic Church and enlisted them in support of his organization. Hague, who despite the fact that he was cold and aloof had the steadfast loyalty of tens of thousands of voters—voters who cast ballots a second or third time as needed, voted for the dead, turned out for whichever party's primary they were asked to, and even stayed at home on Election Day if that's what was asked. Hague, whose name alone was enough to make New Jersey's Republicans cringe because he had stolen so many elections from them and who grinned while watching them moan in defeat, his enemies having forgotten all the past wrongs by their kind, which he was determined to avenge because the Irish Catholics of Jersey City couldn't forget.

Religion and politics are a lethal combination. Key to understanding Frank Hague is the treatment the Irish received at the hands of the old guard WASP Republicans of Jersey City when his kind arrived on the west bank of the Hudson River. It was nasty. That experience forged solidarity among the city's Irish Catholics, making them a force in county and state politics for several decades.

Although Republicans like Arthur Vanderbilt viewed Frank Hague as a malignancy that must be eradicated, Hague's brand of political corruption was organic, entirely natural for his place and time. The Hudson County Democratic organization, seen as a monster by the rest of New Jersey and much of the nation, was a by-product of prejudice. Long before Frank Hague rose to power, a religious war had been waged in Jersey City, and it left behind ugly scars.

The story of Frank Hague's city begins with the events following Alexander Hamilton's fatal duel with Aaron Burr in 1804. Burr didn't just kill Hamilton: as part of his plans for the industrialization of America, Hamilton envisioned a port city on the west bank of the Hudson River to rival New York. Two centuries later, it's clear that location—only location—was what drove the site's selection. The terrain consisted of several large jagged hills sloping down to the Hudson. The hills separated two broad shallow coves and were surrounded by tidal mud flats. Beyond the mud flats was a swamp and beyond that was Bergen Hill, the southern end of the Hudson Palisades, a line of steep cliffs along the west side of the river. These trap rock ridges date back two hundred million years when massive outpourings of lava covered the Hudson River Valley. Erosion and additional volcanic activity created fractures in the earth's surface, resulting in a strip of land shaped much like a jagged key.

This orphaned plot of land was surrounded by water on three sides: the Hudson River to the east, the Kill van Kull to the south (a tidal strait between it and Staten Island), and Newark Bay to the west. The only people living nearby at the time Hamilton and his partners bought the site were farmers at the top of the hills—descendants of the original Dutch settlers. It wasn't until 1838 that the legislature finally named the place "The City of Jersey" (evolving to Jersey City), population 2,500, and granting a municipal charter with the right to elect a mayor and council.

Between the War of 1812 and the Civil War, the United States made huge strides in developing a national railroad system. In the 1850s, as New Yorkers were building their "empire state" and the New York City's entrepreneurs were looking to expand their role in America's economy, the railroads began viewing Jersey City as the doorway to New York City. In short order, plans were being made to create an elaborate infrastructure for thousands of trains and millions of passengers going to and from New York City. In time, the tax revenue generated from the railroads' land holdings would play a major role in the politics of both Jersey City and New Jersey.

Large numbers of unskilled laborers were needed to make the railroads' plans a reality. The work would be dirty, difficult, and dangerous (the "three Ds"). It was crack-the-bones work, crawl-down-in-the-hole work, smash-it-shovel-it-haul-it work. It was exhausting work fit for people one step above slaves; people the WASPs of Jersey City considered subhuman. In the 1850s in the greater New York region the prime candidates for such work were Irish immigrants who had fled starvation in their homeland.

If ever there was an immigrant class ripe for exploitation, it was the Irish. Yet plunking down tens of thousands of uneducated, unwashed, and unholy "papists" in staid Jersey City was traumatic for both the old-timers and the newcomers. Unlike Newark, which recognized the importance of integrating newcomers, Jersey City saw them as little more than animals to be exploited for their labor. A deadly mold, "the blight," had laid siege to the Irish potato and drove the Irish to America. By the mid-1840s famine resulting from the destruction of Ireland's major food crop began in earnest. From 1845 to 1852 Ireland lost one-fourth its population: one million fled the country and another million died of starvation.

There was no Statue of Liberty or Ellis Island awaiting the Irish sailing into New York Harbor in the 1850s. What was awaiting them, except for the most menial of jobs, were signs stating "Irish Need Not Apply" and hostility from both the elite and the working-class Protestants. Native-born WASPs and newly arrived "Micks," a disparaging term for the Irish, were a combustible mixture in mid-nineteenth-century America; think Martin Scorsese's movie *The Gangs of New York*. Long-time Americans feared the competition of cheap immigrant labor and the only work available was the three Ds.

As the Irish arrived in New York, work gangs were assembled in lower Manhattan and ferried across the Hudson River. No sooner had the roughneck laborers landed when hundreds of hastily erected shanties appeared. Most of the immigrants—predominantly Irish, but some Germans and Poles—worked and lived among grimy, sooty machine shops, tumbledown houses, foundries, unpaved muddy streets, garbage-strewn salt marshes, and swarms of unwashed children. Tumbledown houses were soon followed by multistory tenements, and by new Roman Catholic churches, signaling that the immigrants were here to stay.[1] The more permanent their presence became, the greater the chasm between the two cultures.

In the 1850s zoning ordinances and uniform construction codes weren't even thought of. Immigrant homes and workplaces—whether construction sites, factories, or warehouses—stood side by side. Makeshift shanties for newly arrived Irish were built in dockyards and near piers where all nature of menacing industrial freight, livestock, and foodstuffs were unloaded. Discarded cargo—dead animals and rotten food—produced the foulest of odors, creating a climate pregnant with misery, disease, and death. The housing built by contractors friendly with the railroads provided shelter and little more. For the new arrivals, the horrors of the Potato Famine were exchanged for the harsh realities of urban America.

Soon, the railroads were not only welcoming new travelers and splintering neighborhoods by destroying portions of the street grid, but moving the Hudson's shoreline further away, relegating the Irish to these low-lying areas. As described by a reporter from the *New York Times* following a stroll along the city's shore in 1870:

> A walk up to the Long Dock discloses, after you pass large manufactories, oil refineries, etc., that occupy nearly the entire space of dry land, the slimiest, dirtiest shore in this part of the country. When the tide is down, on a hot day, it is absolutely sickening. Old bits of carpet and clothing, ragged baskets, old tin kettles, bottles, and various articles of household crockery, all covered by green slime, are to be seen, suggestive of every nasty thing that lies or crawls in such a stench, including dead cats and dogs, and some other dreaded shapes whose mystery the rising and falling tides reveals. Decaying hulks of vessels are moored in the mud, where rats rush frantically through their gaping seams.[2]

Aggravating further the established community, made up mostly of Protestant businessmen who took the ferry to New York each day, the creation of a modern network of railroads in Jersey City was a catalyst for industrialization. Many enormous, multistory factories, often covering several acres, were built in the city following the arrival of the trains. Straddling streets, blocking the sun, encroaching upon homes, and spewing strange smoke, smells, and sounds: there was no way to escape.[3] Equal to the condition of the immigrant housing were the conditions in the workplace. Safety guidelines, workday limitations, and minimum wages didn't exist. Nor was there workers' compensation; when employees were injured on the job and disabled, they were fired.

But the old guard WASPs had little concern for the immigrants' working conditions. They were focused or containing the spread of "Romanism." To the old guard, the Irish represented a hostile culture, combining peasant values with the Catholic religion. The WASPs were determined to make a stand against these papists.

Not long after the arrival of Irish work gangs in Jersey City and America generally, the American Party, also known as the Know-Nothing Party, emerged. Its guiding principle was "Americans shall rule America." The Know-Nothings were one of many political movements in American history born out of an irrational longing to return to a mythical past that had existed before immigration; what none of them ever grasp is that the United States is a nation of immigrants. In many places the Know-Nothings were a secret organization; when members were asked about their politics, they replied, "I know nothing," which led to the American Party's widely used name.[4]

In Jersey City, as elsewhere, the Know-Nothing movement was more about contempt for the Catholic religion than antiforeign sentiment per se. Yet the Irish were Roman Catholic and the WASPs knew what was best for them and Jersey City. As Jersey City historian Douglas Shaw states, "Native-born citizens worked to change the Irish: to make them temperate, respectful of the Sabbath, and if possible even Protestant." In the eyes of the native-born residents, "the Irish could cure their problems by ceasing to be Irish."[5]

As the Irish population swelled, WASPs responded by creating the Hudson County Bible Society and the Jersey City Mission and Tract Society. The societies were part of a nationwide response to Catholic immigration. As prophesied by the Hudson County Bible Society in its first annual report of 1853, "The foreign element which is so rapidly flowing into this country is destined, at not distant day, to exert an immense, if not controlling, influence in our county affairs, both political and religious." The goal of these pious organizations was to protect wholesome, God-fearing Protestants from the unwashed, ignorant papists by bringing evangelical religion and middle-class morality to these new arrivals to Jersey City; the aim was to convert them. They failed miserably. There was no curing the Irish of their Catholicism. By the end of the nineteenth century there would be a dozen Roman Catholic parishes, with the size of their congregations dwarfing those of the Protestants.

Despite bigoted resistance, the Irish were gaining recognition as voters. Flocking to the Democratic Party—the Republicans were solidly WASP—the Irish became a voting bloc. During the 1860s, as their numbers increased, they targeted two local offices: police recorder, an early form of today's municipal court judge, and chief of police who, within several years, assembled a force filled by Irishmen. The WASPs were outraged. In 1866, with the Irish firmly in control of the police department, the leaders of both political parties went to the state legislature to obtain the appointment of a police commission, which removed the Irish from the department. Not long after appointing the commission, the legislature revised the city's charter to eliminate the position of police recorder, replacing it with two "police justices" appointed by the legislature. But the Irish weren't to be denied.

Although unskilled labor offered little opportunity for grasping a piece of the American dream, there were some who with superior talent, harder work, and more perseverance became part of the city's economic elite.[6] Yet they couldn't shake the stigma of Catholicism as they moved into the WASP world, and in time they had had enough. They began by wrestling for power within the city's Democratic Party, which was controlled by the remains of the Know-Nothing politicians.

Forming groups like the Young Democrats and the People's Party, the new Irish elite worked to arouse a consciousness of political exploitation among the working poor to pry them away from native-born regular Democrats who wanted nothing more of the Irish than their votes. In the first election in which the Young Democrats were active—the 1870 general election—they ensured the election of Republicans by splitting the Irish vote. Yet they had sent tremors through the WASP community.[7] Terrified by the independence that the Irish had shown, the WASPs of both parties joined forces again, heading south for Trenton to demand yet another city charter. Written by the Jersey City Republican leaders, with no opposition from the regular Democrats, this new charter was approved by the Republican legislators, nearly all of whom were rural, native-born WASPs, every bit as fearful of the "Micks" as were Jersey City's WASPs.

Knowing they had the support of the Republican legislators, the Jersey City politicians crafted a new city charter vesting all control of city government in three five-man commissions to be appointed by the legislature and replacing the sixteen wards with six aldermanic districts. These new voting districts concentrated as many Irish as possible into one horseshoe-shaped district. It was a vicious gerrymander, quickly dubbed "the Horseshoe," encompassing the tenement districts along the Hudson River and the railroad rights-of-way together with the swampland shanties at the base of Bergen Hill.[8]

After passing the state senate on March 21, 1871, the special legislation went to Governor Theodore Randolph. Years earlier, Randolph had practiced law in Jersey City and had been elected to the legislature in 1860 by a coalition of Know-Nothings and Democrats. That same coalition had supported him for governor, but despite his disdain for the Irish, he viewed the charter as "anti-republican in form—arbitrary in spirit and purpose."[9] Randolph vetoed the bill as soon as it reached his desk.

Notwithstanding a fight among the Republicans—some viewed the legislation as "a disgrace to the party"[10]—the Jersey City delegation held fast, demanding an override of the veto. At the end of the day, a twisted type of home rule prevailed. If stripping voters of their rights was what the Jersey City delegation wanted, then the state Republican Party would support it. On March 28, 1871, the charter was adopted, taking effect immediately. The WASPs were back in charge.

That spring, elections in the six new aldermanic districts (two aldermen per district) produced ten Republicans—all Protestant—and two Democrats from the Horseshoe, who were treated as if they didn't exist. The spring of 1871 saw the Irish losers in three ways: (1) city government was totally controlled by unelected Protestant commissioners; (2) despite being nearly a majority of the population, their political strength had been diluted through gerrymandering; and (3) native-born Democrats cut them out of power. For the people of the Horseshoe, the rule of law didn't exist.

Self-restraint wasn't a virtue of the city commissioners. They viewed their power not only as an opportunity to crush the "Micks" but also as a license to plunder the public coffers; there was nothing subtle about their larceny. Whether looking at the rising tax rate and city debt or the exploding payroll, it was plain that the new commission government had run amok.

Enter Supreme Court Justice Joseph Bedle. Prior to his appointment to the court in 1865, Bedle had been an active Democrat, and he had no love for Jersey City's Republicans. Bedle was a savvy pol in his own right (later elected governor in 1875) and seized the opportunity to be on the right side of history. In January 1872 he empanelled a grand jury, which was one of the many duties assigned to state supreme court justices, urging them to root out public corruption and stating, "There seems to be a spirit abroad that winks at, if it does not actually encourage official dishonesty."[11] Heeding Bedle's call, the men who served on the grand jury returned 148 indictments against 17 commissioners and 2 police justices. Trials and convictions resulted, with some defendants fleeing the country, followed by more indictments and more convictions. Although there were grumblings that the panel had been stacked with Democrats, a tally revealed that of the twenty-four panel members, there were four independents, eight Democrats, and twelve Republicans. Most telling was the rebuke of the grand jury's work hurled at the legislature.

Not satisfied with merely indicting the commissioners, seventeen of the twenty-four grand jurors signed a public letter to the legislature chastising Republican power brokers for creating the situation. They demanded "relief from the fraudulent and burdensome charter foisted upon the city." Continuing, they wrote, "We are convinced that the true remedy lies in a complete restoration of local government to the hands of the people."[12] The letter was read aloud in the assembly but squelched in the senate as "disrespectful." The indictments and the grand jury's letter received wide attention; the state Republicans wanted out of the glare of Jersey City's politics. Finally, after five years of squabbling, legislation was approved in 1877 preserving the several commissions, all to be elected: one each from the six alderman districts, serving staggered terms. The final bill was signed into law by recently elected Governor Joseph Bedle.

Restoring power to the voters produced change. In little more than fifteen years following the WASPs' power grab, the Hudson County Bible Society's worst nightmare was a reality. By 1885, the "Micks" controlled city government totally; nonetheless, a bitter residue lingered in the Irish community for years—one that bred a hunger for revenge.

Hunger caused by the Great Famine had forced Frank Hague's parents to flee Ireland, arriving in Jersey City amid the religious war. The two of them, making separate journeys, found their way to Jersey City, meeting, marrying, and raising a family in the Horseshoe. As pictured by the historian Steven Hart, "It [the Horseshoe] was a grindingly poor area, jammed with shanties, squatter shacks, and wooden tenements jammed shoulder to shoulder. . . . Livestock—chicken and pigs—often shared space in the crowded houses. . . . There were some forty saloons—virtually one on every corner—and drunken brawls were a common sight. Children grew up fighting and learned early that membership in a local gang was the only guarantee of safety. Waves of typhoid would sweep through the neighborhoods, leaving funerals in their wake."[13]

This was the city within a city in which Frank Hague was born on January 17, 1875, the third son and fourth child of the eight children of John and Margaret. Like most Irish children born in the Horseshoe of the nineteenth century, baby Frank entered the world on a kitchen table. His father—a bank guard who had obtained his job through the ward leader—didn't play much of a role in Frank's life, but Margaret—a demanding mother—was revered by her son, despite the fact that some people in the neighborhood viewed her as "a bitch on wheels."[14] Education didn't count for much in the Horseshoe, and by the sixth grade, Frank's formal education was over. The classroom was no place for his energy, and at age thirteen he was expelled from school, continuing his education on the streets.

There was no such thing as a peaceful election in Jersey City. Politics was a blood sport, with elections often becoming brawls. People able and willing to wield fists, clubs, and bricks were always in demand. It was a rough-and-tumble environment in which Frank Hague thrived, absorbing his political education much the way he absorbed his Irish brand of religion. It was on the streets and in a neighborhood boxing gym that he perfected his "favorite device of persuasion,"[15] namely, to shove his proposal down the throat of anyone who disagreed with him.

Before he left his teens, Frank Hague was exploring the world of politics, and he liked what he saw. For someone of his background there was no other path out of poverty. Becoming a player in a political machine meant power—and a secure income—and power is never dispensed lightly. It's earned, often with guile or force, and Frank Hague had both. Hague learned early that success in politics meant being able to deliver constituent services.

To quote a longtime practitioner of ward politics: "We worked at winning votes 365 days a year. The ward heeler, block leader, and precinct captain knew every person in their voting district and were there to lend a helping hand, no matter what the problem. That's how we got their loyalty on Election Day. It was all about services rendered."[16]

Ward heelers must be ready for duty on a moment's notice. And so it was that Hague could be called from his bed in the middle of the night for any number of situations: to help someone who had lost his home in a fire; to transport a sick child to the hospital; to haul coal to a building where the tenants were cold; or to go to the police station and post bail for someone arrested in a barroom brawl and then follow up with the police justice to have the charges quietly dismissed. Finally, like every other foot soldier in any city organization of his day, he let no one move into his neighborhood without registering to vote.

With the backing of saloon owner Ned Kenny, nicknamed "The Mayor of Cork Row," Frank Hague was elected to his first City Hall position, as a constable, in 1896. Constable, a public office dating back to medieval England, was an arm of the court system, primarily for the enforcement of civil orders. It wasn't much of a position, but it moved Hague into the business of politics on a daily basis.

While in City Hall, Hague made two friendships that proved integral to his career. The mayor's secretary (at the time, many secretaries were male), A. Harry Moore, "was a handsome, charming young man of twenty-nine, full of anecdotes and pleasant banter."[17] A Presbyterian Sunday School teacher, Moore was probably the first Protestant Hague had known personally. He would market Moore to the Irish of Jersey City as a WASP they could trust because Hague controlled him. Harry Moore was a natural-born charmer. A dapper dresser and eloquent speaker, he was as smooth a glad-hander who ever lived. Hague saw instantly that here was a potential candidate: all he had to do was wind him up and point him in the right direction.

Every leader of any political organization of heft needs a consigliere, a trusted legal adviser, and Hague recognized John Milton as a lawyer he could work with. Their relationship would span four decades. Five years younger than Hague and admitted to the New Jersey bar at the age of twenty-two in 1903, Milton was a green but resourceful lawyer working in the city's solicitor's office. He loved the game of politics and saw it as an avenue for gaining clout in his profession. Over the years, Milton became a reliable intermediary for people hoping to make a deal with Hague.

Hague, Moore, and Milton became a trinity in state politics and remained so for nearly thirty years; they made Arthur Vanderbilt and Republicans recoil in dismay. Despite his limited education, Frank Hague was learning important truths that would guide him not only in staying atop this threesome but also in dominating New Jersey's politics. First among his lessons: To acquire and retain power, a leader must reward his friends and punish his enemies. All of Niccolò Machiavelli's teachings can be reduced to this simple maxim and Hague grasped it well. Second, power doesn't corrupt anyone; everyone comes to the game who they are. Power reveals. Third, a leader hoping to remain in power must have control of the force of law, as distinct from the rule of law. At the end of the day, prevailing over one's adversaries is often about having your people in the appropriate garb—whether policemen in uniforms or judges in robes—to vest your authority in apparent legitimacy. Fourth, the good fathers of the Roman Catholic Church could be valuable allies. Finally, Hague understood that most people—the mighty and lowly alike—only turn to government when they need something. The politician who delivers on those needs will see his power grow.

It was during his years as commissioner of public safety that Hague transformed the police department. Prior to Hague, Jersey City's police force had been an embarrassment, having a reputation just a little less frightening than that of the city's criminals.[18] Within days of taking office Hague launched an all-out assault on business as usual, dismissing corrupt and lazy officers. As historian Steven Hart notes, "In his first display of the concern for detail that would make his political machine legendary, Hague cruised the streets of Jersey City checking up on his men. More than one out-of-shape cop found himself confronted by the menacing Horseshoe brawler, who would order him to report back to the chief and 'tell him Commissioner Hague don't want cream puffs on the street.' Hague earned the favor of church leaders by cracking down on prostitution and narcotics trafficking."[19]

While cultivating his image as a reformer, Hague had the added bonus of being in position to grab control of a large number of jobs. Scores of policemen were ruthlessly dismissed for minor infractions. The reduced ranks of the police force were replenished by Hague's young Horseshoe followers, from whom he personally selected an elite squad of plainclothesmen called Zeppelins.[20] The term arose from an early German airship used for spying. Their task was spying on the other officers, weaving a web of secret surveillance around the entire force. The Zepps, as they became known, soon had every cop in the city looking over his shoulder. They eventually became Hague's private gendarmes, answerable to him alone, not only disciplining police officers but also muscling political opponents when necessary.

Hague also recognized the appeal of drama in public life. In his first term as city commissioner he captured the public's admiration in a way other politicians had to envy. On Good Friday of 1916, a bizarre set of circumstances led to the murder of a Jersey City resident, Frank Kenny, son of saloon owner Ned Kenny, by a gun-wielding immigrant Italian best known as a strike-breaker. The Kennys were a very popular family in the Horseshoe and word of the murder sent torrents of grief throughout the community. Worse still, the murderer had escaped arrest and was at large, believed to be Newark.[21]

As commissioner of public safety, Hague could have dispatched his men to work with the police in Newark. Instead, he took charge, publicly vowing personal responsibility for the investigation and promising the Kenny family that he would not rest until the murderer was caught.[22] Having received a lead on the murderer's whereabouts in Newark—his name was Michael Rombolo—Hague and his men sped to the address where Rombolo was believed to be hiding. The house was empty, and Hague left the others to watch things as he set out on foot to explore the area. As chance would have it, in the first shop Hague entered he saw a man answering the killer's description. Spooked, Rombolo drew his gun and ran for the rear exit with Hague running after him. What happened next is best told by Jersey City historian Bob Leach:

> Pedestrians purposely blocked Hague's chase, but he managed to see Rombolo duck into a playground. Hague went around the block, climbed a fence, and came from behind upon Rombolo, who was crouched behind a fountain with drawn revolver, awaiting Hague from the other direction. Hague leaped on Rombolo's back, subduing him after a struggle.
>
> When Hague's car, with Rombolo shackled in the back seat, crossed the Hackensack River Bridge into Jersey City, the Zepps were waiting in full array. Hague was greeted by a motorcade of police wagons, motorcycles, and private autos, which escorted his car to headquarters in a noisy caravan of horns and whistles.[23]

That night there was a swearing-in ceremony for a new class of policemen at Saint Michael's parish hall, with Hague administering the oath. The new officers gave their chief a standing ovation, and when he left he was swarmed by a huge crowd, "hoping to touch his garment."[24]

For weeks after the arrest, the local newspapers featured stories of the murderous Italian thug and Hague's heroics. It was a "publicity bonanza." An example was the banner headline of the *Jersey Journal* that sang his praises: "HAGUE FACING DRAWN REVOLVER OVERPOWERS AND CAPTURES KENNY KILLER." Even the *Hudson Observer*—no friend of Hague—cheered him on

saying, "Director of Public of Safety Frank Hague, who arrested the slayer in
Newark, is the lion of the hour, and the members of his department, as well as
the general public are loud in their praise of his bravery."[25] New York's papers
covered the story as well; the name and face of Jersey City's public safety
commissioner were everywhere.

Legends are born from less. Frank Hague was now a celebrity. After two
appeals and a second trial, Michael Rombolo was sentenced to life impris-
onment. During a twenty-four-month period, hundreds of news articles
about the Kenny murder appeared in print. Hague's daring in handling the
arrest made good copy and propelled his stature to dizzying heights. Kenny's
murder was so deeply personal to the Irish community that the fearlessness
shown in hunting down his murderer made Hague a lifelong hero to tens of
thousands of people who were always ready to reject attacks by his critics.
Long before the term was applied to American politicians, Frank Hague had
charisma. The following year he was elected mayor, a position he held for the
next thirty years.

Yet, 1916 was marked by another pivotal event besides the Kenny murder: it was the year Hague murdered the progressive wing of the New Jersey Democratic Party. Woodrow Wilson had inspired a whole generation of
young politicians throughout the country. In Jersey City, one of his followers, successful grocer Otto Wittpenn, had been elected mayor in 1907. Hague
had supported Wittpenn in 1908 and was rewarded with the position of City
Hall custodian—a job with more to offer than the title indicates. With a salary of $2,000, it was the best-paying job he had ever had. More important,
it enabled Hague to dispense patronage positions of his own—two dozen
janitors—to the people helping him get out the vote, awarding some of them
with the title of "deputy custodian." One, a pal from the Horseshoe, John
"Needle Nose" Malone, would later be Hague's alter ego, serving as deputy
mayor. It was from the position of City Hall custodian that Hague ran for a
seat on the city commission.

Another change in the law coming out of Trenton during Wilson's years
as governor prior to the Kenny murder was the Walsh Act of 1911. It permitted city governments to abandon their large city councils and replace them
with city commissions made up of five members, who would then select a
mayor from among themselves. Hague quickly saw that a five-man commission would be much easier to control than a city commission of eighteen
members. He was now a full-fledged progressive, yearning to restore trust in

government, and he joined the effort to change the city charter at a special election to be held in April 1913. In 1913, ninety-three candidates ran for five city commission seats. Among them were Frank Hague and A. Harry Moore. They finished in the top five; the top vote getter, former mayor Mark Fagan, was selected mayor and Hague was named commissioner of public safety.

Incumbent mayor Otto Wittpenn had his sights set on becoming governor and chose not to run in the special election of 1913; come 1916, he got a rude awakening. The Republican gubernatorial primary of 1916 was hotly contested between two successful businessmen, Walter Edge of Atlantic County and Austin Colgate, heir to the toothpaste fortune. Edge had money, but his pockets weren't as deep as Colgate's; he needed help, and it came through a deal struck between Hague and Atlantic City Republican boss Enoch "Nucky" Johnson.[26] Both men were branching out, looking for alliances outside their own counties. Each understood it was useful to have friends in the other party to help on issues affecting their city. For Otto Wittpenn and Austin Colgate, the timing couldn't have been worse.

There was no contest in the Democratic gubernatorial primary, yet Hague saw that Wittpenn was serious about reforming government at every level, and he wanted none of it. Getting himself into power was all the change in government Frank Hague wanted. At Nucky Johnson's urgings and with a pledge of cooperation from Walter Edge, Hague instructed his people to "cross-over," with thousands of "Republicans for the day" voting for Edge in the Republican Party. Hague then abandoned Wittpenn in the general election, with many thousands in Jersey City's Second Ward staying home. Edge won handily. Wittpenn never saw it coming. From then on, Otto Wittpenn and the progressive wing of the Democratic Party were no longer a factor in Frank Hague's political calculations.

Between 1896 and 1917, during twenty-one tumultuous years marked by daring, persistence, ruthlessness, and paying attention to details, Frank Hague had climbed every rung of the local political ladder—crushing anyone who got in his way and earning advanced degrees—on the streets of Jersey City—in psychology, sociology, and political science, gaining complete control of his city. Every step of the way he was mindful of taking care of his own. Despite his gruff ways, Hague made time for "my people." He was ever-present at funerals following the death of a member of his organization. He was there to throw out the first pitch at ball games. He would stay at weddings long enough to hug the bride and hand her husband an

envelope with cash. And while making his daily rounds he might visit a
tenement where there had been complaints of no water or heat. Beware to
the landlord who failed to do anything in response to the needs of a Hague
supporter. It didn't happen a second time.

Pliable to Hague's prompts, the Irish Catholics of Hudson County placed
tens of thousands of votes at his disposal. With each election Frank Hague's
shadow over New Jersey politics loomed larger. And as his might grew,
Republicans throughout the state began seeing him as a force for evil. But
what they failed to grasp was that for Hague and his followers it wasn't politics, but rather a religious war not of their own making that motivated them.

Revenge can get ugly. When people who have been oppressed for generations get the upper hand, it's difficult to restrain them. This is especially true
when religion rears its head. Often the extent to which revenge plays out is
commensurate with the indignities inflicted by the oppressors. That people
become fierce in settling scores is no surprise. What is surprising is the belly-
aching of the former oppressors when the time arrives for balancing the scales
of justice. The Republicans had made it easy for Hague to paint the world of
ward politics in black and white. Despite their indispensable role in building
Jersey City, the Irish had to fight WASP Republicans for recognition as part of
humanity. Once they had won the fight, they were eager to control the process.
Yet mastery over voting results—the likes of which Hague had developed—
came only through an outsized effort, overseen by a brilliant mind.

Long before computers were used to keep track of how people behave,
Frank Hague had his own technology to ensure success on Election Day.
Covering the wall of his office was an enormous chart of columns and rows
containing the numbers necessary to assess the vitality of his organization.
Jersey City was made up of 12 wards and 306 voting districts, with each
district broken down into precincts—totaling nearly 600—to which were
attached names of block leaders and ward heelers responsible for a getting
out the vote. Hague knew every one of them intimately—their hopes, their
fears, and their vulnerabilities—plus the total number of votes they were
responsible for. There were also countless files, updated regularly, on the reli-
ability of individual voters: who could be depended on to get their entire
family out to vote, who was indebted for a recent favor, who needed a ride to
the polls, and, finally, who had died recently but had yet to be removed from
the eligible voter rolls.[27]

Every home in each precinct was under the watchful eye of ward heel-ers working at the direction of precinct captains; the precinct captains, in turn, answered to ward lieutenants, who in turn reported to the ward boss, with every ward boss answering to Hague. Hour by hour throughout the day votes were compared to results from prior elections and any falloff was quickly seized upon, with additional workers dispatched to precincts where the count was light. If a precinct worker failed to deliver, his career with the organization was over. There were no second chances: someone was always ready to move up in the organization.

There was a fervor for politics in Hudson County unlike almost anything that exists today anywhere in America; perhaps the only contemporary phe-nomenon that compares is the passion of professional football fans. Under Hague, nothing was left to chance. As not only mayor of Jersey City but also chairman of the Hudson County Democratic Party and later vice chairman of the Democratic National Committee, Frank Hague, along with and his cohorts, toiled daily to ensure huge victory margins in every election. His crew of workers—numbering in the thousands of city and county employees—wove themselves into the fabric of the community. They organized ward clubs, social groups, parades, excursions, and family outings; they distributed food, cloth-ing, and coal to the needy and found jobs for many of them. They also served as intermediaries with the police over nonfelony charges and handled neighbor-hood complaints such as garbage pickups, much like a "Scandinavian ombuds-man."[28] And everyone grasped the quid pro quo—votes.

Another player on Hague's team also came to expect quid pro quos. In exchange for hiring priests as city chaplains and contributing generously to the church coffers—and later helping to establish a monastery in Bergen County—the hierarchy of the Roman Catholic Church was an important ally. It wasn't uncommon for local politics to become part of Sunday services.

Each November, and in primary elections as well, the Sunday before the election Hague met with hundreds of his leading party workers in Jersey City's Grotto Auditorium (appropriately, home to many boxing matches), where he exhorted them to get out the vote. His pitch was basic. "Three hun-dred and sixty-four days you want favors from me, now one day in the year I come to you."[29] They delivered year after year; the numbers were stagger-ing. At the height of Frank Hague's reign, of approximately 375,000 eligible voters in Hudson County, Democrats could boast that 345,000 (92 percent) were registered to vote. In a typical general election, as many as 300,000 (more than 85 percent) purportedly made it to the polls to cast their ballots, often making the difference for Democratic candidates in a statewide contest.

When it came to electing a governor, making the difference is where Hague excelled. Hudson County's power to sway New Jersey elections became apparent in the gubernatorial election of 1919, less than two years after Hague was chosen as Jersey City's mayor in 1917.

One of Hague's early moves as mayor to balance the scales with the WASPs was on city property tax assessments. His initial attempt to revalue properties of the railroads and utilities had been frustrated. Before Hague became mayor, railroads were assessed at a mere $3,000 per acre, compared with other commercial real estate at $17,000 an acre. Tax valuations on Standard Oil and Public Service Corporation, the utility, were likewise pitifully low. Knowing none of these companies could leave Jersey City, Hague raised the assessments on the railroads' parcels by 240 percent, from $67 million to $160 million; Standard Oil from $1.5 million to $14 million; and Public Service from $3 million to $30 million.[30] His victory was short-lived. The new tax assessments were overturned on appeal to the State Board of Assessments, which was dominated by Republicans. That couldn't stand. Hague was determined to have a governor of his own who would appoint the right people to seat on the tax board. State Senator Edward "Teddy" Edwards, who was also president of the First National Bank of Jersey City, would be his candidate in the 1919 election.

Despite opposition to Edwards's candidacy from Democrats in Essex County, Hudson County's Primary Day workers made the difference, and from there it was on to the general election. The Republican candidate was Newton Bugbee, a successful engineer and contractor from Mercer County. Edwards versus Bugbee wasn't the only issue in the campaign. The Eighteenth Amendment to the U.S. Constitution—"Prohibition"—was scheduled to go into effect the January following the election. Edwards was strongly anti-Prohibition, proclaiming himself "as wet as the Atlantic Ocean." Though he was a social drinker, Bugbee maintained that Prohibition must be enforced because it was the law of the land. When the votes in twenty of New Jersey's twenty-one counties were counted, Bugbee had a margin of 21,008 votes. Yet late in the evening word came out of Hudson County that Edwards had won there by more than 35,000 votes.

Edwards's election proved decisive to Frank Hague's plans for balancing the city's tax assessments, assuring Hague the revenue he needed to hire political supporters and implement his social service programs in City Hall. Hague also had the governor's ear on key appointments. Edwards dismissed the entire state highway commission, replacing the former members with people chosen by Hague; likewise, the attorney general and Hudson County prosecutor, John Milton, were Hague men; and finally, openings in the judiciary were filled with people handpicked by the mayor.

With Edwards unable to run for reelection and eyeing the U.S. Senate, Hague had two campaigns to run in 1922: Edwards for senator against popular incumbent Joseph Frelinghuysen, and someone for governor. Hague settled on Circuit Judge George Silzer of New Brunswick as his candidate. Edwards won his election easily. Yet with twenty of twenty-one counties reporting, Silzer trailed Union County state senator William Runyon by nearly 34,000 votes in the gubernatorial vote. Arthur Vanderbilt was Runyon's campaign manager, and they were hopeful. Nonetheless, when the votes were tallied in Hudson County, Silzer had won there by more than 46,000 votes. It was one of many statewide elections in which Hague smiled as the WASP Republicans howled at being cheated.

Governor Silzer had an independent streak, and not long after taking office dismissed the members of the highway commission, citing graft in the letting of highway contracts. Three years of Silzer were enough, and in 1925 a Hague puppet, the smiling Harry Moore, was elevated from city commissioner to the governor's office. His opponent was a wealthy Morris County state senator, Arthur Whitney, who barnstormed the state making "Hagueism" his rallying cry. Whitney carried eighteen of twenty-one counties, and until the ballots in Hudson County were counted, he was leading Moore by 65,000 votes. When the votes were counted, the ever-popular Harry Moore had carried his home county by nearly 105,000 votes, winning election as governor the first of three times.

New Jersey's Republicans were incensed. The state Republican committee presented the county prosecutor with overwhelming proof showing that many of Hague's people had voted multiple times and that dead people had cast ballots. In one voting precinct, the number of votes cast exceeded the number of registered voters, and in a precinct where Republicans could prove their supporters had gone to the polls, the official tally showed Moore receiving 100 percent of the recorded votes. Hague's pal John Milton was

Hudson County prosecutor. Needless to say, the Republicans' evidence of voter fraud never saw the light of day.

Despite their humiliation, the Republicans weren't going away, and several months before the next gubernatorial election in 1928, they decided it was time for Hague to go to jail. Too bad none of them had ever spent New Year's Day in Jersey City. If they had, they might have had a better understanding of what they were up against.

CHAPTER 6

The Celtic Chieftain

People stood in line down the length of the hall and out the building. The scene at City Hall on New Year's Day in Jersey City was reminiscent of a feudal lord summoning his serfs to his castle yearly, pledging his continued protection in exchange for their payment of land rents. Each January 1, despite the fact that local government reorganized every fourth year—in May at that—Frank Hague received his subjects, "my people" as he called them, even when it meant returning from his home in Florida to winter's cold.

Yet there was nothing cold about the greeting from the people in line. Although there were the usual politicians on the make, vendors hoping for contracts, and litigants pleading for him to get the ear of a judge, many more were eager supporters ranging from municipal employees beholden for their income and hospital patients thankful for free care to residents grateful for help when they were down on their luck. Everyone wore their finest threads and waited for hours to shake hands and speak briefly with His Honor. Always, the inner circle of Moore, Milton, and Deputy Mayor Malone was on hand, ready to receive people passed on to them by Hague. For thousands of local residents, New Year's Day in Jersey City was a sacred ritual.

Frank Hague knew that rituals are part of the glue that holds society together. Early man dwelled in superstitions: those fears spawned myths and legends that became the basis for religion and a shared understanding of the universe. Hague's organization provided its members with the rationale they needed to make sense of the world. The backbone of the organization was Irish, and for many of them, Democratic politics under Frank Hague was all the religion they needed. Every player in the Hudson County Democratic organization—including, or especially, the judges—knew the role expected of them.

For most Irish people in Hudson County, Frank Hague's Democratic organization was the "One True Faith," providing its members with all the abiding truths they needed to make sense of their world. Recalling growing up in Jersey City as the son of the Hudson County sheriff, the historian Thomas Fleming put it this way: "By the time I was ten, I was a complete convert to the Hague Organization's politics. I fervently believed it was the Catholic Democrats of Jersey City against the Protestant Republicans in the rest of New Jersey. These Protestants used to run Jersey City before Mayor Hague took over. They did not care if Catholics lived in tenements with no running water or only cold water. They lived in big houses in the suburbs and owned railroads and banks and factories where they paid Catholic workers as little as possible. The Republicans were out to get us."[1]

With the ability to manipulate the votes of the Irish Catholics, Hague could decide who won elections not only to statewide office but also on occasion in Republican primaries. With tens of thousands of loyal Irish Catholic voters willing to help him make mischief within the party politics of the WASPs, Republican politicians grew to hate him, and as their hatred grew so did their frustration.

Not long after New Year's Day 1928, the Celtic Chieftain began making plans for the upcoming gubernatorial election. The Republican establishment had handpicked a highly regarded attorney, former judge, and progressive reformer Robert Carey, to be the candidate. By all accounts he was serious about reforming state government, particularly the antiquated judiciary. With Harry Moore unable to seek reelection, and no Democrats whom he trusted, Hague decided, as he had twelve years earlier, to have a talk with his friend from Atlantic City, Nucky Johnson. The two bosses reached an agreement to support Republicans Morgan Larson for governor and Hamilton Kean for U.S. senator. Both were elected.[2]

After the election, a U.S. Senate committee conducted a formal investigation into a charge that before the primary Kean had given Johnson a signed blank check that was cashed for $200,000 and the money used as a slush fund to buy votes. The check was never found, but the primary was noteworthy because it was another one in which the Democrats in Hudson County crossed over into the Republican primary. The orders went out from Hague, and thousands of Irish Catholic Democrats invaded the Republican primary to vote for Larson and Kean. Even Democratic election officials themselves voted in the Republican primary. The investigating committee estimated that more than 20,000 Hudson County Democrats had crossed over to vote into the Republican primary. In the Horseshoe alone, 1,300 votes were cast to nominate Morgan Larson, with a similar number for him in the general election.[3] Although Larson was no friend to Hudson County, he wasn't a reformer either. Nonetheless, Hague's manipulation of the election had denied Carey the nomination and infuriated the Republicans.

State Senator Clarence Case (his nephew, Clifford, later served four terms as U.S. senator) viewed Hague's power as an affront to civilized society. Case was born in Jersey City in 1877, the year after Hague, but in a different solar system; his family later moving to the village of Somerville, where Republicans could breathe easy. From Case's vantage point, the Hudson County Democratic organization was un-American. Knowing there was no hope that Hudson County Prosecutor John Milton would ever act on charges against Hague, and that the state attorney general, who had little power, would not do so either, Case wrote directly to U.S. Attorney General John Sargent.

John Garibaldi Sargent was a longtime Republican, but he wasn't from the progressive wing of the party. He was from Vermont, and having been appointed by fellow Vermonter President Calvin Coolidge, Sargent wasn't the type to go looking for trouble. In a letter dated June 29, 1928, Case implored Sargent to launch an investigation. Portraying Hague as "the dominating figure in Hudson County politics" and the "controlling personality in Democratic politics in New Jersey," he cited "two abortive investigations" of Hague's organization, pleading for help. Concluding his plea, he told the attorney general that exposing "the true Hudson County situation" would be of "incalculable value . . . to the State of New Jersey and to good government in general."[4] Case's pleas were for naught. There's no record of any type of reply from Attorney General Sargent.

With no help coming out of Washington, Senator Case was prepared to go after Hague on his own. Case and his WASP Republican cohorts in Trenton were confident that they could kill the slithering Hudson County Democratic organization by ripping off the head of the snake. Frank Hague was a thief and a thug. They wouldn't rest until he was behind bars.

Their revenge would come, or so Senator Case hoped, through an inquisition that would lay bare "Boss" Hague's sins against democracy. Case planned to scrutinize Hague's finances publicly, hoping scrutiny would lead to the indictment, conviction, and disgrace of Jersey City's mayor. Hague wasn't rattled, even a little; to him, Case and his investigation were an annoyance, nothing more. Probing into Hague's public and private affairs, the legislature created a joint committee comprised of members of both the senate and the general assembly, calling more than 300 witnesses and receiving several thousand pages of testimony. The result was a litany of offenses for which there was no end: Hague's corrupt ways were a perpetual work in progress.

At the risk of oversimplifying, what follows is a sampling of transactions scrutinized by Case's committee to demonstrate how far an annual salary of $8,000 could take His Honor.

1. In 1921, he purchased 150 shares of stock in the First National Bank of Jersey City (Governor Edwards's bank) for the sum of $37,500, paid for in cash.
2. The following year he acquired 100 shares in the Trust Company of New Jersey at the price of $34,500, again paid for in cash.
3. In 1926, he was assessed $12,000 as a shareholder in the Duncan Company. It was paid by John Milton's personal check and Hague reimbursed him in cash.
4. The same year Hague purchased beach property in Deal, New Jersey, in John Milton's name for $65,000 and reimbursed him in cash. Milton also wrote checks to contractors working on Hague's new oceanfront home for another $60,000, which likewise was satisfied in cash.
5. During the six years preceding Case's investigation, there were other cash transactions totaling more than $300,000—approximately $4 to 5 million in cash today—on a contemporary salary of $120,000.[5]

Also attracting the committee's attention were several land conveyances involving one Mr. H. S. Kerbaugh. Between 1915 and 1922 the mysterious Mr. Kerbaugh, who refused to leave New York City to testify before the joint committee, was involved in multiple land transactions in Jersey City. Given the location of the properties, the timing of the purchases, and the profits upon sale, Mr. Kerbaugh was either clairvoyant or plugged into Hague's City Hall. For example, in 1915, Kerbaugh purchased a large vacant lot in Jersey City for the sum of $60,000. Four years later, it became the site of a new Hudson County government services building, selling for $386,215. In 1921 he bought a large tract of land included in the Jersey City watershed in Morris County at the price of $125,000 and conveyed it to the city the following

year for $325,000. Finally, in 1922 he acquired a tract of land that eventually
became part of the city's key commercial center, Journal Square, for $218,000,
assigning it to a corporation controlled by Hague. Two years later, the county
condemned one-twelfth of the land and agreed to pay $320,000, with the
remainder eventually being sold to private parties with fair market value having been established by the county.[6]

One of the condemnation hearing officers who determined the price to be
paid by the city and/or county on these sales was State Civil Service Commissioner Theodore Smith. The Case Committee concluded that the fees he
earned helped him look the other way while people on the city and county
payroll: (1) never took the required exams; (2) worked without job specifications; or (3) didn't work at all, that is, were no-show political employees who
came to work on payday only.[7]

Hague's payday never had to wait, and while his investments bespoke graft,
shakedowns, and insider deals, his lifestyle was conspicuous for the entire
world to see. Senator Case's inquiry into Hague's life revealed that he and
his wife Jenny, and children, Frank Jr. and Peggy, lived in a fourteen-room
penthouse apartment on the top two floors of the lavish Duncan Apartments
in the posh Bergen Hill district overlooking the Hudson River and the New
York skyline. The family lived rent-free because Hague had paid $75,000—
in cash—for the land on which the high-rise was sitting. The investigators
suspected that he owned the building, but it was titled to a corporation about
which no one was talking.

Employing two maids, a chef, and chauffer-valet-handyman to drive Mrs.
Hague in her Cadillac, this was a family on the move. Each May the Hagues
left Jersey City for their enormous beachfront home in the stylish resort town
of Deal, fifty miles south. The Deal residence had two gardeners to tend to
the lawns, shrubbery, and sunken gardens, plus five house servants to cater
to sleepover guests and house parties. After several months at the beach and
commuting to the city, Hague usually took his family abroad to Europe, traveling first-class on the most popular ocean liners of the day. Upon return in
late summer, it was back to the Duncan until frost set in, and then, sometime
between Thanksgiving and Christmas, it was off to Florida where the family
spent most of the winter in either Biscayne Bay or Miami Beach. Overlapping
these residences was a suite at the Plaza Hotel in Manhattan, where Hague
had lunch most days when he was otherwise in Jersey City. His was a life of
splendor befitting the Celtic Chieftain.

Having the likes of Hague rub their nose in the political dirt was more than the Republicans could bear. Their investigation produced documents and testimony, raising questions that had to be answered. They demanded Hague appear before the Case Committee and testify under oath.

Confrontations were something Frank Hague relished. If circumstances had permitted, Hague would have likely stuffed the subpoena he received down Senator Case's throat. Initially, he was summoned before the committee and asked a series of ten questions regarding his personal finances, all calculated to show that the cash used to reimburse John Milton and others couldn't possibly have come from lawful sources. Hague refused to answer any of them.

Case upped the ante, calling for a joint session of the state legislature, resulting in a second subpoena. Appearing before the members of the senate and general assembly, the overwhelming majority of whom were WASP Republicans, Hague was asked the same ten questions. Again, he refused to answer any of them. The Republicans adopted a joint resolution holding him in contempt and issued a warrant for his arrest, stating that he was to be confined in the Mercer County jail "until such time as he should make known to the chairman of the joint committee in writing that he was willing to answer the questions already recited."[8]

Hague was at home when the legislature's sergeant-at-arms attempted to arrest him. The sergeant-at-arms quickly found himself under arrest by Hague's Zepps. The following day, Hague presented himself for arrest at John Milton's office, which happened to be adjacent to Vice Chancellor John J. Fallon's chambers. Hague's lawyers, Thomas Brogan of Jersey City and Merritt Lane of Newark (Vanderbilt's rival in Newark), immediately petitioned the Chancery Court for a writ of habeas corpus, which was granted. Fallon, a former Hudson County assemblyman, county counsel, and loyal judge, wasted little time finding that "the arrest of Hague was without legal justification and ordered him discharged."[9]

Case and the Republicans were outraged that Fallon would dare to hear the petition. They went to Chancellor Walker demanding disqualification, complaining not only of Fallon's past alliances but also the fact that his tenure as Hudson County counsel had been scrutinized by the joint committee. Worse still, in September 1928 Fallon had given the *Jersey Journal* a statement assailing the motives of Case's committee. The chancellor was unimpressed.

Walker was an old-line Democrat from Mercer County who had been appointed a vice chancellor more than twenty years earlier. Born during the Civil War, he was truly a nineteenth-century legal thinker: he may have heard of Louis Brandeis and Roscoe Pound but it's unlikely he ever read them. Issuing a ruling refusing to remove Fallon from the case, Walker found that the only interest that could disqualify a judge was "a direct pecuniary one." Continuing, he said, "But prejudice growing out of business, political, or social relations is not sufficient to disqualify a judge. And prejudice against the cause or defense of a party is not a disqualifying prejudice. Generally it is held that an interest which a judge has in common with many others in a public matter is not sufficient to disqualify him."[10] As for the arrest of the legislature's sergeant-at-arms, that was "entirely collateral."

Free to act, Vice Chancellor Fallon reinforced Hague's writ of habeas corpus with a formal opinion. Berating the legislature, he ruled that they had "pursued a course of investigation designed ostensibly to pry into the petitioner's private business affairs, to besmirch his character and reputation, to stigmatize him before the public. . . . It bristles also with clear manifestation of partisan activities of the investigators."[11] Finally, Fallon's caustic opinion plowed new ground in New Jersey's common law: he announced a "constitutional right of privacy as to his personal affairs" something the U.S. Supreme Court didn't get around to expressing until thirty-five years later in *Griswold v. Connecticut*.[12] Hague's crony Jack Fallon was a legal scholar blazing trails in constitutional law.

Sensing this was their last best chance at ending Hagueism in New Jersey politics, Clarence Case and the Republicans pressed on, appealing Fallon's decision to the E & A. They got clobbered. On May 10, 1930, by a vote of ten to one, the state's highest court rejected their arguments. They viewed the entire matter as political sour grapes. And as we shall learn in chapter 8, the author of the court's decision wasn't a Hague cohort.

Before leaving the Case investigation, it's worth noting two areas left unexamined by his committee: "rice pudding" and waterfront money.

Widely known, but unexamined by Case's committee, was the fact that Hague's organization took its cut from the payroll of what eventually became a very bloated municipal workforce. Every employee was required to kick back 3 percent of his or her salary in a monthly ritual known as "rice pudding day." The term "rice pudding" was used by Irish bartenders in the greater New York area for the coins left on their bar by customers—either too drunk or not paying attention—which the bartender would snatch when wiping the counter.[13] Yet rice pudding was only the beginning of Hague's income stream. As historian James T. Fisher observed, "Frank Hague's many critics on the outside never understood that kickbacks from Jersey City's public employees paled next to the bounty pouring forth from the docks, especially from the loading racket, a system that guaranteed income from every exchange made between rail cars, trucks and barges."[14] The waterfront and the roughneck stevedores who worked there were a world unto themselves (much like *On the Waterfront*), and Hague had a close alliance with them. As Fisher recounts, one of Hague's links to the waterfront was a neighbor in the luxury high-rise on Hudson Boulevard. Cornelius "Connie" Noonan was tied to the Irish underworld and "a menacing waterfront figure in his own right."[15] Hague and the Second Ward leader, John V. Kenney, were deeply involved in the affairs of Terminal Workers Union Local 1730. It's hard to believe that Clarence Case and his committee knew nothing of "rice pudding" and the waterfront money. It's easier to believe they simply avoided those issues. The rice pudding would have been messy. The waterfront money would have been dangerous. The stevedoring trade was filled with scary people, the type Hague could prevail upon to break legs. For whatever reason, Case didn't go to City Hall or down to Jersey City's docks.

Once again, Frank Hague had prevailed. Clarence Case and his WASP Republican pals could sulk in defeat, while this "Mick" was going to spend time at his beach house and then set sail by luxury liner to vacation in Europe. In Hague's mind, the money, homes, minions, and travel were the spoils of war. To Hague's way of thinking, the WASPs had looted the public treasury and humiliated the Irish, so why shouldn't he do the same? So what if he was better at it than they were? That was their problem. He had vanquished the enemy and earned his plunder. Finally, within eighteen months after defeat in the courts, the Republicans were humiliated further by, yet again, the election of A. Harry Moore as governor: his winning margin coming from carrying Hudson County by more than 100,000 votes. All was well in Frank Hague's empire.

Yet there was more to Hague's empire than feasting on the booty of political combat and crushing WASPs throughout his life. Hague empathized with poor kids from the street. As recounted by the noted political reporter Clayton Gilbert, writing in a series of articles in the *New York Evening Post* in October of 1925, Hague had a strong commitment to the children of the working poor.

Gilbert spent several days with Hague and in one instance reported on film footage he saw of the goings-on in a sick-baby clinic. Hague noted one of the children in a crib and reported sadly that the child had died. According to Gilbert, "It seemed as if he felt that his efficiency, his powerful will, his hospital ought to be enough to thwart the fate that preys upon babies; that death in the face of it all was unbelievable. He could have told me the name, the age, the exact circumstances of the child that died on him, so comprehensive is every-thing that goes on under him."[16]

Not long after becoming mayor, Hague established the Mothers' Insti-tute with an eye toward assisting new mothers in caring for their children. When the time came for the city to purchase a building to house the insti-tute, Hague found a property up for auction and scared off any other buy-ers, purchasing the property for a song. It was Hague's interest in children, particularly juvenile delinquents, that was the foundation of the phrase that virtually became Hague's middle name as used by journalists and historians for the past seventy-five years.

Historians know that context matters, and Hague's classic utterance "I am the law" was said in a context unmentioned, and unknown, by the people who now use it.[17] According to numerous reliable sources, the true context of Hague's notorious utterance is as follows: Two twelve-year-old boys viewed as total incorrigibles by the police were on their way to a youth detention facility when Hague intervened on their behalf. Following a brief discussion with the boys—both of whom reportedly told him they'd rather go to jail than to school—Hague decided he was going to put them to work, quite literally, using them as free labor doing difficult work for the city in the hopes they would get the message. Over the objections of the correc-tion officers and the school superintendent who cited the law requiring these young boys to either be in the detention facility or in school, Hague replied, "In this case, I am the law." Unfortunately for Hague, the first time he repeated this story in public was at a Methodist church in November 1937. It didn't take long for Jersey City's Methodists to spread the word and the phrase "I am the law" quickly made its way into the newspapers.

Despite being corrupt, Hague's administration was efficient. As reported by Clayton Gilbert, "The leader has a recipe that is better than any recipe that any boss ever has had. It produces a municipal administration such as not even the purist of reformers has ever given, and a machine such as the most powerful of bosses never dreamed of. You admire one and fear the other."[18] But it wasn't just a newspaper reporter who thought Hague administered an enlightened, people-friendly City Hall. Long after he had reason to throw bouquets, none other than his Republican rival, former governor Walter Edge, had this to say, "Although I consistently battled with Mayor Hague politically, justice compels me to correct the impression created by his many critics that he is the incarnation of all evil. True he is a cold, calculating, and ruthless political boss, but he is at the same time an able administrator with strong humanitarian qualities, and Jersey City is in many ways a well-managed municipality."[19]

Hague also was a leader for women's suffrage, and not long after women earned the right to vote through the adoption of the Nineteenth Amendment, Hague anointed a forty-eight-year-old widow, Mary Theresa Norton, as his chosen female candidate, ordaining her election to the Hudson County Board of Freeholders. A year later, in 1924, she was the first Democratic woman elected to the U.S. Congress; she served thirteen consecutive terms until retiring in 1951. Congresswoman Norton returned Hague's support by using her position, and ultimately seniority and committee chairmanships, to garner federal funding and patronage for Hudson County.

Finally, Hague had a passion shared by all American progressives. He had a vision for battling a primal fear of every person in a civilized society: going it alone when good health abandons us. Frank Hague wanted to care for the sick and dying, treat the ill and injured, and welcome babies into the world on clean sheets in a hospital bed—not on a kitchen table.

As the nation's economy expanded, medical care for the casualties of American industry was an afterthought. Regardless of the profits coming from business or the tax revenue flowing to government, there just never seems to be enough money to make quality health care available to all. Frank Hague knew the plight of the working poor and decided medical care shouldn't be a privilege but a right. He wielded his power to guarantee that every resident of Jersey City in need of medical treatment received it.

There was nothing in the United States quite like the hospital Frank Hague built for the people of his city. And he made it happen despite hard times for his city and America. The story of Hague's hospital requires some background.

Few people remember the Great Depression fondly, but Frank Hague probably did. Upon gaining a foothold in the Democratic National Committee, Hague quickly became the go-to guy in New Jersey for any Democrat hoping to run for president. Hague had his heart broken in the 1928 presidential campaign, supporting his friend New York governor Al Smith, the Happy Warrior. Largely forgotten today, Smith's loss in that election was a bitter pill for all Irish Americans. The campaign was marked by fierce anti-Catholic, anti-Irish bigotry, which Herbert Hoover watched in silence, knowing he would benefit at the polls. Come 1932, with the nation's economy in dire straits, Hague would have liked nothing more than to see Smith take another shot at Hoover, but alas, it was not to be. Franklin D. Roosevelt, then governor of New York, had the talent, charisma, and money needed to ensure victory, and after the national convention in June, Hague got on board his campaign.

Ever the quick study of people, Franklin Roosevelt knew that Frank Hague had his own agenda. Hague would have to prove himself to the Roosevelt campaign. To rebuild bridges damaged at the 1932 Democratic convention Hague wooed Roosevelt's campaign manager, James Farley, telling him that if FDR would launch his campaign in New Jersey, he "would provide the largest political rally ever held in the United States."[20] Sometime in July, Hague spoke directly with Governor Roosevelt, who committed to being in the seaside community of Sea Girt, about sixty miles south of Jersey City, on August 27.

Rallies were where the Hague organization shone. For years, his people had been organizing parades, festivals, and neighborhood political parties. Bringing people in by trains, buses, and cars, Hague staged what politicians and newspapers alike termed a "monster rally," generating enormous respect for Hague with Roosevelt's people. More than 100,000 people turned out to applaud, hoot, and holler for FDR's initial campaign speech. It was like nothing anyone had ever seen and formed a lasting bond between Hudson County and Roosevelt's political people.

Things got better. Come election time in 1932, it was full throttle. Hague's organization produced a winning margin for FDR in Hudson County of 184,000 to 66,000. Again, Hudson County made the difference, pushing FDR into the victory circle in New Jersey by a vote of 806,000 to 775,000. Not long after FDR's inauguration, Hague ingratiated himself with Harry Hopkins, head of the Work Projects Administration (WPA). It proved to be a blessing for Hague's dream of babies in Jersey City being delivered in beds, on clean sheets.

Harry Hopkins, a graduate of prestigious Grinnell College, known for turning out social activists, was an apostle of progressivism. Frank Hague, the sixth-grade dropout, infamous for corruption and bullyboy ways, had

choked progressivism to death in Jersey City. Nonetheless, they found common cause in the need to put people to work in capital projects benefiting
the public. Despite the fact that WPA funds were officially to be distributed
through the offices of America's governors, things were different in New Jersey. The money went to Hague. During the five years Hopkins was director
of the WPA—with Congresswoman Norton serving as Hague's eyes and ears
in Washington—$50 million poured into Jersey City. Add to that another
$17 million from the Public Works Administration, Frank Hague had nearly
a $1 billion in today's dollars at his disposal. Even while using this bounty to
reward his friends, priority number one was the hospital.

   In many of America's cities in the late nineteenth and early twentieth centuries, clinics served the masses. The first clinic in Jersey City was a pesthouse,
used to quarantine people with contagious diseases. The first more broadly
defined hospital opened its doors in 1868. Known as the Jersey City Charity
Hospital, it was soon overwhelmed by the needs of the growing Irish population. Once he had power, Frank Hague decided things had to change. Efforts
toward building a modern medical center began early in his second term
as mayor. In 1921, with his power over both city and county politics growing, Hague persuaded the Hudson County Board of Chosen Freeholders to
approve a $1.6 million bond (more than $20 million today) for the construction of new facilities. From there it was one small step after another until the
Great Depression when money flowed into Jersey City thanks to FDR.

   With unlimited resources, the hospital grew into a sprawling art deco
complex, dominating the skyline along Bergen Hill and becoming the trophy
of Hague's career. As described by a noted Hague biographer, "The [medi-
cal] center reflected Hague's obsession with health—growing up in the pest-
hole of the Horseshoe had made him a life-long hypochondriac—but it also
reflected good politics. By the time of its completion in 1941, the center was
the third largest medical facility in the world, with 1,800 beds and a top-
notch staff whose services were rendered effectively free of charge."[21]

   No expense was spared; that was reflected in everything from terrazzo
marble floors and Cadillac ambulances to the hospital's staff of topflight physicians. On October 31, 1931, the first building in the complex, the Margaret Hague Maternity Hospital, opened its doors. Hague biographer Leonard
Vernon notes, "At its peak of operation in the late 1930s, more babies were
born there than in any other hospital in the nation—the total for 1936 was
5,088. Of the 6,906 mothers admitted that year, only 20 died—a maternal

mortality of about 0.33 percent. The infant mortality was 2.50 percent. Both figures were well below the national average."[22] Nationally, the mortality rate for infants was 5.5 percent. The maternity hospital could accommodate up to 400 mothers and babies at once; it featured a stainless steel chandelier in the delivery room and brass and bronze fixtures throughout, along with a movie theater on the top floor.

On October 2, 1936, five years after the opening of the Margaret Hague Maternity Hospital, the mayor declared a public holiday and the entire city was invited to the dedication of the new medical center complex. More than 200,000 people turned out for dedication of the new additions to hear President Roosevelt sing the praises of his good friend, Frank Hague.

When the crowd was gone, the mayor remained. He spent more of his waking hours in the medical center than he did in City Hall, even having a mahogany-paneled office built. He was ever-present, known to prowl the medical center's halls, ready to pounce on bits of litter or any cigarette butts. He even went to different parts of the city and called in false alarms in order to record the response time of the ambulance crews. Beware to the ambulance driver or physician who appeared to be dragging his feet. At best, he could expect "a good bawling out";[23] at worst, a punch in the face from His Honor the Mayor.

Despite his obsession with the medical center, Frank Hague's mastery of Hudson County and control of state government continued. His political juggernaut had strengths beyond cranking out lopsided vote margins; it had tentacles capable of retrieving valuable information. An example came in the gubernatorial election of 1934.

With Harry Moore unable to succeed himself as governor—Hague orchestrated Moore's election to the U.S. Senate that year—the only Democratic candidate acceptable to Hague was the lackluster William Dill, mayor of Patterson. There was little to no enthusiasm for Dill's candidacy, and he was defeated by Republican Harold Hoffman. Frank Hague appeared to have lost his grip on state government. Yet to the consternation of the Republicans, Hague and Hoffman got along just fine. The mayor still controlled every state contract, patronage position, and judicial appointment coming out of the governor's office that might affect Hudson County or any of his allies throughout the state. As leader of the progressive Essex County Clean Government movement, Arthur Vanderbilt confronted Hoffman, telling him to his face that "he had no judgment and no character."[24]

An important footnote to Hoffman's tenure as governor came twenty years later. When he died in 1954, Hoffman left behind a deathbed confession admitting he had embezzled $300,000 (nearly $4 million today) from state government.[25] Some historians believe that Harold Hoffman "permitted Hague to boss him because the mayor had come upon his secret."[26] The next gubernatorial election in 1937 was a free-for-all, and again Hoffman behaved more like a Hague ally than a Republican governor.

Through it all, across Newark Bay from Jersey City, Arthur Vanderbilt's stature as one of New Jersey's preeminent attorneys was increasing and his prominence as the state's most powerful Republican was growing. Vanderbilt had built a political organization of his own, and he was determined that 1937 would be the year he had a governor of his own. Frank Hague couldn't help but notice.

CHAPTER 7

Clean Government versus Hagueism

Vanderbilt's Clean Government Republicans were anxious to take their reform agenda to the entire state. Although they had made progress on a range of legislative issues, Frank Hague remained a hurdle to any serious measures for fulfilling Arthur Vanderbilt's quest to reform the state's judiciary. The Jersey City mayor's relationship with whoever occupied the governor's chair was an inevitable roadblock for the progressives. From 1921 onward, the governor's appointment of people to the more than eighty agencies, boards, and commissions of state government, plus the posts of attorney general, county prosecutors, and judgeships, a striking number of whom were from Hudson County, was always done with Hague looking over his shoulder.

Vanderbilt and his allies were fixated on marginalizing Hague's role in state government. By 1937, Essex County's new ruling class was determined that the next election wouldn't be stolen by a lopsided vote in Hudson County for a Frank Hague candidate. Newark, the city of grandeur, aimed to bring gritty little Jersey City to heel.

Few state elections in American history have produced the passion and venom that spewed from the battle for New Jersey governor in 1937. With the stature attained by Vanderbilt's Essex County organization throughout the state, Hague knew that he couldn't manipulate the selection of the Republican candidate. He prepared accordingly. The campaign featured a Presbyterian minister, Lester Clee, as the Republican candidate, versus a Presbyterian Sunday school teacher, Harry Moore, as the Democratic candidate. Hague had summoned Moore home from the U.S. Senate, forcing him to resign so he could run for a third term as governor. Word was that "poor old Harry" was deeply disappointed; he wanted to stay in Washington, but he had no say in the matter. Despite being a retread, Moore was Hague's best hope for holding on to control of the governor's office. And Hague knew it would be a tussle.

Lester Clee was the real deal; a true believer and genuine heir to the Progressive movement, he was seeking to transform New Jersey's government and bring it into the twentieth century. Like Vanderbilt and Frank Sommer, Clee was a Teddy Roosevelt–style Republican, seeing a central role for government in uplifting society. While having nothing like Moore's résumé—many viewed that as a strength—he was the dynamic and widely respected pastor of the large Second Presbyterian Church of Newark. He was closely identified with Vanderbilt.[1] As an early ally in forming both the Republican League and Clean Government movements, Clee was elected first to the assembly, where he served briefly as speaker, and then state senator. Intelligent, articulate, and a tireless campaigner, Lester Clee was an adversary who wasn't going away quietly.

Reruns are rarely exciting but this round of the New Jersey Republicans versus Hudson County was an exception. As had occurred repeatedly in prior gubernatorial elections, with twenty of twenty-one counties reporting, the Republican candidate led by a healthy margin—more than 84,000 votes. Predictably, many hours after the polls had closed elsewhere, word came from Hudson County that of the 221,000 votes cast there, favorite son A. Harry Moore had received more than 75 percent, with a margin of nearly 120,000, making him the next governor, yet again.

Clee knew he'd been robbed and wasn't backing away from a fight. The total vote in Jersey City alone was 145,000. Granting the city every benefit of the doubt, Clee's campaign advisers figured that, if as many as 90 percent of all eligible voters had registered and 90 percent of the registered voters had voted, Jersey City could have produced at most a vote of 119,336.[2] While Clee, Vanderbilt, and the key players of Clean Government were crying foul, Hague taunted them, issuing a public challenge: "Ever since I have been in politics . . . all I have heard from Republican leaders is fraud and corruption in Hudson County. . . . I say to Senator Clee and his cohorts: Now is the time for your recount. I dare you to come into Jersey City."[3]

Clee accepted the dare but it came with a steep price tag. Chief Justice Thomas Brogan required the Republicans to deposit $9,795—roughly $160,000 today—with the Hudson County clerk before the recount could proceed. Brogan was a longtime Jersey City solicitor who had represented Hague on his writ of habeas corpus when the legislature tried to arrest him in 1929; Harry Moore had appointed him to the state Supreme Court during has second term as governor. Hague knew he could count on Brogan's loyalty. Busy attacking Hague on another front, Vanderbilt was not part of Lester Clee's legal team. That was handled ably by Robert McCarter. He may have been jealous of Vanderbilt but Hague had a way of uniting Republicans of all stripes, except those like Harold Hoffman who had been co-opted by Frank Hague.

By the first week of December the money had been paid and the process begun. The Essex County Republicans were invading Jersey City. With just six miles to travel from Newark, Clee's supporters arrived daily, becoming a disquieting presence, making no sign of leaving until their man was declared the winner. Although small errors in precinct tallies and dubious ballots were found, in most instances the Hudson County Board of Elections smugly ruled that the mistakes favored Harry Moore. Clee, Vanderbilt, and Republicans throughout the state were seething with indignation.

Next was a petition by Clee's lawyers to examine the poll books themselves, and they had ammunition the Democrats never saw coming. Unknown to Hague, less than two weeks after the election Charles Stroebling, the Republican Hudson County commissioner of registration and the person officially responsible for the books, let down his guard. On Saturday, November 13, Clayton Freeman, chairman of the Republican State Committee, met quietly with Stroebling in his office and had an opportunity to carefully examine the voter registration books of a single polling place.[4]

Stroebling was a longtime Jersey City person; with Hague's approval, Governor Harold Hoffman had appointed to him to this statutory position, which normally went to the party controlling the governor's office. From Vanderbilt and Clee's perspective—and just about everyone else's—Stroebling and the Hudson County Republican Party were a wing of Hague's organization. For reasons we'll never know, Stroebling agreed to meet with Freeman and several people from the Clee campaign. The single set of voting records that Stroebling permitted Clee's supporters to review confirmed their suspicions. Needless to say, once Hague learned of the Freeman-Stroebling meeting, none of the records for any of the other voting districts were available.

Yet in the one precinct alone, there were ample voting irregularities to warrant a lawsuit. Clee and his supporters took their proofs to the court, revealing: (1) a rabbi who had left Jersey City three years earlier was shown as having voted, and confirmed by an affidavit that he hadn't; (2) patients in a mental hospital had voted; (3) dead people had voted; (4) ballots had been destroyed; and (5) several ballots clearly showed signs of alteration. Robert McCarter's pleadings appeared to make a strong case for going to the next step, namely, physical examination of all the voting poll books via comparison of signatures.[5] McCarter's adversary was Jersey City attorney Ed O'Mara, and although O'Mara was in fact an able advocate, he never had to break a sweat; he and Tom Brogan were on the same team, both alumni of the Jersey City solicitor's office.

On this initial confrontation, Chief Justice Brogan gave scant attention to the arguments of Clee's lawyers, ruling that the court had no authority to permit a complete examination of the voter registration books prior to a trial between Clee and Moore contesting the official results as stated by Hudson County. He concluded, "I am of the opinion that there is a lack of power in the court to permit the requested examination in advance of trial."[6]

Frothing with anger at being spurned by a Hague crony in robes, the Republican-dominated legislature held a special session to empower an investigative committee to retrieve the pollbooks from Jersey City. The committee members demanded to meet with the voter registration commissioner. In a tough break for the Republicans, Charles Stroebling had suddenly fallen ill and wasn't receiving visitors. Dr. Robert Stockfisch of the Jersey City Medical Center, who was treating him, was so concerned for Stroebling's health that he wasn't permitting visitors. As an added measure of protection, the Jersey City Police Department had both Stroebling's home and office placed under twenty-four-hour guard so no one would disturb his rest or tamper with his records while he was ill.

Clee and his supporters were infuriated. The special legislative committee implored Attorney General David Wilentz, to do something. Wilentz had previously been Democratic Party chairman of Middlesex County and was as cagey a lawyer-politician as ever lived. At the time, Wilentz was something of a celebrity, known nationally as the prosecuting attorney in the Lindbergh baby kidnapping trial in 1935—dubbed by newspapers as the "trial of the century." A Hague ally, Wilentz had been appointed attorney general four years earlier in the final year of Harry Moore's second term as governor. At Hague's urging, Governor Harold Hoffman had dutifully reappointed him as the state's head lawyer. The Republicans beseeched Wilentz to dispatch the state police to Jersey City to take possession of the pollbooks from Stroebling to ensure their safekeeping. Wilentz respectfully declined to act. The attorney general was of the opinion that absent the issuance of a court order, a request for help from the mayor of a city, or the direction of the governor, the state police had no authority to enter a municipality that had its own police force. Wilentz wasn't buying into the urgency of the situation, and Governor Hoffman was mum. The state police weren't going to Jersey City to safeguard the pollbooks.

Lester Clee, Vanderbilt, and the Clean Government Republicans were watching their victory slip away. Three weeks after the first court hearing—and precious time passing—Robert McCarter had no choice but to petition Chief Justice Brogan a second time, demanding a trial to prove voter fraud. Again, he was met by Ed O'Mara, who was now on the attack. In essence, Clee and the Republicans charged that the election officers in the 519 districts were so derelict in the performance of their duties that all 200,000-plus votes cast in Hudson County were suspect. Nonetheless, for purposes of his pleadings, McCarter argued that a minimum of 55,000 fraudulent votes were cast for Harry Moore. O'Mara moved to dismiss the Republicans' lawsuit.

Brogan began his analysis by citing Harry Moore's clean hands. "At the oral argument of this motion, it was expressly admitted by counsel for the contestant that he had no thought of intimating that the incumbent was in any way responsible for the alleged derelictions of which complaint is made."[7] Continuing, he gently reproved McCarter for overstating his case by commenting on the number of people who would have to have been involved in the fraud, a minimum of 2,076 election officers in 519 voting districts. According to Brogan, to say that so many people throughout Hudson County had "failed utterly in even a single instance to compare signatures, as required by law, imposes a strain upon one's credulity."[8] Referencing the state election statute, dating back to 1876, Brogan said that it was the burden of the challenger to name the people involved by identifying the voters in question, the people who cast votes in their name, and the poll workers who permitted it, as well as specifying in which districts the fraud occurred and establishing that the total number of fraudulent votes cast would alter the results of the election. And if that information was provided there was a final obstacle to relief: "Of course, it is palpable, even assuming illegal votes were cast, that no one can truthfully say for whom they were cast."[9]

In essence, Brogan viewed McCarter and Clee's charges of election fraud as overly broad and too vague to warrant convening a plenary hearing to receive testimony on their claims. And, as every lawyer knows, fraud cannot be established by offering conclusions: such charges must rely upon specific facts, recited in detail. Because the Republicans had seen the books of only one voting district, conclusions as to the other 518 districts were insufficient. A recount of the election results by the Hudson County Board of Elections had been properly conducted and that was all the Republicans were entitled to. Examination of the pollbooks of all 519 districts in Hudson County could not be granted because the findings of one polling district were not an indicator of what the other 518 districts would reveal, no matter that dead people and a rabbi who had left town three years earlier had allegedly voted. Showing his knowledge of Latin, Tom Brogan finished his ruling stating, "The maxim *quod non apparet non est* applies to the situation before us."[10] Translated: what appears not does not exist.

Chief Justice Brogan's ruling was issued on January 11, 1938, two weeks after oral argument and less than a week before Harry Moore was scheduled to be sworn in as governor. Efforts to get the E & A to take the matter up on short notice were to no avail—apparently not everyone was back in town from the holidays. The inauguration ceremony went forward as scheduled.

To Lester Clee and his allies it was like being mugged in an alley. All the efforts of Vanderbilt's Clean Government movement were for naught. Harry Moore was off to the statehouse for his third term as governor. His first act in office was to appoint Hague lawyer and Hudson County prosecutor John Milton to serve out his term as U.S. senator. From his perch in Jersey City, Frank Hague was pleased with the outcome: the WASP intruders had been repelled. Harry Moore was back in Trenton, John Milton was in Washington, and Jersey City's Celtic Chieftain was secure on his throne. Through it all, Vanderbilt was exasperated, but he wasn't quitting. Aggressively waging war against Hague on another front, he aligned himself with people whom Hague hated as much as WASP Republicans.

Despite the national Democratic Party's emerging alliance with organized labor, Hague rarely showed anything but contempt for the labor movement. Two obvious theories are plausible. First, Hague didn't want anyone competing with him for organizing anything or anyone in his town. The Democratic Party in Jersey City was the one true unifying force in the community. As the overlord of Hudson County politics, Hague knew what was best for his people, and no one was going to vie with him for leadership. Second, throughout its early years, organized labor was seen by many as part of, connected to, or influenced by Bolshevism—the "red menace," that is, Communism. Rather than snuggling up to the labor movement, Hague saw political advantages to confronting it. He would out-American the Republicans by showing what a fierce patriot he was, defending against forces undermining the American way.

Yet something personal likely added to Hague's hostility to organized labor. The construction of the Jersey City Medical Center and the Margaret Hague Maternity Hospital had taken on an importance in Hague's life like nothing else, and the only serious obstacle he encountered in building the hospital came from a labor union. The story begins in the fall of 1931, when a Newark contractor, Leo Brennan, was hired to construct a backup power plant, ensuring that electric service to the hospital wouldn't be interrupted. To keep peace with Ironworkers Local 45 in Jersey City, Brennan was willing to hire union men for his work crew. But he refused to accept workers from the select list of men controlled by union boss, Teddy Brandle, who could be every bit as belligerent as Frank Hague. The two of them weren't exactly pals, but they were partners in corruption, using one another to swipe tax dollars.

Brandle was no mere thug; he was an enterprising thug. He had formed a bonding company that issued performance guarantees that reaped huge fees through state and county contractors steered to him by Hague. There is no way to learn how many dollars flowed to Hague from Brandle, but the two men's understanding was a solid one. So much so that the Jersey City Police Department had a hands-off policy toward any strike called by Ironworkers Local 45. Because Hague had not first run the power plant contract by him, as he had done on other jobs, Brandle was perturbed with both Brennan and Hague. He felt his partner had reneged on their understanding.[11]

Brandle's instincts took over, and he retaliated by calling a strike. Brennan refused to stop work, and Brandle upped the ante, bringing in his goons to smash heads; several of Brennan's men were beaten badly, requiring hospitalization. Although the temporary shutdown of construction sites and fights among workers in Jersey City were fairly common, this project was Hague's obsession, a maternity hospital named for his mother. Trying to prevent more violence—and more important, any further sullying of the hospital's public image—the Jersey City police shut down the work site. Hague was trying to get everyone to calm down. He failed. Brennan wasn't just tough, he was smart, and he had resourceful lawyers. Within days he went to court, obtaining an order permitting work to resume.

Brandle threatened to shut down the entire project—not just the power plant. Hague had an enormous mess on his hands and was forced to do something that no one saw coming. He cut a deal with Brennan to take him out of the picture and let the job go forward with a contractor willing to hire from Brandle's list of union workers. The fly in the ointment for Hague was the fact that Brennan was demanding full payment for the job. With a second contractor on board, the county would have to pay for the same work twice. Hague couldn't handle this one with his walking-around money and was forced to go to the Hudson County Board of Freeholders for payment of a cost overrun. There was never any doubt they would approve the money, but it was all embarrassing for Hague.

Failed partnerships oftentimes turn into lifelong grudges. After the power plant debacle, Frank Hague and Teddy Brandle were at each other's throats whenever they were in one another's presence. The rancor permeated Hague's thinking to such an extent that what had previously been a negative disposition toward the labor movement mutated into a hate-filled crusade against all unions. In time, Jersey City became one of the most inhospitable places in America for organized labor. And in the autumn of 1937, while he was battling Vanderbilt's Clean Government candidate, Hague decided to wage war with the Committee for Industrial Organization (CIO), a labor group with whom the national Democratic Party was making moves toward building a political partnership.

Established in 1935, the CIO, later the Congress of Industrial Organizations, was an umbrella organization for many unions. Quickly gaining notoriety through successful sit-down strikes in several tire factories in Ohio, the CIO had created a new wrinkle for factory owners. Prior to the development of this tactic, striking workers seeking to organize unions had formed picket lines outside factories, bringing operations to a halt. The problem was that management brought in scabs to replace them, work resumed, and the strikers were fired. With the sit-down, employees stayed in their places within the factory, refusing to work. This strategy meant that sending in new people to continue the job was off the table for factory owners. Management was afraid to bring in private security forces to remove the striking workers for fear of the violence that might unleash.

When the CIO announced in November 1937 that it had targeted Hague's town for a mass recruiting effort, he viewed it as a declaration of war, every bit as critical as Clee's election challenge. There weren't going to be any sit-downs in any of Jersey City's factories. With Hague pal Tom Brogan covering his back in the courts, Hague wasn't troubled by Clee's voter fraud lawsuit. That meant he could direct his energies toward putting down the invasion of his city by people he viewed as union punks who the Zepps had told him were on the way to town.

Several weeks following the election, on November 23, 1937, the *Newark Evening News*—no friend of Hague—trumpeted the arrival of the union organizers. The article's headline read, "C.I.O. Prepared for Invasion—Mass Drive by 3,000 to be Launched Monday in Jersey City." The news article reported that Bill Carney, the CIO regional director, was planning a membership drive in Jersey City and that he relished a "show down" with the mayor of that fine city. Carney was quoted as saying, "We will go to Jersey City to organize in a peaceful manner. Whether this will be possible in the face of denials of civil rights in that city I am unable to say at this time."[12]

Around 6:00 a.m. on November 29, CIO organizers arrived, filtering through the streets, setting up stations near factories, and preparing to form informational picket lines. Frank Hague was ready for them. To his way of thinking these un-American troublemakers had no right to agitate in his town, and the Zepps were out in force. Without warrants or any basis for probable cause, the union members were stopped, searched, and their handbills seized before any were distributed to factory workers. Many months later a federal trial court would find that the city had acted against the CIO organizers through a "plan and conspiracy" to "harass and molest" them in total disregard of their rights as American citizens.[13]

As termed later by the federal court of appeals, dozens of the organizers were "deported" from Jersey City. They were dragged down to the waterfront and placed them on ferries to New York City or thrown into the back seat of police cars and driven beyond the city's boundaries, dumped on the street and threatened with beatings if they ever returned. No amount of protest or pleas for reason got them anything but rougher treatment. Others were arrested, promptly tried, and convicted the same day by a police justice, who sentenced them to five days in jail for the illegal distribution of handbills.

While all this was occurring, there was a second wave of the invasion by these unwelcomed "Bolshevik" agitators. Representatives of the CIO, ACLU, the American Whig Cliosophic Society of Princeton University, the progressive *Catholic Worker*, and, finally, perennial Socialist Party presidential candidate Norman Thomas all filed applications with Public Safety Director Daniel

Casey. Thomas was represented by none other than Arthur Vanderbilt. Each applicant was seeking a permit to address the public in Journal Square on the rights of workers to organize for collective bargaining with management. No sooner were their applications filed than the Chamber of Commerce, the Sons of Poland, the Catholic War Veterans, the Lions Club, the Board of Realtors, the Ladies of the Grand Army of the Republic, and the Italian War Veterans all wrote to Casey protesting the issuance of permits, expressing grave concerns for the well-being of the city's residents and property.

In denying all the requested permits, Director Casey asserted "the necessity of preserving peace and good order" in the city, citing the "possibility of riot, strife and injury of the speakers and the citizens of Jersey City."[14] As the legal challenges to the city's brazen defiance of the law made their way through the federal court system—with Hague losing and appealing each time—the facts were reported to the public in greater detail and Hague's role in the "plan and conspiracy" to "harass and molest" became more obvious. This wasn't the community rising up to ask the city to protect them from out-of-town troublemakers; this was a carefully orchestrated brutal assault of the civil rights of CIO organizers, with His Honor the Mayor serving as the maestro.

Barely able to restrain their indignation, the three-judge panel of the Third Circuit Court of Appeals politely mocked the notions that the local police force could not have maintained the peace and that there was a community-wide outcry over fear for life and limb. The court said: "The evidence is incontrovertible that he [Hague] was the spearhead of the movement to keep the appellee labor groups out of Jersey City. . . . The record indicates that the calling together of these organizations [the Chamber of Commerce and the others] was done upon the instructions of Mayor Hague and that he himself actively collaborated in" getting local residents to barrage Public Safety Director Casey not to permit the use of Journal Square by violence-prone "reds."[15]

Hague's belligerence took him all the way to the U.S. Supreme Court. The several written decisions from the trial level to the Supreme Court only get shorter, the inevitable result flowing from facts and law that would have been obvious to a junior high school civics class.

In February 1939, with oral argument on Hague's appeal to the U.S. Supreme Court only days away, Governor Harry Moore dutifully announced the appointment of Hague's son, thirty-four-year-old Frank Jr., as a lay member of the

E & A. Frank Jr. had dawdled away eight years attending Princeton, the University of Virginia School of Law, and Washington and Lee University School of Law without receiving a degree from any of them. The vacancy permitting Frank Jr.'s appointment was orchestrated by Dad. He persuaded a sitting member of the high court, Thomas Glynn Walker, a former Democratic assembly leader from Hudson County, to resign in exchange for an appointment to the federal bench, an appointment that FDR delivered in December 1939. There was fierce opposition to Frank Jr.'s nomination. Vanderbilt's personal files at Olin Library at Wesleyan University reveal that he was galvanized by this event. He viewed Junior's appointment to the E & A as an affront to the very idea of an independent judiciary. The fight on the floor of the state senate was led by Essex County Clean Government Senator Frederic Colie, but when the votes were counted, Hague got his way. Yet the mayor wasn't going to get his way with the nation's highest court.

Four months after oral argument in *Hague v. The C.I.O.* the decision was announced. Justice Owen Roberts ruling made it clear that "[t]here is no competent proof that the proposed speakers have ever spoken at an assembly where a breach of the peace occurred or at which any utterances were made which violated the canons of proper discussion or gave occasion for disorder."[16] Continuing, Roberts stated, "Citizenship of the United States would be little better than a name if it did not carry with it the right to discuss national legislation and the benefits, advantages, and opportunities to accrue to citizens therefrom."[17] Finally, commenting on the challenged ordinance and the city's fears of unrest beyond the control of the local police department, Justice Roberts wrote, "It enables the Director of Safety to refuse a permit on his mere opinion that such refusal will *prevent riots, disturbances or disorder assemblage.* It can thus, as the record discloses, be made the instrument of arbitrary suppression . . . for the prohibition of all speaking will undoubtedly *prevent* such eventualities."[18] Needless to say, the U.S. Supreme Court found the Jersey City ordinance unconstitutional.

Making Hague's manhandling of the CIO organizers all the more disturbing to most people was the fact that the labor wars were supposed to be over. Somehow, Frank Hague hadn't received the news. From the late nineteenth century into the 1920s there had been many instances of violence against workers trying to organize. With acceptance of the need to protect workers' rights growing each year among both progressive Republicans and enlightened northern Democrats, in 1933 Congress adopted the National Labor

Relations Act (NLRA). The NLRA greatly expanded government's right to intervene in labor relations by guaranteeing all workers the right of self-organization and, most critical, the right to bargain collectively through representatives of their own choosing. Despite the controversy created by the new law, FDR put the full weight of his administration behind enforcing it.

Although there were union leaders affiliated with both national political parties, the Democrats were consciously creating alliances with organized labor. In most northern states productive partnerships were being formed between the local Democratic leaders and trade union members, with the adoption of the NLRA serving as a major impetus. Hague was out of step with his fellow Democrats. Deporting the C.I.O. organizers was a blunder. The political ripples spewing from the ugly clash in Jersey City were making Frank Hague the skunk at the garden party.

There's an interesting footnote to the goings-on in federal court. Parallel to that litigation was the state court challenge brought by Arthur Vanderbilt on behalf of Socialist Party leader six-time candidate for U.S. president, Norman Thomas. Hague found Thomas particularly annoying, and whenever he came to Jersey City to speak for the right of workers to organize the Zepps were out in force to greet him and he was promptly "deported." It had to have galled Hague to learn that Vanderbilt represented Thomas. Needless to say, his application for a permit to speak in Journal Square had likewise been denied by Director Casey.

Predictably, the New Jersey Supreme Court saw things differently than the U.S. Supreme Court. A three-judge panel composed of Justices Bodine, Heher, and the ever-loyal Tom Brogan ruled that the city's ordinance was lawful and had been competently enforced. "No one is justified in obstructing a public street by collecting therein a large assemblage of people for the purpose of delivering an address to them. The common highways of the state are not designed for the purpose of holding public meetings therein, and anyone who attempts to do this, without having first obtained permission from the public authorities commits a public nuisance." The court concluded by paying lip service to Casey's justification for denying the permit: "Often a public speaker is subjected to rough handling even in this country. When opposition to a speaker's views runs high, no reason exists for subjecting the speaker and innocent bystanders to dangers of assault."[19]

Vanderbilt appealed the state Supreme Court's holding to the E & A, but before the appeal was decided, Justice Roberts's ruling in *Hague v. The C.I.O.*

was issued. No matter, when the E & A finally got around to ruling, nearly six months after the U.S. Supreme Court, it unanimously affirmed the state Supreme Court's holding.[20] Why/how? Well, now that the ordinance had been voided by the federal courts, the question on the issuance of the permit had become moot. With the ordinance gone, Public Safety Director Daniel Casey could no longer be compelled to grant the permit. Even in defeat, Frank Hague could count on his chums on the bench never to lift a finger against his interests.

Arthur Vanderbilt and his client probably could have pursued the issue further by seeking damages for violation of Thomas's civil rights in federal court, but they chose not to. The "two-bit Hitler on the Hudson," as Vanderbilt referred to the mayor, was shown for the tyrant he was and that was the best Vanderbilt could hope for.

Frank Hague had been rebuked on the national stage. Sprinkling salt into the wounds, his perennial critic, the *Newark Evening News*, spread the word to all twenty-one counties in New Jersey. A lesser ego would have wilted. If there had been any doubts about Hague being the nastiest bully of political bossism in America, they had been permanently dispelled. It's hard to understand how his instincts hadn't warned him.

There was something else to which his instincts had not alerted him: the extremes to which he was goading Vanderbilt. Vanderbilt's need to remove Hague as a barrier to his quest for judicial reform would reveal a side of Arthur Vanderbilt that his supporters, and Frank Hague, never suspected. Despite his prominence as the state's most powerful Republican, his national stature as a scholarly lawyer, and his personal wealth, a sixth-grade dropout had dashed his hopes of electing a progressive governor in 1937. Hague's dominance gnawed at him, driving him to a devilish undertaking.

CHAPTER 8

Box 96

ARTHUR AND DAVID

David Dayton McKean. Three generations later the name is tied tightly to Frank Hague, quoted in hundreds of historical works and news articles. The first place historians, journalists, and screenwriters turn to when then want to know about the bad old days in Jersey City under Hague is McKean's book, *The Boss: The Hague Machine in Action.*[1]

No one did more to sully Frank Hague's name in American history than David Dayton McKean. Thanks to McKean's book, Hague's image in twentieth-century urban history is beyond rehabilitation. How could an Ivy League scholar who lived in New Hampshire and had no ties to Hudson County gather so much information and make so much trouble for the mayor of Jersey City? He had help.

Before joining the faculty at Dartmouth College, Professor McKean was on the staff at Princeton University, where he taught speech. From all reports he was an excellent instructor. During those years, 1932 to 1938, McKean was active in New Jersey politics; he ran for and won two terms in the state assembly. While in Trenton he got to see Frank Hague pulling strings up close, observing that no key appointment by the governor or any critical vote in the legislature was beyond Hague's reach. McKean concluded that the biggest hurdle to lifting state government out of its swamp of corruption was Frank Hague.

Not long after leaving Princeton for New Hampshire, McKean became interested in writing a book about Frank Hague and the Hudson County Democratic machine. History doesn't tell us who reached out for whom but we do know that sometime in 1938 or 1939, the Warrior Lawyer from

Newark and the speech professor from Dartmouth began their collabora-
tion on what was to be one of the great biographical hatchet jobs in American history. Delivered in a breezy tone yet presented as a serious study of
a big city mayor's life and times, the book and its author(s) had an agenda,
namely, the political assassination of their subject.

Their alliance began before the first words were written, when Vanderbilt
advanced funds to McKean to carry him between the spring and fall semes-
ters, enabling him to get the research and writing process under way. Vanderbilt would handle much of the research. He was eager to get started working with David and had no qualms about his anonymous role in a deceitful
enterprise, once writing to a friend about the project: "It is rather difficult to
keep sweet when you know definitely that you have had at least two gubernatorial elections stolen in the last fifteen years."[2]

Vanderbilt valued the difference between the spoken and the written word.
He knew that ink on paper has greater force, wider reach, and more authority than a single person's voice, regardless of the speaker. Although there had
been articles critical of Hague in major newspapers and national magazines
over the years, none inflicted lasting damage. In truth, Hague enjoyed the
notoriety, and his supporters weren't troubled by the negative reports as long
as he kept delivering. Publicly referring to the mayor of Jersey City as the
"two-bit Hitler on the Hudson" might let Vanderbilt vent his disdain but it
didn't faze Frank Hague.

Arthur Vanderbilt needed more. Hague had to be battered, and since that
couldn't happen through the election process or the courts, the Warrior Lawyer
would do it with the written word. Vanderbilt couldn't beat Hague in a street
fight, so he would stab at him from the shadows. The mannerly progressive
who fretted over a court system in which only the well-connected could count
on fair play wasn't troubled by his covert undertaking. He was determined to
have a full-length book damning Hague, a book scholarly in appearance yet
calculated to destroy any aura of respectability remaining after the debacle with
the "deportation" of the CIO union organizers and Hague's theft of the 1937
election from Lester Clee.

Vanderbilt wanted a book that would be read not only in New Jersey but
also distributed nationally, so the book had to be placed with a major publisher with outlets in all forty-eight states. After all, the mayor of Jersey City
was also vice chairman of the Democratic National Committee, and it was

only fitting that his friends nationwide should have a chance to learn more about his career. Again, history doesn't tell us precisely when McKean and Vanderbilt began their work but we know the first fruits of their labors were delivered for Vanderbilt's review in January 1940.

Safely tucked away in the archives at the Olin Library of Wesleyan University are Vanderbilt's voluminous personal files.[3] Very few lawyers today can review the records of his infinitely broad client base, nationwide contacts, or the varied legal and political issues he pursued throughout his career without feeling like small-time players. The archival catalog alone is imposing, and although delving into the records is a daunting task, it's engrossing, a window into the mind of an extraordinarily accomplished person. Vanderbilt was a blur of motion. He not only juggled four careers but also found time to keep a record of his exploits. The exceptional effort and care that went into maintaining more than forty years of documents from his public life tell us that Arthur Vanderbilt was someone who believed he had earned a place in history. Long before his death he knew he had made his mark on America's legal system.

Significantly, the Vanderbilt archives are the only place one will find Republican Arthur Vanderbilt linked to Democrat David McKean. Only by exploring a clue left behind by the late Judge Alfred Clapp of Essex County did the footprints of their conspiracy come to light.[4] Box 96 reveals the Newark lawyer and the Dartmouth professor gleefully conspiring like a pair of mischievous schoolboys. The Wesleyan records contain numerous letters between Vanderbilt and McKean and smash any pretense of an even-handed look at Hague's career. In reading their correspondence, one can almost hear them chortling like giddy pranksters.

Arthur and David's efforts were only *semi*-scholarly. They were far more intent upon destroying Frank Hague's character by means of what lawyers and judges term an ad hominem attack than upon dispassionately portraying in context one of the largest figures in New Jersey's history, a figure whose life spoke much about the times he lived in and the dominant role he played in the state's politics for more than three decades.

Putting it kindly, Box 96 confirms that the president of the American Bar Association—so committed to truth and justice—was not above cherry-picking the public record in libeling Frank Hague. He was very selective in weaving a story that was mostly accurate yet decidedly misleading. Vanderbilt also personally drafted multiple revisions to McKean's book—far greater than mere editing, akin to being a coauthor—which made their way into the final manuscript, all contrived to appear like serious history, with portions deliberately distorting the truth of several important events in Hague's career.

In March of 1940, Vanderbilt wrote McKean a three-page letter containing nine numbered paragraphs in which he recites very detailed changes he believed were needed to a particular chapter.[5] A week later, in commenting on a portion of a chapter analyzing the Boss's personal finances, Vanderbilt discusses Hague's relationship with Jersey City union thug Teddy Brandle, promising to do needed legal research: "I will try to dig out for you the list of New Jersey cases and get some dope for you on the Hudson County Bar Association, which is a story in itself."[6] One conspicuous fingerprint is the number of citations to court decisions. Even the casual reader is likely to notice them. In the same letter in which he promises to do legal research, Vanderbilt continues, "Another item that might strengthen the chapter is a reference to the outward manifestation of Hague's wealth: his ownership of the Duncan Apartments, his suite of rooms in New York, his palatial home at Deal, and his extravagant display of automobiles—all on an official's salary."[7] In another letter Vanderbilt remarks, "Meantime, I have read Chapters II ["The Boy in the Horseshoe"] and III ["The Rise to Power"] with increasing enjoyment."[8]

McKean's solicitation of Vanderbilt's thoughts, including rewrites, is readily apparent from their correspondence. In one letter McKean comments, "This particular chapter seems to me a bit weak, and I'd be glad to have the most trenchant criticisms you would care to make. I am perfectly willing to rewrite the whole thing, and if you would like to make your comments right on the copy that would be all right."[9] In the same letter McKean recalls a recent weekend stay at Vanderbilt's home, expressing his fear that he may have left a virus behind, hoping that none of Arthur's children caught his cold.

Notably, the exchanges between these accomplices show that Vanderbilt replied promptly to McKean's latest drafts and queries. No matter how busy he may have been with any one of his four careers, Arthur always found time to help David with his research and writing. He even clipped newspaper articles and submitted them unsolicited, pointing out their value at giving the history a more current flavor. In one such instance he wrote to McKean on the "Bozzo matter," which involved a racetrack in Passaic County and what Vanderbilt viewed as corruption of the Racing Commission by Hague. "The whole race track situation literally smells to the high heaven."[10]

There was substance to much of what Vanderbilt complained about and urged exposing. Hague was a huge target. He had committed many crimes. He had run roughshod over many lives. Nonetheless, the mix of life experiences in his personal history that incited his conduct was complex and warranted a thoughtful examination. The contents of Box 96 reveal two Ivy League professors plotting against an alumnus of the Horseshoe with all the sophistication and subtlety one would expect of a pair of twenty-first-century smash-and-trash talk radio hosts.

Later in the winter of 1940 David submitted a draft chapter on "socialized medicine" to Arthur, stating, "I hope you will feel free, as before, to comment. I also hope you find this amusing."[11] When one reads the mocking criticism of Hague's feat of extending universal medicine to Jersey City's residents, the coauthors' cynicism is palpable. Health care for the poor, particularly pregnant women, was a cornerstone of the progressive movement, yet in McKean's book the hospital was all about politics. In chapter 10, "Turning Hospital Beds into Votes: Socialized Medicine under the Hague Machine," McKean lambastes Hague's life's work:

In his recognition of the political possibilities of hospitalization Hague stands unique among American bosses: he alone has seen the way that lavish medical care can be used to disarm criticism, and that it is practicable to have children literally born into the organization, obligated to it from the first squalling moment. Cared for during the recurrent illnesses of youth, they come to associate health itself with the generous political party that has guided their city for decades; they will no more vote against Hague than against life.[12]

In an attempt to minimize Hague's cherished trophy, McKean recounts a sanitized history of Jersey City's public hospital system, suggesting that the medical center wasn't a new idea but rather the latest installment of the city's continuing effort to provide health care to its citizens, which Hague put a stranglehold on for his political ends. McKean leaves out an important point—the fact that the Irish were shunned, shooed, and discriminated against by the early WASP-operated health clinics.

As I noted earlier, the first public clinic in Jersey City was the pesthouse where Irish people with contagious diseases were quarantined. The first more broadly defined hospital, the Jersey City Charity Hospital, was little more than a bandage for the growing Irish population that had come to town to work at the three Ds, namely tasks that were dirty, difficult and dangerous. Many workers were injured building the railroads and tunnels and working in the city's fetid factories. Completely ignored by the lawyer and the professor is the fact that it wasn't until 1921—when Hague was consolidating power in his second term as mayor—that anything in the way of serious health care for the working poor was provided. The WASPs neglected the obvious health care needs of the immigrant class, and it took Hague to make things happen. And he did it on a grand scale.

Jersey City Medical Center was gigantic, made up of seven towers and several hospitals: the Medical Building, providing what might be called urgent care today; the Tuberculosis Hospital, battling a scourge on American society that devastated millions of families; the Psychiatric Hospital, creating a safe place for the mentally ill; the Hospital for Infectious Diseases, quarantining and treating patients with transmittable illnesses; and most prominently, the Margaret Hague Maternity Hospital, the first to open. For the Irish of Jersey City the maternity hospital was a giant step up from being born on a kitchen table. In its prime, the hospital named for Mom was unsurpassed in the nation in its low rates of maternal mortality and infant mortality. Yet in *The Boss* all this was reduced to a place where Jersey City's residents were "born into the organization, obligated to it from the first squalling moment."[13]

Was the Medical Center grandiose and ultimately unsustainable? Yes. Did Hague and his allies benefit from it in innumerable ways? Yes. Was the Celtic Chieftain obsessed with his own handiwork? Yes. Nonetheless, for nearly fifty years the Medical Center welcomed all comers—no matter their ailment— and cared for everyone free of charge. History tells us, as do most religious teachings, that the hallmark of a civilized society is how well it looks after the weak and vulnerable; it's a strong thread sewn into the Holy Bible, enhancing Hague's stature with the hierarchy of the Catholic Church. The residents of Jersey City knew that if good health abandoned them they weren't alone; Hague's hospital was there. Vanderbilt and McKean might scoff at the Medical Center as no more than political pandering, but only someone who cared deeply about his constituents would pursue such a vision.

One portion of *The Boss* that surpassed most of the other inquiries into Hague's machine up to that time was the manner in which Arthur and David exposed Hague's sway over the judiciary. With obvious input from Arthur, David—quite cogently—gives the reader perspective on how Hague had filled key positions in the court's upper echelons in taking control of the judiciary with his own people. Speaking of Hague's homegrown judges, McKean said:

> [T]hey tend to be Irishmen, who, after finishing their legal education, or even while completing it, get into politics. Soon they get elected to the Assembly, where they spend two or three years, rising to be Democratic floor leaders, or going to the Senate for a term or two. Their legislative records are perfectly regular; that is, obedient. Then they leave state affairs for a while to be counsel to their home city or county, prosecutor, or county judge. This period may last ten years or more, and since there are never enough places on the highest courts, many never get in the way when the lightning finally strikes.
>
> The long period of testing and training has proved its worth in the justices and vice-chancellors who have survived. *In re Hague* is perhaps the most outstanding case in point, elsewhere discussed in these pages; in that, the Court of Errors and Appeals held that the legislature had no right to ask Mayor Hague questions about his wealth.[14]

In re Hague was "outstanding" but not quite in the way McKean would have the reader believe. It was this litigation discussed in *The Boss* that provoked this historian's curiosity and raised doubt in my mind about the book's evenhandedness.

Shortly after the 1928 Republican gubernatorial primary, Somerset County Republican state senator Clarence Case declared war on Hague. As recounted in chapter 6, that was the primary in which party-endorsed reform-minded Judge Robert Carey went down to defeat as result of 20,000-plus Hudson County "Republicans for the day" voting for Morgan Larson in accordance with a deal struck by Hague with Nucky Johnson.

Enraged by Hague's manipulation of the selection of their candidate, Republicans launched an inquisition of Frank Hague's finances. His Honor the Mayor was summoned to Trenton from Jersey City and ordered to answer questions about the assets he had compiled over the previous twenty years. He declined their request. A nasty confrontation ensued. The litigation arising from Hague's refusal to answer questions on his finances posed by Case's committee was recounted in *The Boss* by David with obvious help from Arthur.

Emphasizing the farcical nature of a mayor being able to amass a fortune while receiving an annual salary of only $8,000, McKean assailed Hague's ill-gotten wealth. Tracing funds and cash payments, identifying Hague's

partners in crime and connecting the dots to show the intersection of politics
and money, McKean told this story more clearly than most chroniclers of the
time. Whole sections of the senate committee's record are expertly refined to
their essence, reading much like the brief of an able attorney. Although the
details of Hague's corruption are consistent with the Case Committee's findings, that's only part of the story.

Unraveling Vanderbilt's quilt of partial truths in McKean's discussion
of *In re Hague* requires a somewhat broader discussion of those legal proceedings than David and Arthur presented. When the legislature issued a
warrant for the arrest of Frank Hague, the mayor's lawyers petitioned the
Chancery Court seeking a writ of habeas corpus; literally in Latin "you have
the body," or as generally understood in the courts, "bring forth the body."
Habeas corpus connotes the ancient rule in the Anglo-Saxon tradition of the
law whereby any citizens held against their will have the right to seek a court
order requiring that they be brought before a judge to determine whether the
government has the right to continue detaining them. Although Hague was
never physically incarcerated, that threat existed, and his lawyers wanted to
dispose of it immediately before raising the other issues involved in Hague's
rights of privacy versus the legislature's right to inquire into his finances.

Hague pal and longtime Hudson County politician Vice Chancellor
John J. Fallon was the judge Hague's lawyers, Tom Brogan and Merritt Lane,
petitioned. Fallon wasted little time in granting the writ and finding that "the
arrest of Hague was without legal justification and ordered him discharged."
The Republicans charged that Fallon had a conflict of interest and were outraged by his willingness to hear Hague's petition. Both Fallon's refusal to
recuse himself and his order voiding the arrest warrant were challenged by
Senator Case and the Republican legislature; the lawfulness of the arrest was
preliminary to a full hearing on the merits on the main issue of the legislature's power to compel a citizen to answer questions about his finances.

Fallon's refusals to step aside and to nullify the warrant quickly made their
way to the E & A. Each side knew that regardless of how the state's high court
ruled, there still had to be a trial and a final ruling on the legal question of
whether or not the legislature could compel Hague to answer their questions.
As described in *The Boss*:

> The committee naturally was curious about the sources of all this cash
> money, but Mayor Hague "declined to answer." The committee then

brought him before the whole legislature, where he still declined to answer. He said that the questions were personal and beyond the right of legislative inquiry; he was arrested for contempt [note to reader: he was *not* arrested], but he immediately applied to Vice-Chancellor John J. Fallon, former Hudson County assemblyman and county counsel, who granted a writ of habeas corpus on the ground that the legislature was usurping a judicial function in asking questions that were designed to show a criminal conspiracy. The state appealed to the Court of Errors and Appeals, which, by dividing evenly six to six, upheld the vice-chancellor. Mayor Hague said in a public statement: "I am very much pleased and satisfied with the decision. It is exactly what I expected."

The decision cut the ground from under the Case Committee; they were never able to explain the Mayor's great affluence.[15]

There are problems with this recitation. The full story is a lot more than a "six to six" vote. Vanderbilt had to know that there were a total of five court decisions ruling on the issues raised by *In re Hague*. McKean cites only one of those decisions, and the court citation used is for a different ruling than the one that yielded the six-to-six vote; he never discusses the fifth and final decision of the E & A.[16] McKean would have the reader believe that the final vote of the high court was a tie, but the six-to-six vote merely dealt with the preliminary question of the propriety of the warrant for the arrest. The six-to-six ruling came down on April 18, 1929, and because it was a tie, Fallon's decision to halt the legislature's attempt to arrest Hague and place him in a jail cell was upheld.

Not discussed by McKean and Vanderbilt was the fact that following that ruling the litigation continued and a final determination was made on the legal authority of the legislature to compel Hague to answer their questions about his personal finances. That decision came down thirteen months later on May 19, 1930. By a vote of ten to one, the state's highest court rejected the Republicans' arguments. But that's only part of it: the judge who wrote the opinion chiding the legislature was a lifelong Republican and no friend of Frank Hague, and he was someone before whom Arthur Vanderbilt had appeared on numerous occasions.

Chief Justice William Gummere was the dean of New Jersey's legal community. His personal history and role as one of the most enlightened jurists in an antiquated system made him a fabled figure among the state's lawyers.

Born in Trenton in 1850 to a prominent Quaker family, he was the son of a well-known lawyer who was a leading member of the New Jersey bar. Gummere's career in the law was fast-tracked by his family. After attending the Lawrenceville School he was off to Princeton, receiving his diploma in three years, graduating several weeks prior to his twentieth birthday.

Many of Gummere's peers remembered him fondly for his role as captain of the Princeton football team that faced Rutgers in 1869 in the first intercollegiate football game played in America. To this day, Gummere's athletic presence on the gridiron, playing a game that more closely resembles a combination of rugby and soccer, is preserved in sepia tone. He also starred in baseball, and legend has it that he was the first player to hook-slide into second base to avoid being tagged.

Not long after graduating from Princeton, Gummere began carving out a presence in the law. From 1870 to 1873 he studied law with his father and was admitted to the New Jersey bar, immediately developing an active practice. Two years later, in 1875, he relocated his practice to Newark, going into partnership with his uncle Joel Parker, a former governor who had led the reform of the state's constitution in 1844. Toward the end of the 1880s he returned to Trenton to represent the mighty Pennsylvania Railroad Company, handling the details of the railroad's expansion in New Jersey. In 1895 Republican governor George Werts appointed Gummere to the state Supreme Court. Six years later, Democratic governor Foster Voorhees named him chief justice, a position he held until his death in 1933.

William Gummere revered the rule of law. He wasn't the least bit impressed with the Republicans' arguments, all of which he viewed as cheap political grandstanding. He took Senator Case and the entire legislature to school.

Cogently summarizing the record, Gummere chided the legislature for failing to respect the separation of powers. It's one thing for a legislative committee to make inquiries in furtherance of adopting laws that address statewide public policy issues with an eye toward drafting legislation, but quite another to use the might of its subpoena and investigatory power to zero in on the affairs of a single citizen.

By refusing to answer the joint committee's questions, "Hague was exercising a legal right and this being so, the legislature was without power to punish him for such refusal." As expressed by Gummere, Frank Hague was firmly in the right. "No person can be punished for contumacy as a witness before the legislature unless his testimony is required in a matter into which the legislature has jurisdiction to inquire." Noting that even if the legislature had been legitimately exploring the need for legislation, Gummere concluded that it was still out of bounds. "Any compulsory discovery by extorting the party's oath to convict him of a crime is contrary to the principles of a free government. It is abhorrent to the instincts of an American. It may suit the purposes of despotic power; but it cannot abide the pure atmosphere of political liberty and personal freedom."[17]

Vanderbilt's spin on the case law coming out of *In re Hague* and what was to be learned from it fell far short of how he would have treated it were he lecturing on the investigatory powers of a state legislature in his class at NYU. As a result of the information fed to him by Vanderbilt, McKean portrayed Hague as escaping punishment on a tie vote. McKean shortchanged the reader, and popular history was deprived of knowing that Chief Justice Gummere thought the Republican legislators had behaved no better than the bully they had condemned.

As the exchange of correspondence and draft chapters of McKean's manuscript arrived in Newark, it becomes apparent from his letters that Arthur is growing anxious about David's efforts at finding the right publisher—a publisher with clout, a publisher whose stature would guarantee the book would be reviewed nationwide. The accomplices also hoped to have the book serialized, or portions published in national magazines. The magazines they targeted, the *Saturday Evening Post* and the *Atlantic*, both declined. As confirmed by materials in box 96 of the Vanderbilt Papers at Wesleyan, it was understood between the conspirators that Vanderbilt had assured McKean that he could guarantee any would-be publisher that a minimum of five hundred copies would be pre-purchased, something all publishers are delighted to learn.

Finally, the prestigious Houghton Mifflin Company of Boston offered McKean a contract and all was well with the plans for publication. There was only one snag; the publisher didn't like the proposed title—suggested by Vanderbilt. In late August of 1940, David wrote to Arthur lamenting, "I have lost the battle over the title of the book."[18] The title urged by Vanderbilt was *The Compleat Boss*. Few people other than Arthur would have suggested such an arcane variant—meaning "quintessential"—of the word "complete." The title settled on by McKean and Manley Jones of Houghton Mifflin was *The Boss: The Hague Machine in Action*.

We'll never know just how much angst all these contrivances caused Vanderbilt but we know that they did. Despite having ink up to his elbows in the writing of McKean's book, Vanderbilt started to have second thoughts. The first indication of that comes with a letter from Vanderbilt to McKean in which he declines to be acknowledged in *The Boss*. Vanderbilt is honored but doesn't want to see his name in McKean's book. "I can't begin to tell you how much I appreciate your suggestion of expressing your appreciation to me in the preface for what little assistance I have been able to give you. I think you will agree with me that as long as I hope to stay in active politics in New Jersey my interest in the matter had better remain *sub rosa*."[19] The emphasis appears in Vanderbilt's original letter.

While Arthur's refusal to permit an acknowledgment of his involvement probably came as both a surprise and disappointment to David, what came next—by way of angst—borders on hysteria. Whether it was fear of involvement in a libel lawsuit, supposed concerns over ripples through the Republican Party, or merely unease at having his cover blown, Arthur dispatched one of his allies in the Newark legal community off to Boston to meet with the people in charge at Houghton Mifflin.

Box 96 contains a long-winded memo that can be read as either a somber delivery of bad news, or as a farce, or maybe both.[20] The memo from "D.A.C. to A.T.V." is etched in frustration. "D.A.C.," Dominic A. Cavicchia, was a Newark lawyer and former student of Vanderbilt's at NYU. Professor Vanderbilt had now given him an assignment he could never have imagined when he was sitting in a classroom years earlier. Cavicchia's offices were in the Essex Building, where Vanderbilt's law firm was also located. In November of 1940, he wrote to ATV reporting on his meeting with Houghton Mifflin's executives at which he confirmed Vanderbilt's desire to fade into the woodwork.

Apparently there had been communications of some sort between Vanderbilt and a Mr. Brooks, an executive with Houghton Mifflin, shortly before Cavicchia traveled to Boston. "'I understood' I said [Cavicchia speaking to people at Houghton Mifflin], 'from the hurried conversation I had with Mr. Vanderbilt last night that his request would be granted. I'm sure that under the circumstances he had no doubt about it.'" Whatever those exchanges were, letters or telephone discussions, they didn't achieve the understanding Cavicchia had been led by Vanderbilt to believe had been achieved.

Essentially, what Vanderbilt wanted was for the publisher to remove his name entirely from its files. He wanted all his prior correspondence vouching for McKean and playing down the potential of a libel lawsuit by Hague returned to him. He also wanted "the two original memos Fuhrman sent you regarding publicity procedure" returned with Cavicchia. Joseph Fuhrman was a publicist from Newark and an ally of Vanderbilt, helping with public relations in his political wars. Finally, Vanderbilt wanted the original invoice for his purchase of five hundred books returned and re-created to show his emissary as the book buyer. Cavicchia quickly learned that wasn't going to happen.

Trouble was apparent from the outset. Mr. Brooks was nowhere to be found and Cavicchia was led from one office to another. His memo recounts his meeting with the billing department, stating, "'Did you understand me, Mr. Warren?' I asked. 'I'd like the records stripped of the billing to Mr. Vanderbilt and my name substituted.'" Mr. Warren referred him to Mr. Jones on another floor, who kept him waiting. Jones never appeared, and Cavicchia noted, "While I waited, however, there was a sudden liveliness about the place that struck me as being too energetic for so staid a House. The coming and going of imposing men convinced me that conferences were behind closed doors, and that plainly my visit had upset the House of H-M."

Cavicchia was then escorted to a conference room where he was told that Mr. Brooks was away and nothing could be done in his absence. Cavicchia persisted, and he was then taken to Mr. Greenslet. "Down to Greenslet's sanctum we marched . . . Introductions . . . New faces. (To these B.B.B.B.'s the name Cavicchia was a tongue-twister. That made me more determined to be smooth and suave.) Now, like a well-planned football play beautifully executed, this group in Greenslet's den gyrated in such manner that by the time presentations were completed all around, I was left with Greenslet" and two other executives who "constituted the directors of the board relating to trade."

"A polite battle of wits began. Greenslet, nervously twitching his head and clearing his throat (as he did throughout the conference) called for the file. Despite his pretense of examining it for the first time that day, I was certain that he had seen it while I had been upstairs." As the conversation progressed Greenslet told Cavicchia that complying with Vanderbilt's request "would mean the delivery to me of virtually the entire file because throughout it there is repeated reference to yourself in one form or another." One letter in particular from McKean to his publisher was seized upon by Greenslet: one in which David quotes Arthur, stating that he "has read the manuscript and says that it is safe to publish it." Greenslet told Cavicchia that, in light of

Vanderbilt's pleas to remove his name from the file, he "treasured" the letter, viewing it as "tantamount to a legal opinion from you."

As for altering the invoice and company records on the purchase of five hundred books, that wasn't happening either. "On the question of the order for the books, they could see no point in changing the billing, which they certainly couldn't do honorably anyway, they said; it isn't the first time some- one has ordered books for distribution, is it? And should they make such an alteration and the matter ever come to light, how much more damaging would it be in view of the payment received in cash, they said."

While the memo sometime fawns over Vanderbilt, fair reading shows that Dominic Cavicchia fought the good fight and lost. Trying earnest pleas, veiled threats, and bluster, he couldn't gain traction with the executives at Houghton Mifflin. He even tried arranging a telephone conversation between Greenslet and Vanderbilt, but "[t]wo attempts to get you through the H-M operator failed." Even if he had made contact, it's unlikely the conversation would have been productive because of Greenslet's comment, as preserved in the memo: "'I suggest Mr. Vanderbilt write me,' said the dope. 'His phone may be tapped. Doesn't Hague tap wires?'" Whether read as comedy or drama, the memo concludes much as it begins, with frustration.

Box 96 doesn't tell us Vanderbilt's thoughts on the events in Boston; there's no reply memo from A.T.V. to D.A.C., but we have to conclude that Arthur knew he was at a dead end with Houghton Mifflin. He knew it was time to move on to the next phase—distributing *The Boss* throughout New Jersey and the nation. He excelled at that.

Joseph Fuhrman was Vanderbilt's go-to guy when it came to strategizing the marketing of McKean's book. The two of them had worked together in reforming the Republican Party in Essex County and respected one another. One of the items Cavicchia had hoped to retrieve on his trip to Boston was a memo from Fuhrman to the marketing people at Houghton Mifflin advising them about newspapers that would be happy to receive McKean's book. It was Fuhrman who worked with Vanderbilt to create a mailing list and develop the road map for placing *The Boss* in the hands of journalists who could be counted on to review it favorably for the major newspapers across the nation.

Vanderbilt didn't want to miss out on any of the mischief he was creating, and one of the first things he did before Houghton Mifflin distributed the book was to enter into a contract with Burelle's Press Clipping Bureau, Inc., of New York City. Burelle's duties were to "Take all references to the book 'The Boss—The Hague Machine in Politics.'"²¹ We don't know how much time Vanderbilt spent reading all the press clippings assembled by Burelle, but box 96 contains numerous clippings of reviews and news articles about McKean's book. Some are more sensational than others, but Hague doesn't fare well in any of them.

In addition to newspapers in New Jersey and New York, reviews of McKean's book appeared in papers in Connecticut, Massachusetts, New Hampshire, Maine, Pennsylvania, Ohio, Indiana, Illinois, Wisconsin, Michigan, Minnesota, Maryland, Virginia, Tennessee, North Carolina, Texas, Louisiana, Colorado, California, Utah, Arizona, and Washington, D.C. McKean's goal was to sell books. Vanderbilt's goal was to reach as many potential national Democratic leaders as possible in order to taint Hague in their eyes. He succeeded.

One after another the reviews forwarded to Vanderbilt by Burelle's Press Clipping Bureau, and ultimately finding their permanent home in box 96, spoke of McKean's work in glowing terms. An example of the gushing reviews reads: "*The Boss* is a masterpiece in suave mayhem. It is an indictment against Hague and for all things that he stands. It charges him with nearly every political crime listed in the politician's handbook. . . . It is the story of a political party operating on a broad scale, which sort of makes Tammany Hall and all other political machines look like worn-out and antedated vehicles."²²

With the release of *The Boss* in 1940 following the U.S. Supreme Court decision chastising Hague's manhandling of the CIO organizers, the mayor's prestige as vice chairman of the National Democratic Party had taken a huge hit.

Despite Vanderbilt's hopes that *The Boss* might help the gubernatorial campaign of Republican Robert Hendrickson in 1940, it didn't. Vanderbilt's candidate lost. That wasn't good news for the mayor of Jersey City, though. For nearly twenty-five years Hague had been used to having a say in all political patronage positions coming out of Trenton and he had grown accustomed to his governors appointing judges from Hudson County to key positions on the bench; things were about to change. The next governor would be a Democrat hostile to Hague's reign—an inventor's son, intent on reinventing New Jersey's government.

CHAPTER 9

The Inventor's Son

Frank Hague was always on the lookout for a candidate he could control, especially one for statewide office. He hoped that the inventor's son was one. With Thomas Edison his father, Charles Edison's name and lineage would make him a potent candidate for any public office he sought in New Jersey. Hague wanted him to be U.S. senator and was willing to meet with Edison on his home turf in Essex County.

Llewellyn Park is little more than eleven miles from the Horseshoe, yet it's a different world. Situated on 450 lushly wooded acres in West Orange, the private enclave of approximately 150 exquisite homes—many with names of their own—was like something out of a Hollywood movie. The Park is believed to be America's first planned residential development. Its landscape design is reminiscent of New York's Central Park, replete with winding paths, bubbling brooks, ponds, and rare ornamental trees. From the time of its founding in 1857 to Charles Edison's era, Llewellyn Park was home to people of impeccable résumés, elegant wardrobes, and extraordinary means—basically the hoity-toity WASPs Frank Hague despised. Dinner at Glenmont, a twenty-three-room Victorian mansion on thirteen manicured acres, purchased by Thomas Edison in 1886, is probably the only time the mayor of Jersey City entered the gates of Llewellyn Park. It made enough of an impression on Edison for him to recount it in his memoirs.

Toward the end of 1935, FDR and the Democrats in New Jersey were searching for a candidate to run against the incumbent, Senator W. Warren Barbour. They wanted someone friendlier to the New Deal. Despite being a Republican—a Theodore Roosevelt/Frank Sommer/Arthur Vanderbilt type of Republican—Charles Edison had strong ties to FDR's administration through his efforts to assist the economic programs of Roosevelt's administration. There was intense speculation among political watchers that the inventor's son would challenge Barbour; everyone wanted to know his next move.

What hardly anyone had considered was Edison's handicap. Like his father, Charles had sustained a serious hearing loss—in his case following a bout with typhoid as a child. Thomas always claimed his hearing loss followed being "yanked by my ears" onto a train when he was a boy, but most physicians believe it was caused by scarlet fever. As had occurred with Thomas, Charles's hearing worsened as he aged. According to Charles, "large chambers, of varying acoustical properties, filled with many voices, left me at a distinct disadvantage, even with the help of a hearing aid."[1] Although he had little trouble working one to one or in small groups, Charles decided that he wasn't suited to serve in a legislative body. Hague thought otherwise: "That deaf little SOB only hears what he wants to hear." Edison's hearing problems didn't deter Hague from trying to recruit him. Nonetheless, there came a time when the mayor must have regretted wooing the inventor's son.

Edison's memoirs don't tell us who arranged the dinner meeting on December 9, 1935, but Hague was his usual self. "Hague, stern-visaged and imperious, used the occasion to corner me outside the earshot of others to offer me the Democratic nomination for the United States Senate." Hague wasn't taking no for an answer, and he pressed the point. "One of Hague's mannerisms when he wanted to put over a point consisted of rigidly extending the index finger of his right hand and punching it soundly against the chest of his victim—an irksome, if not painful, form of physical punctuation. Even after I explained to him why I chose not to be a candidate, Hague persisted; and, with his extended finger tattooing my chest, he said, *This is Frank Hague asking you. Me, Frank Hague. People don't say no to me.*"[2]

Amazingly, Hague repeated the same tactic on Mrs. Edison, trying to recruit her to persuade her husband. She was appalled. Needless to say, Charles Edison said no, and their relationship only got worse after that evening. And from the history of his life prior to the dinner with Hague it's hard to imagine anyone less likely to align himself with Frank Hague or a more unlikely path to the governor's office of New Jersey than the one trod by Charles Edison.

Charles's father, Thomas Alva Edison (1847–1931), was one of a handful of geniuses who drove the industrial and technology agenda of the modern

world. He was all of twenty-four when he arrived in Newark in 1871, coming to town with the reputation of being an eccentric genius. He also had a
$40,000 advance from Western Union (comparable to $2.5 million today) to
underwrite the costs of creating an improved stock ticker. "Needing space to
manufacture 1,200 tickers immediately, Edison leased the top floor of a four-
story building at 4–6 Ward Street."[3] He advertised for workers "with light fin-
gers," and within a short time he employed more than seventy men. Thomas
Edison's march into the future began in Newark.

Vital technologies taken for granted today—electric lighting, recorded
sound, and moving pictures—all had their genesis between his ears. Edison's
mind was a torrent of ideas leading to hundreds of patents for new gadgets
and gizmos, large and small. His creative energy made him an international
celebrity, until that time equaled only by Benjamin Franklin at the height
of his career. The "Wizard of Menlo Park" cast a large shadow on both New
Jersey and his son.

For America's greatest inventor, a formal education would have been an
impediment. Too brilliant for ordinary schools—considered addlebrained by
one teacher, who was probably overwhelmed by him—Thomas was homeschooled in Michigan by his mother, who saw his genius at an early age. He
was a voracious reader and a lifelong learner in many fields beyond science.
Since Edison had little need for formal schooling himself, it was predictable
that his own children would receive an unorthodox education.

Thomas was a loving father and had six children by two wives—his first
wife, Mary Stilwell, died from a brain tumor at age thirty. His second wife,
Mina Miller, was the daughter of another prominent inventor, Lewis Miller
of Ohio, inventor of the first efficient combine—a harvester-reaper machine
that was critical to increasing America's agricultural output. In 1874, Miller
was cofounder of Chautauqua, a nonprofit educational center in western
New York that thrives to this day. Solidly grounded on the four pillars of
the arts, education, religion, and recreation, Chautauqua epitomized the progressive thinking of the day. It was ecumenical long before that term had
common usage. Mina Miller brought that view of the world to her marriage
and parenting.

Mina wanted her sons and daughter educated differently than the first
three Edison children, who were essentially homeschooled, studying with
tutors and reading books assigned to them by Thomas. While Charles (born
August 3, 1890) and his sister, Madeleine (two years older), and brother,

Theodore (eight years younger), had a French governess who lived in the home, they all received a formal education in private schools from kindergarten through high school. A broad range of readings assigned by their father together with family dinner conversations supplemented their learning. Additionally, portions of every summer were spent at the camp meetings of Chautauqua, where they were exposed to music, painting, literature, and philosophy. After attending the Carteret Academy in West Orange, Charles attended the Hotchkiss School in Connecticut and then enrolled in Boston Tech, today's Massachusetts Institute of Technology. He later said he went to college because "Father wanted me to be able to read a blueprint,"[4] but he left in 1912 prior to receiving a degree. From there he went to work, briefly, at the Boston Edison Company, an electric utility company founded by his father.

After Boston, Charles headed west to the Rocky Mountains, the Grand Canyon, and the Pacific Ocean and traipsed up and down the West Coast. Visiting Los Angeles and staying for a time in San Francisco, he eventually made his way home and was attracted to New York's Greenwich Village, where his sister Madeleine was living with her husband. Discovering Greenwich Village in 1914 opened doors to interests Charles had only touched upon during summer stays at Chautauqua. With the safety net of a position with one of his father's businesses, he decided to explore the bohemian lifestyle.

Although, as he said, "I went on the payroll as an assistant to father, with general duties he hadn't bothered to define too clearly,"[5] Charles's assignment was to work on development of the company's new phonograph records. There were recordings to be made, demonstrations for prospective customers, and "tone tests" of the new "Diamond Disc Phonograph using virtually indestructible plastic records, approximately quarter-inch thick and a real diamond stylus."[6] Charles was energized by the people and goings-on of Greenwich Village and decided that some of the demonstrations and tests of the system should occur there.

With his famous name, striking good looks, dapper attire, stature, an amiable personality, and the resources to pursue his interests, it wasn't long before Charles was involved in the founding of a theater, The Thimble Theatre, and a magazine, *Bruno's Weekly*. Although the theater never made any money, it gave aspiring playwrights and actors a place to be heard and extended Charles's circle of friends. Involved in both ventures was a new friend he had made in Greenwich Village, Guido Bruno, a gregarious Serbian expatriate, fluent in several languages and with a flair for promoting the arts.

In his prime as a private practitioner, Arthur T. Vanderbilt employed as many as seventeen associates, all working under his direction; none ever became his partner. Courtesy of Arthur T. Vanderbilt II.

Newark High School, 1905 class officers; Florence Althen was secretary and Arthur president. Arthur and Floss were teenage sweethearts. Courtesy of Arthur T. Vanderbilt II.

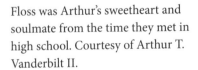

Floss was Arthur's sweetheart and soulmate from the time they met in high school. Courtesy of Arthur T. Vanderbilt II.

Roseville's Prodigy during his college years at Wesleyan University. There's no way of calculating which—the school or the student—made a greater mark on the other. Courtesy of Arthur T. Vanderbilt II.

Arthur, Floss, and their three daughters on the Boardwalk in Atlantic City. They frequently spent Thanksgiving weekend in the resort. The Vanderbilts' two sons are not pictured. Courtesy of Arthur T. Vanderbilt II.

For most of the thirty-four years Vanderbilt taught at NYU's law school, classes were held on the top two floors of the American Book Company. The building was an embarrassment that Vanderbilt set about changing shortly after he was named dean. Courtesy of Arthur T. Vanderbilt II.

The Vanderbilt homestead in Short Hills, Essex County, New Jersey. It was purchased shortly after the fees he collected in handling the Virginia Carolina Receivership. Courtesy of Arthur T. Vanderbilt II.

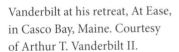

Vanderbilt at his retreat, At Ease, in Casco Bay, Maine. Courtesy of Arthur T. Vanderbilt II.

November 1937. Vanderbilt's client, Norman Thomas, being "deported" from Jersey City by Hague's Zepps. Courtesy of Arthur T. Vanderbilt II.

Governor Alfred Driscoll was a master of the art of compromise and blazed the path to reforming New Jersey's government. Courtesy of Tennessee State Library and Archives.

First Fruit

No one worked longer, harder, or with more persistence than Arthur Vanderbilt to reform New Jersey's corrupt court system. Courtesy of Arthur T. Vanderbilt II.

Administration of the oath to Vanderbilt as district court judge by Frank Sommer. The judgeship was a prerequisite to being appointed to the new state supreme court. Courtesy of Arthur T. Vanderbilt II.

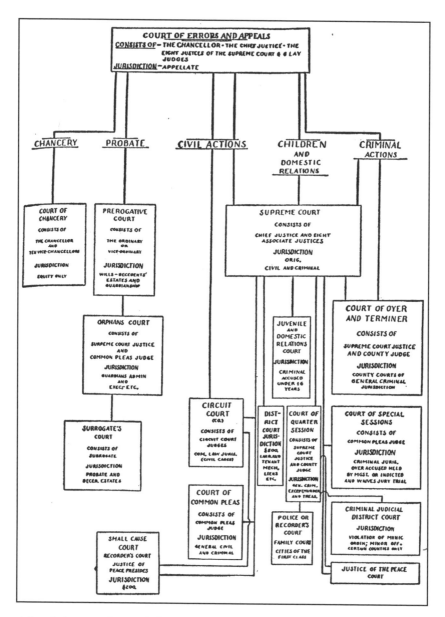

A "tree" showing the tangled roots and hodgepodge of courts of New Jersey's pre-1948 court system. Courtesy of Arthur T. Vanderbilt II.

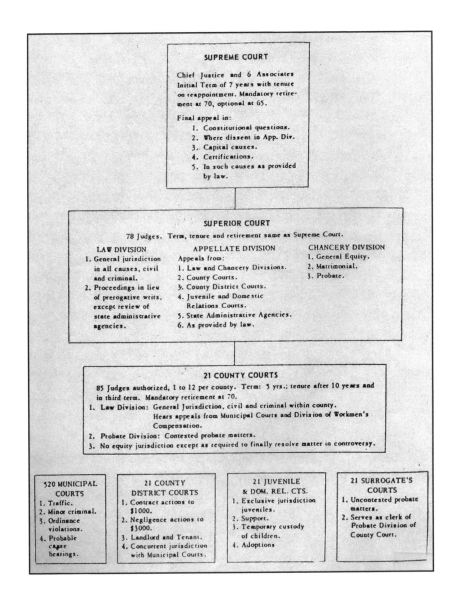

New structure of the court under the 1948 constitution. Courtesy of Arthur T. Vanderbilt II.

The original members of the new state supreme court in 1948.
Courtesy of Arthur T. Vanderbilt II.

"The Horseshoe Takes Care Of It s Own"

Frank Hague was born in the Horseshoe in January 1876. It was a rough-and-tumble world where children survived by their wits and fists. Courtesy of Jersey City Free Public Library.

Hague in 1917, the year he first became mayor, a position he held for the next thirty years. Courtesy of Jersey City Free Public Library.

Each ward of Jersey City had its political club, which provided needed social services to the working poor, building a loyal voter base. Courtesy of Jersey City Free Public Library.

New Year's Day: Jersey City residents line up by the thousands to pay homage to the Celtic Chieftain. Courtesy of Jersey City Free Public Library.

The Jersey City Police Department. Hague understood that control of power often meant having his people in the appropriate garb, whether policemen in uniforms or judges in robes. Courtesy of Jersey City Free Public Library.

Hague and Babe Ruth. Hague enjoyed baseball, golf, and boxing, and he relished being around celebrities. Courtesy of Jersey City Free Public Library.

The Hague family with Shirley Temple. In 1930, Jack Warner, the Hollywood producer, visited Hague, seeking repeal New Jersey's blue laws, which among other things banned showing films on Sunday. The quid pro quo was a meeting between Hague's daughter, Peggy, and Shirley Temple. Not long after, Hague supported a referendum that repealed the Sunday prohibition on movies. Courtesy of Jersey City Free Public Library.

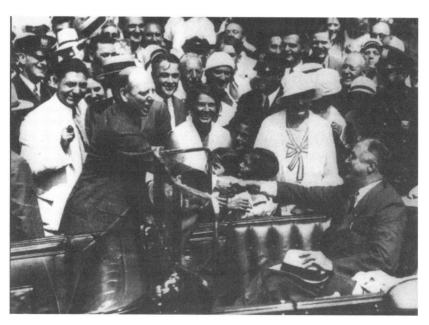

Frank Hague and FDR at the "Monster Rally" in Sea Girt, New Jersey, August 27, 1932. There were nearly 200,000 people in attendance. Courtesy of Jersey City Free Public Library.

Hague and Governor Harry Moore with President Franklin Delano Roosevelt at Hague's home in Deal, New Jersey. In all four of FDR's presidential election victories, Hudson County provided the winning margin in New Jersey. Courtesy of Jersey City Free Public Library.

The Margaret Hague Maternity Hospital. At its peak of operation in the late 1930s, more babies were born there than in any other hospital in the nation: the total for 1936 was 5,088. The hospital had one of the lowest infant mortality rates in the nation. Courtesy of Jersey City Free Public Library.

Under Frank Hague, Hudson County worked to help children get off to a good start in life. Courtesy of Jersey City Free Public Library.

The Hague residence on the beach in Deal, New Jersey. It was purchased in 1920 for $125,000 ($1.5 million in today's dollars). Hague's reported salary never exceeded $8,000 annually. Courtesy of Jersey City Free Public Library.

Unlike Vanderbilt, Hague considered himself a sportsman, traveling to Florida and California frequently for golf. Courtesy of Jersey City Free Public Library.

With Charles's financial backing it wasn't long before *Bruno's Weekly* was publishing works by the like of Oscar Wilde, Stephen Crane, and Edna St. Vincent Millay. Charles was rubbing elbows with everyone from poets and novelists to songwriters and painters. According to Charles, it was in his presence—at a coffeehouse in Greenwich Village, Romany Marie's—that Millay penned the verse for which she is best remembered, on the back of an envelope he gave her.[7]

> My candle burns at both ends;
> It will not last the night ;
> But ah, my foes, and oh, my friends—
> It gives a lovely light![8]

Surviving less than three years, at its peak the magazine had a circulation of four thousand and sold for twenty-seven cents a copy. For the purposes of our story, *Bruno's Weekly* is best remembered for publishing the works of "Tom Sleeper."

Literature abounds with authors known by their pen name: Mark Twain was Samuel Clemens, George Eliot was Mary Ann Evans, O. Henry was William Sydney Porter, and Dr. Seuss was Theodore Geisel. And then there is the poet Tom Sleeper, the nom de plume of Charles Edison. Charles's memoirs reveal that poetry and music were a big part of his life; years after his father's death, Charles published a book of poems entitled *Flotsam and Jetsam*. Not surprisingly, Thomas Edison didn't take much of an interest in his son's poetry—little of it is memorable—yet one poem in particular speaks to the world Charles knew, especially as the son of someone who had played a pivotal role in transforming American society. "Ad Infinitum" reads:

> Worry, worry, fret and trouble.
> Nothing's right and all is Change.
> Facts are but a phantom bubble;
> Truths today—tomorrow strange.
> Changes bring but other changes;
> Progress runs in Error's ring;
> Plans are made but Change deranges;
> Hail the master; Change is king.[9]

Thomas Edison was the king of change in America and, when the United States entered World War I President Woodrow Wilson asked him to assist the Department of the Navy. He couldn't refuse the president's request, but nonviolence was central to Edison's moral views and he agreed to help the war effort provided he worked only on defensive devices. The results included such items as a device for detecting submarines, a technique for camouflaging ships, and underwater searchlights. As a result of the time Thomas devoted to the war effort, Charles, at age twenty-seven, whose hearing loss prevented enlistment in the army, was drafted out of Greenwich Village by his father and assigned greater responsibilities in Edison's far-flung network of enterprises; thus did Charles's flirtation with the bohemian lifestyle come to an end.

Charles's performance during the war years must have impressed his father, because he was the one—not his older brothers Thomas Jr. or William—Thomas anointed as his heir apparent. Charles immersed himself in the business, and working at his father's side after the war, the two grew very close; so much so that several years prior to his death Thomas granted Charles complete control of the family's far-flung business interests. While his creativity was in the arts rather than science, Charles proved himself a shrewd businessman, managing the many Edison companies successfully for the next thirty years.

Like his father, Charles had a sense of obligation to the nation, and when President Franklin Delano Roosevelt came calling during the Great Depression he was eager to serve. In 1934 Charles was named compliance director for the National Recovery Administration in New Jersey. After that he became assistant secretary of the navy, forcing him to leave Llewellyn Park for Washington, D.C. Realizing war was inevitable, Edison successfully pushed for the development of a fleet of swift battleships; one of these became the USS *New Jersey*.

When Secretary of the Navy Claude Swanson died in late 1939, Edison was elevated to that job but didn't stay in Washington long, deciding six months later to run for governor. The story of how he became the candidate of the Democratic Party in 1940—despite being a lifelong Republican—is pretty much that that's what President Franklin D. Roosevelt wanted and Charles answered the call of duty, or, perhaps he wanted out from his father's shadow and grabbed at the chance to be someone more than his father's son.[10] Either way, an interesting footnote that preceded the announcement of his candidacy was a visit from Russell Watson, one of many lawyers involved in Vanderbilt's Clean Government movement, who encouraged him to run as a

Democrat.[11] Still smarting from the theft of Lester Clee's election in 1937, the state's progressive Republicans were hedging their bets, Edison speculated. They were fearful that Hague might support former Governor Harold Hoff- man in the primary by unleashing his "Republicans for a day" in Hudson County. At the time, his father's footprints were everywhere in New Jersey, and once Edison announced his candidacy, no one dared oppose him in the Democratic primary.

Charles Edison was Frank Hague's nightmare; he was beyond being bought, couldn't be manipulated or intimidated, and wasn't wowed by Hud- son County's dominant role in gubernatorial elections. If he was going to be governor, it would be on his terms, not Hague's. As things turned out, Gloucester County state senator Robert Hendrickson beat Hoffman in the Republican primary, and as the campaign went forward it was obvious that Vanderbilt and Clean Government were the winners regardless of who the next governor might be.

From the outset, Edison sent the message that he didn't need Hague. "My campaign was financed entirely by contributions from a few friends and relatives and from my own funds."[12] Then, almost as if to rub the Jer- sey City mayor's nose in the new reality, candidate Edison appeared at one of Hague's "monster rallies" in Sea Girt—with more than 100,000 people in attendance—and delivered a speech distancing himself from Hague. "It is my happy privilege to be able to stand here and tell you that if you elect me you will have elected a governor who has made no promises of preferment to any man or group. I want to make perfectly clear: you can be sure that I will never be a yes-man except to my own conscience."[13] This was no puppet. At the general election, Edison defeated Hendrickson by 64,000 votes, "a margin considered to be somewhere between slim and comfortable. It was not a landslide."[14]

Statehouse legend has it that early in 1941, while setting up headquarters in the governor's office, Edison ripped out the telephone line that had pro- vided Hague with direct access to Harry Moore when he was governor.[15] Worse still, David Dayton McKean was on board. Edison's memoirs don't tell us how he came to know the Dartmouth professor, but they tell us that "McKean was referred to within the Edison camp as Exie or Mr. X inas- much as his real name was anathema to Frank Hague."[16] The Dartmouth professor was one of Edison's key campaign advisers and served as deputy finance commissioner in the new administration, a position that placed

McKean within a small circle of people advising Edison. We can only imagine Hague's rage.

For the first time in nine elections spanning more than twenty-five years, the mayor of Jersey City was unwelcome in the governor's office. The first test for both men came within days of Edison taking office. An aging state Supreme Court justice, Thomas Trenchard, was in ill health and announced his resignation. Trenchard had presided at the Lindbergh baby kidnapping trial in 1935 and was respected for both the fairness and the soundness of his rulings over a career on the bench spanning more than a quarter century. Tradition held that the vacancy should be filled with a Republican because Trenchard was Republican. As ever, Hague had a nominee of his own and pressed Edison to name that person, Vice Chancellor Wilfred Jayne—a former Republican state senator and stalwart of Hague ally Ocean County Republican boss Tom Mathis.

Edison had someone else in mind, and in a move that Hague could only view as a barb, Edison nominated Clean Government state senator Frederic Colie. It was Colie who had led the unsuccessful opposition to Frank Hague Jr.'s appointment to the E & A in 1939. Hague viewed Colie's appointment as a slap in the face. It was also the benchmark for the end of Hague's control of patronage coming out of the governor's office; his anger was to no avail. Colie was widely respected by both parties as brilliant, honest, and independent. Edison got his way and sent a message that the courts mattered to him.

Judicial reform was high on the new governor's agenda. Like Vanderbilt, he took to the hustings at every opportunity to spread the word of the need for judicial reform. One of his opening lines was to remind the audience that you didn't need to be a lawyer to understand the importance of the rule of law. "I am not a lawyer, but I think that non-lawyers, whose lives, properties and rights are subject to the Courts, ought to have something to say about the machinery for providing justice. There is a suspicion . . . that certain lawyers are not enthusiastic about constitutional revision, because they feel they have a vested interest in the obscurities and complexities of our court system, which they think that they alone understand."[17] Little did Edison realize at the time the lengths to which the old guard would go to preserve their vested interests.

Relying on his passion for the arts, he would quote lines from a comic opera by Gilbert & Sullivan, satirizing British government and law:

The law's the true embodiment
Of everything that's excellent.

It has no kind of fault or flaw,

And I, my Lords, embody the law.[18]

He was particularly critical of the confusion relating to the court in which a lawsuit had to be presented. "When a professor of law in a New Jersey law school admits that his students come out of the study of our court system more confused than when they went in, I am sure you will not expect a mere Governor to explain their system clearly. . . . In many cases not even the best lawyers can tell their clients where their cases belong, in law or equity. They often face the chance that they may have to bring two actions, with two sets of fees and two sets of costs. Cases shuttled back and forth from law to equity, delaying and therefore denying justice."[19]

Edison had witnessed Arthur Vanderbilt's frustration in his role as chairman of the state bar association's Judicial Council. Time and again, reform legislation written by Vanderbilt was passed in the assembly, only to see it die in the senate without a vote being taken; there was even a measure approved by the senate, defeated in the assembly. It was almost as if Hague was toying with the WASP do-gooders. And then it got personal.

On June 23, 1941, state bar association president Milton Unger publicly announced the reappointment of Vanderbilt as chairman of the Judicial Council. He had been chairman for two five-year terms dating back to 1930. Days after Unger's announcement—much to his surprise—Unger learned that three weeks earlier, outgoing bar president Sylvester Smith Jr., a Hague ally from Warren County, had replaced Vanderbilt with someone else.[20] Vanderbilt had been serving as a holdover for several months and it never occurred to anyone that Smith might secretly name a new chairman of the council before leaving office. It caused a firestorm among the Clean Government types but no one else—the rank and file of the bar had little interest in reform. The effect was to gut the council. But the governor had moves of his own.

Edison needed Vanderbilt as an ally for constitutional reform, and much to Hague's annoyance, the new governor countered by pushing through the legislature an act establishing a state-sponsored Commission on Revision of the New Jersey Constitution. Its purpose was to draft a model constitution and begin a public dialog that it was hoped would lead to a referendum. As approved by the legislature, this new commission had seven members: two appointed by the president of the senate; two appointed by the speaker of the assembly; two appointed by the governor; and the final member selected by the commission members.

Both the senate president and the assembly speaker were Republicans, but they viewed the Clean Government movement as a threat to their way of doing business. They appointed four knowledgeable people, none of whom was Arthur Vanderbilt or anyone allied with him. The Republicans were relying upon Governor Edison's two appointments going to Democrats. "My old friends in the Legislature thought they had it arranged so that I would not be a member of the Commission," Vanderbilt wrote years later, "but Governor Edison, then a Democrat, fooled them by appointing me, a Republican, to the Commission, a stratagem for which the Republican majority of the Legislature never really forgave him."[21]

While President Roosevelt's motives in encouraging Edison to run for governor are murky, today's perspective confirms that Charles Edison's single term in Trenton was the third cut at whittling Frank Hague down to size. Following the U.S. Supreme Court decision in *Hague v. The C.I.O.* on the "deportation" of union organizers, and Vanderbilt's and McKean's handiwork in *The Boss*, Edison's efforts propelled the momentum that was building to reshape Hague's world. The members of the new constitutional commission who hoped to have a hand in reshaping New Jersey were Edison's opponent in the general election, Senator Robert Hendrickson (chairman); Senator Crawford Jamieson; Judge Walter J. Freund of Essex County; Judge Walter D. Van Riper of Morris County; James Kearney Jr., editor of the *Trenton Times*; Professor John F. Sly of Princeton University; and Arthur T. Vanderbilt.

"When we first convened," Senator Hendrickson recalled, "I had never met seven members with more divergent views on the theory and principles of government, and that applies to all branches of the government, judicial, executive, legislative, and administrative."[22] Nonetheless, the members of the Hendrickson Commission, as it became known, listened to one another and committed to a diligent schedule of meetings. After five months of proposals and counterproposals made at weekend-long meetings in the privacy of one of the quiet meeting rooms of the University Club in Manhattan, the commission members unanimously agreed on the submission of a draft Constitution that provided for a dramatic reorganization of the courts, which had existed in its present structure since 1844, and much as it was in 1776.

Unlike the state bar association's Judicial Council, which, for more than ten years, had tried in vain to woo the leaders of the bench, bar, and politicians through a watered-down amendment process, the commission members put aside the idea of individual amendments. They simply drafted a new constitution, substantially enhancing the status of the judiciary. Yet most members of the bar association were content with the cozy relationship among bench, bar, and politicians and had little enthusiasm for reform. They viewed themselves as part of the ruling class. For many lawyers in New Jersey, being asking to change the system by which they earned their livelihoods was like asking them to commit financial suicide. Integral to the organized bar's efforts to undermine the efforts of the Hendrickson Commission efforts were editorials in the *New Jersey Law Journal (NJL)* the longtime weekly newspaper for the state's attorneys.

Thematically, the objections were based upon the ever-reliable tactics of conjuring up fear and appealing to devotion to the American way. On March 20, 1941, the *NJL* featured an editorial predicting what a constitutional convention would look like. According to the author, William Evans, it would be dominated by "highly organized minority pressure groups" and that the public could "expect to witness such an exhibition of log-rolling and horse trading as would result in such a hodge-podge of principals which might undo at one fell stroke much of our progress in industrial, social, and economic fields." Evans forewarned that a constitutional convention had "infinite possibilities for damage." In concluding his attack on the process, he spoke reverently of the 1844 Constitution, saying, "It may be compared to the Ten Commandments whose principals are fixed and unchanging."[23] He ended his essay quoting from the King James Bible, the Book of Thessalonians (5:21) stating, "Hold fast to that which is good."

Several months later, in July 1941, Robert Carey picked up the theme of the need to remain loyal to tradition. "Our present Constitution is now almost 100 years old—over 50 years younger than the Federal Constitution. Incidentally, have you heard of anyone advocating a new Constitution for the United States? We have heard people advocating most wholesome respect for it, but we haven't heard a sane voice raised in favor of discarding it." Carey concluded his editorial by stating "It is a bad time for experiments."[24]

Interestingly, although Vanderbilt had critics and enemies, none of them challenged him directly in any of their public statements. Throughout 1941 and into 1942 the *NJL*'s official editorial page remained a forum for critics of reform. On May 18, 1942, the commission formally presented its report to Governor Edison and the people of New Jersey that included a draft of a completely new constitution. Included in the commission's report was its proposal for a public referendum to be held in the upcoming primary election in September. The goal was for the voters to authorize the legislature to finalize the draft constitution and then formally submit it to vote of the people at the general election in 1942.

Frank Hague watched with interest as Vanderbilt and his allies went about their work; he then went into action. With Hudson County senator Ed O'Mara serving as point man, Hague's people pulled together all of the Democratic members of the senate and assembly, creating a wall of opposition to what was now being called the Hendrickson Constitution. Hague also knew how to work across party lines and picked up allies among Republican legislators from rural New Jersey who feared that the new constitution would result in reapportionment of the legislature's districts, weakening their powers, particularly in the state senate. Working together, Hague's allies on a joint legislative committee sidetracked the proposed referendum by altering its timetable. A decision was made that no further action should be taken to amend the state's constitution until after World War II, and New Jersey's citizens in uniform were home.

Vanderbilt and Edison weren't retreating. The following year, under the leadership of Vanderbilt's erstwhile Boston emissary, Dominic Cavicchia, who was now in the assembly, a bill was passed in April 1943 submitting the constitutional referendum at the November election of 1943. With Governor Edison approaching the end of his three-year term, Clean Government was anxious to find a candidate willing to continue Edison's work for constitutional reform and someone strong enough to run against Harry Moore should Hague decide—yet again—that Moore should run for governor.

There weren't a lot of options for Clean Government. Name recognition can be decisive in an election. There's no truer adage in elective politics than "you can't beat somebody with nobody." At that point in New Jersey's history no candidate was better known statewide than A. Harry Moore; it would take a somebody to beat him. Hague, Moore, and the traditional Hudson County shenanigans in counting votes struck terror in the heart of everyone supporting constitutional reform. Vanderbilt and the Clean Government movement decided they had no choice but to run a retread of their own, former governor Walter Edge.

Yet the former governor and onetime ambassador to France was no ordinary retread. Seventy-year-old Walter Edge, who had made his fortune in marketing, advertising, and the newspaper business in Atlantic City, was the distinguished elder statesman of New Jersey's Republican Party. His first election as governor in 1916 was the product of a deal struck between Hague and Atlantic City boss Enoch "Nucky" Johnson. The Celtic Chieftain had no use for the progressive Democratic candidate, Otto Wittpenn, and after helping Edge win the Republican primary against the wealthy Austin Colgate, Hague instructed tens of thousands of Hudson County voters to stay home that November, enabling Walter Edge's election. But Edge was a climber and left Trenton to run for U.S. senator in 1918 before completing his term as governor.

Walter Edge moved in powerful circles on the national level, and, as an intimate of Warren G. Harding, he narrowly missed becoming vice president in 1920. He was reelected to the Senate in 1924, and five years later he was named by President Herbert Hoover as ambassador to France, holding that position until 1933. Following his ambassadorship, Edge spent most of the next decade traveling and relishing his role as elder statesman. Although he didn't have the same commitment to constitutional reform as Edison, Edge knew that the state's charter was in need of a major overhaul. Edge was prepared to pick up where Edison left off. Equally important, he was the best candidate the Republicans could hope for to match up with Hague puppet Harry Moore.

Always the astute politician, Edge recognized the wrinkles separating rural Republicans from Clean Government. Prior to going public with his plans, Edge convened a meeting of the Republican state senators and told them that unless the senate approved the bill sponsored by Assemblymen Cavicchia and Feller calling for a referendum authorizing the 1944 legislature to approve a final draft of a constitution for submission to the voters, he would not run for governor. Although the rural Republican senators were deaf to Edison's reform measures, they heard Edge loud and clear. They were more fearful of a fourth term of Harry Moore than they were of Clean Government's efforts to rewrite the constitution. Edge's move proved decisive, and the Republican senators agreed to back the legislation so that they would have a candidate capable of defeating anyone proposed by Frank Hague.

Much to everyone's surprise, several months before the election Harry Moore developed a spine; deciding that he'd had enough of having his strings pulled by Frank Hague, he retired from politics. Hague had no one to replace him as a candidate other than union leader Vincent Murphy, mayor of

Newark. The Republicans campaigned with scare tactics, warning voters that a Murphy victory would lead to domination of "labor leaders, communists, and Hagueism." Edge won by a margin of 127,000 votes. According to the biography written by Vanderbilt's grandson, "It was a combination of this event [Moore's decision not to run], the ability of the various factions of the New Jersey Republicans to rally behind Edge, and the introduction of voting machines in New Jersey with the passage of a bill sponsored by Clean Government Assemblymen after the Clee Defeat in 1937 that let Edge emerge the victor of the 1943 Gubernatorial Election."[25]

Edge's victory was accompanied by voter approval of the referendum authorizing the legislature to sit as a constitutional convention in order to prepare a document based on the model constitution drafted by Vanderbilt and the commission members. Vanderbilt was elated. "It [election day] was a great day for the Republicans in this state and, particularly, in this county." For the first time since he had entered politics more than twenty-five years earlier, "the Gubernatorial Election had not fallen under Mayor Hague's magical spell."[26] On the public question of revision to the constitution, Essex County had provided a majority of 65,000 votes out the statewide majority of 130,000.

Hague wasn't going away gracefully, and he had a straw man, John Borg, file a lawsuit to overturn the referendum results. The complaint charged that the constitution could not be "rewritten" but had to be amended through the process spelled out in the New Jersey Constitution of 1844. Everyone knew Borg was acting for Hague; one of Walter Edge's first acts after taking his oath as governor was to name Vanderbilt as a special assistant attorney general to defend the referendum results. The litigation fizzled quickly and the decision of *In Re: Borg* made no new law.[27] In the eyes of Justice Porter speaking for the state Supreme Ccourt, this was a "political" question rather than a legal one. The state's voters had authorized the legislature to sit as a constitutional convention, and there was nothing the courts could do to sidetrack that procedure.

Within weeks of the court's decision, the legislature began its work. Through several provisions discussed early on, Vanderbilt and the Republicans sent Hague the message that things were about to change. Judges had to have ten years of legal experience prior to appointment; there would be no more lay judges at any level; the legislature would have broad power to investigate any municipal official; the governor's powers would be strengthened;

and, critical to Hague's cash flow in Jersey City, there was to be a new method for taxing railroad property. As to investigating municipal officials, Edge didn't wait for a new constitution; he dispatched his attorney general, Walter Van Riper, to Jersey City to look into the many gambling operations flourishing in plain view of the local police department. It was a major irritant to Hague's organization. From Hague's perspective, the Republicans had declared war on Hudson County. The proposed constitution was writing new rules for the game and no one from Hague's team had been consulted. Without a seat at the negotiating table in the process of deciding the powers to be exercised by the three branches of state government, Edison, Edge, Vanderbilt, and the Hendrickson commission had succeeded in alienating Hudson County. Worse still, the Republicans were oblivious to the animosity they had created among Irish Catholic Democrats.

Hague and his allies appeared before the legislature on the final day of the hearings to take one last shot at the Hendrickson Constitution. Despite their broad-ranging and detailed criticisms of the new constitution, the same refrain was repeated by nearly every objector—an emotional plea not to change the constitution "while the boys are away at war." Voting strictly on party lines, the Republicans had enough votes to place the referendum on the ballot at the general election of 1944. Vanderbilt was elated. Yet the Celtic Chieftain still had a card that the Warrior Lawyer never saw coming. Religion was in play.

CHAPTER 10

The Archbishop Shows His Gratitude

Sunday before Election Day. The timing was murder. Two days before the vote on the public referendum that Arthur Vanderbilt believed would propel New Jersey in a new direction, Roman Catholics heard from the pulpit that bingo was in jeopardy. A mindless game of chance involving random numbers matched to preprinted cards, the odds were long and the bets were short—pennies, nickels, and dimes. Tacitly illegal under existing law, it was played in church basements and parish halls throughout the state, while local police departments looked the other way. Bingo was a fun night out once a week for thousands of voters, and more important, it was a major money-maker for the Catholic Church. Losing it would hurt.

Rumored to be authored by the archbishop of Newark, an anonymous letter was delivered to every Roman Catholic church the week before the election. The letter instructed each parish priest to tell his congregation to vote against the new constitution. The unsigned letter read, "The proposed revised constitution should not be supported. Why? Remember the school bus bill. Vote 'no.'"[1]

In urging a no vote, some priests personalized their message. Depending upon the parish, church members heard the letter and no more, or they were warned of various dangers created by the proposed state charter. It was a threat to the priest-penitent privilege, the tax-exempt status of church property, and—somehow—the institution of marriage. Many were also told that gambling of all kinds would be prohibited, endangering the cash flow from bingo and raffles, so critical to church finances. And finally, as the letter instructed, church members were reminded of a state Supreme Court ruling in September that had struck down the "Bus Bill" that had provided funding for busing children to Catholic schools.

Voters from Cape May to Sussex went to the polls on Tuesday, November 7, 1944, and killed any hope of reforming New Jersey's government. Hague hammered Vanderbilt's plans, defeating the referendum by a margin of 126,000 votes out of the 1.4 million cast; the proposal defeated in twelve of the state's twenty-one counties. The plurality of no votes in Hudson County exceeded 87,000. Reform had been routed.

Vanderbilt's plans were a casualty of the religious war begun in Hudson County nearly a century earlier; and it wasn't quite over. Grudges die hard among the Irish, and there was no one better than Frank Hague to rally the Church hierarchy to vanquish the WASPs one more time. For decades there has been speculation regarding the role of Archbishop Thomas J. Walsh in the 1944 referendum. Through it all—at the time of the election and ever since—the Church has remained mum. Yet as with box 96, occasionally dead men speak from their graves.

St. Paul of the Cross Church in Jersey City was where Monsignor Ralph Glover got his start as a priest, serving as an assistant pastor.[2] It isn't clear whether he was one of Hague's "city chaplains," but he was someone interested in the politics of both church and state. After long service to the Church, the archbishop tapped the Reverend Ralph Glover to be his personal liaison in dealing with state government; one of his several titles was chairman of the Catholic Legislative Council (CLC) of New Jersey. He made full use his position to ensure that Catholics had a role in the legislative process, carefully reviewing the work of the reformers.

During his term in office, Governor Edison had been instrumental—together with the League of Women Voters and a new group known as the New Jersey Taxpayers Association—in the creation of a nonpartisan reform group named the New Jersey Committee for Constitutional Convention (NJCC), which was intended to be an umbrella organization for anyone interested in reforming the state's constitution. Later in his term, Edison worked with the NJCC in helping to secure funds for its efforts through another group he helped create known as the New Jersey Constitutional Foundation (NJCF).

Given the general lack of support among politicians and lawyers—plus fierce opposition from nearly every sitting judge in New Jersey's court system—Edison and Vanderbilt knew they had to expand their base. The goal of both groups created by Edison was to spur grassroots support for a

new constitution through educating the public about the need to bring New
Jersey's government into the twentieth century. During the 1943 referendum
campaign and again in 1944, Edison was the public face of the reform movement, lending his name, credibility, and resources to the effort. Even as a
private citizen, Edison was as potent an ally as Governor Edge and Vanderbilt
could hope to enlist in their efforts.

As part of the campaign for the 1943 referendum authorizing the legislature to sit as a constitutional convention, there were several mass mailings.
That fall Monsignor Glover received a letter from the NJCC and decided he
needed to know more about the proposed constitution. "Monsignor Glover's
papers in the archives of Seton Hall University [discovered half a century
later by a historian, Nicholas Turse] reveal his keen interest in revision of the
constitution. From the beginning of 1944 through Election Day, Glover compiled a voluminous file of newspaper clippings on all aspects and opinions
about the constitutional question from no less than ten papers."[3]

In January, Archbishop Walsh, presiding in Newark, reached out to the
bishops of the dioceses of Trenton, Camden, and Paterson seeking their help
"in defending Catholic interests with reference to the proposed revision of the
constitution of New Jersey." He asked them to submit names of "suitable Catholic lawyers" to serve on the CLC under Monsignor Glover's direction. The
archbishop wanted to be prepared. Throughout much of January and February
the legislature sat as a constitutional convention to prepare a document based
largely on the model draft prepared by the Hendrickson Commission during
Governor Edison's term in office. With the legislators' work completed and a
draft constitution circulated by the final week of February, the reformers got to
work, but so did the monsignor.

Glover conducted the initial meeting of the CLC on February 25, 1944. He
defined the task to CLC members as one clarifying the need to "make a defi-
nite study" of the proposed constitution so that everyone involved knew "what
stand we [the Church] are going to take."[4] At that meeting a plan for proceed-
ing was established. According to Nicholas Turse, "it was decided to divide the
various sections of the revised constitution into Rights and Privileges, Legislative, Executive, and Judiciary committees for intensive study. Each diocesan
delegation became responsible for one committee and pledged to issue a report
at the next meeting."[5]

At the next meeting of the CLC, on March 3, the members reported on their
review of the various portions of the draft constitution. Newark mayor Fred

Gassert (Rights and Privileges) went first. "I have examined it. I find nothing harmful to the Church." Next was Francis Reps of Trenton (Legislative) who stated, "[There is] nothing in the proposed revision that would in my opinion effect [sic] us one way or another."[6] Camden prosecutor Gene Mariano reported on gubernatorial powers and opined without hesitation, "I see nothing which affects the Church." Finally, the Paterson diocesan delegation reported as a committee, stating that with the exception of "the possibility that members of other committees wished to discuss section three, article four [the "maintenance and custody of children"], "there is nothing that will require any action by this body."[7] As uncovered by Turse, the CLC's records reveal that without exception, the several committees agreed that the new constitution would do no harm to the interests of the Catholic Church. Read objectively, the reports are tantamount to an endorsement.

Ever critical to the Church was the continued tax-exempt status of its property. That issue was analyzed for the CLC by Judge John Rafferty of the Trenton diocesan delegation. On April 28, 1944, Judge Rafferty reported on the language of tax-exemption statutes. Within the language of the constitution itself, the only tax-exempt property was that of veterans of the armed forces, causing fears that this might lead to Church property being taxed.[8] The review by Rafferty's committee found that the tax-exempt status of Church property would remain unchanged if the proposed revisions to the constitution were approved

Next up for Glover's committee assignments was the question of divorce and how matrimonial litigation would be handled under a new court system. At a meeting on May 12, 1944, the CLC's members discussed provisions dealing with transferring matrimonial actions from the Chancery Court to a new Law Court; this issue divided the committee. Judge Rafferty argued that the transfer of such matters to law courts would make divorce easier. Committee member Nolan replied that there was nothing in the new constitution regarding divorce except that jurisdiction would be transferred from the equity courts to the law courts. Nolan matter-of-factly informed the others that the authority of law courts to decide matrimonial cases was common practice in other states. Nolan further stated that "so far as Catholics are concerned, this constitutional revision makes no difference to them one way or another."[9] By the end of May, the CLC had pretty much completed its work.

May was also the month in which Hague and the New Jersey Democrats issued their party's platform. It was a blistering attack on the proposed constitution, targeted to diverse clusters of voters likely to be offended by some portion of the new state charter.[10] The tax clause was presented as a giveaway to the railroads and a threat to churches. The lack of a collective bargaining guarantee helped rally organized labor. The elimination of the Chancery Court—where all divorce actions were heard—drew vocal criticism from conservative lawyers and various church leaders as somehow making divorce easier. Women's groups and Negro leaders were reminded that there was no antidiscrimination clause. Finally, Hague—with help of Hudson County newspapers—took a very complicated problem involving the demise of America's once mighty railroad system and advanced a "conspiracy theory" of the constitution: it was all the work of rich Republicans and the railroad magnates.[11] Legislation approved under Edison and defended by Edge granting tax relief to railroads, whose finances had been ravaged by the Great Depression and the rise of cars and trucks, was, according to Hague, part of a conspiracy among wealthy WASPs to restore the railroad's tax breaks and give them a second life under the new constitution, robbing the public of sorely needed tax revenue from the railroads.

Spreading the "anti" message were allies of Hague working through statewide groups. The former Democratic senator from Hunterdon County, David Agans, was now the leader of the New Jersey State Grange and he encouraged farmers of New Jersey—most of whom were Republicans—to vote no. Police and firemen in Jersey City were instructed by Hague to reach out to their brothers in the Police Benevolent Association and the Firemen's Mutual Benevolent Association by "sending out anti-revisionist literature to their comrades in the rest of the state."[12] Finally, where needed, new groups were created. To counter the League of Women Voters and the other women's groups active in the pro-reform effort, there spontaneously appeared groups such as the Women's Nonpartisan Committee Against the Proposed Revised Constitution, supposedly headquartered in Trenton. One group Hague stayed away from was the CLC.

As the months wore on, every issue with the potential to impact the Church was examined by the CLC and its committees, and nothing was found harmful to the Church. Despite his need to know "what stand we are going to take," Glover wouldn't permit any type of public announcement—pro or con. He was biding his time. An issue critical to the Church was pending in the New Jersey court system: a legal attack on funding for busing children to Catholic schools.

Challenging a statute known as the Bus Bill was Arch Everson, a taxpayer in Ewing Township. Everson was also the executive vice president of the New Jersey Taxpayers Association, a key organization in the pro-reform movement. By all accounts, Everson was motivated by principle. With a background in business, he was the original founder of the association and was combative in his pursuit of efficiency in government. He understood what a mess New Jersey's court system was and eagerly joined the reform effort. The sums spent on busing Catholic school students weren't large—in Ewing Township the budgeted amount was a mere $357—but Everson believed that the government should never use any tax funds for private religious purposes. His lawyers argued that the school bus legislation amounted to aid to religion in violation of the establishment clause of the First Amendment of the U.S. Constitution, and likewise violated the New Jersey Constitution of 1844. Everson's lawsuit was a gift to the Celtic Chieftain: a constitution revision spokesperson attacking a law benefiting Catholic families. Hague couldn't have scripted it any better himself.

That September, in the matter of *Everson v. B.O.E of Ewing Township*, the state Supreme Court invalidated the Bus Bill.[13] In a perfunctory, almost tactless, seven-paragraph decision, the court struck down the law without ever addressing: (1) the state's requirement of compulsory education; (2) the fact that children were transported only via previously established bus routes; and (3) that it was the children and their parents who benefited from the law, not the Catholic Church. Arch Everson's lawsuit was a contentious, high-profile, and potentially volatile issue pitting the Knights of Columbus and the Catholic Daughters of America against the New Jersey Taxpayers Association and the League of Women Voters. *Everson* eventually made its way to the U.S. Supreme Court, resulting in a landmark decision ruling that public funding to transport children to religious schools did not violate the First Amendment to the U.S. Constitution, but that didn't help for November's election.

In politics, as well as in life, perceptions are the reality from which people work. As word of the *Everson* decision spread—reported at Sunday mass that September, little more than six weeks prior to Election Day—many New Jersey Catholics perceived the ruling as Catholic families getting short shrift from a WASP judge on a lawsuit brought by one of the proponents of the new constitution. Much to the frustration of everyone, there was no way the far-reaching issues raised by Everson's lawsuit could be finally resolved prior to Election Day.

While denying money to bus Catholic kids to school was at first viewed by the reformers as little more than an unexpected stone in their shoe, it proved to be a boulder. For New Jersey's Catholics the court's ruling was a stink bomb and, ultimately, a rallying cry against the referendum. "From this point forward religion would play a major role on both sides of the constitutional fight."[14] The week following the state Supreme Court's ruling, looking to seize the moment, "the Frank Hague-friendly *Jersey Journal* ran an editorial titled, 'Blow at Hague Hits Clergy, Doctors, Lawyers and Press.'"[15] Over the years, first by bullying and later with revenue from full-page ads, together with goodies such as lucrative government appointments to editors, Hague had been assured of the *Journal*'s editorial support. The fact that clergy was placed first in the editorial emphasized the growing turmoil over the state's religious divide. The newspaper argued that the revised constitution, which it called "dangerous" and referred to as "political scheming," would be opposed by "every clergyman." Following the *Everson* decision through to Election Day, the *Jersey Journal* and other Hague-friendly papers became megaphones for Hague's opposition to the new constitution.

Ever the savvy politician, Walter Edge recognized that enough angry Catholics could scuttle his plans. He couldn't sit in office and pray that the Bus Bill ruling had no effect on the referendum. Although concealed from the media, within two weeks of the Supreme Court's decision striking down the funding to bus Catholic children, on September 27, Governor Edge journeyed from Trenton to the Newark Chancery building (the Church's headquarters in New Jersey) to meet with Archbishop Walsh. The governor was joined by his attorney general, Walter D. Van Riper, and his chief of staff, Edward M. Gilroy. There are no records of the 1944 referendum among the archbishop's permanent papers, which might suggest an effort to sanitize his files, but it is evident that he wasn't the one who asked for the sit-down. In his autobiography, *A Jerseyman's Journal*, Governor Edge writes that the meeting with the archbishop could "not in conscience be called a discussion." Edge's memoir presents a view of Walsh "as a man who had already made up his mind about the issue."[16]

As a successful businessman, two-time governor, and former ambassador to France, Walter Edge had the bearing and tactfulness needed to woo an archbishop. Edge had moves he never shared in his autobiography, leaving

historians to speculate on the true story behind the Horatio Alger–style pab-
lum that flows from his memoirs. In his rise to power Edge had rubbed elbows
with the two most corrupt New Jersey politicians of his generation—Nucky
Johnson and Frank Hague—and came away unscathed. If anyone could have
charmed the archbishop it was Edge; all he lacked was being a Roman Catholic. At the meeting, Edge explained that in his view the proposed constitution
wasn't a threat to the Church; he assured the archbishop he would not stand
in the way of an amendment to the constitution for bus transportation, and
he let him know he could support such a bill.

During their meeting Edge brought up a troublesome concern: frequent
public statements by priests hostile to the new constitution. He cited inflammatory public comments made by Father Farrell of Asbury Park and Monsignor Peter O'Connor of North Arlington as examples of "unfair" clerical
opposition and asked that such comments "be curbed." Walsh curtly refused.
In Edge's recounting of the meeting he states that he "point by point . . . went
over the revised constitution," that Van Riper expanded on several legal points
about the issue of divorce, and that Walsh listened "attentively" but mostly in
silence. When Edge and his colleagues completed making their case, Walsh
"stood up and the audience was ended."[17]

It's unlikely that Edge, Van Riper, or Gilroy left that meeting with any
illusions about Walsh's support. The best they could hope for from their
audience with the archbishop was to get him to think twice about active
opposition. The several Catholic lawyers on the CLC were all well known
and respected and there was no reason for them to be silent on their findings
on the proposed constitution. It's likely—despite the cool reception—that
Edge was hopeful that the advice of those lawyers would discourage Walsh
and Glover from working with Hague.

Yet the Presbyterian governor failed to factor into his strategy an obvious
reality: the Irish Catholic mayor of Jersey City had been tithing his entire
career and was one of the Church's loyal Christian soldiers. Hague never had
to request an audience with Thomas Walsh.

When the archbishop arrived in Newark in 1928, he learned that his predecessor had purchased a mansion in Darlington, Bergen County, for the
creation of a diocesan seminary, but hadn't been able to raise the funds
needed to develop a campus. Walsh's official biography states that the bishop
"recognized from the first" that the present structure was ill suited for a seminary and made the Seminary of the Immaculate Conception his pet project.[18]

Unfortunately for Walsh, the Great Depression made raising an estimated $1,500,000 (more than tenfold that number in today's dollars) a major hurdle.

Walsh's biography states that he established the "Bishop's Associations of the Clergy, of the Religious, and of the Laity" to raise the necessary funds. Hague, who was a founding member, "personally pressured city and county office holders into making generous contributions to a fund for . . . [the] . . . seminary."[19] As Thomas Fleming observes, "Hague helped Archbishop Thomas Walsh of Newark raise millions for Darlington Seminary." Fleming also notes that "at least fifty-four priests, ministers, and rabbis were on the government payroll as chaplains to hospitals, police, fire, and other city and county departments."[20]

Burnishing his credentials with the Church is the fact that during most of the 1920s and 1930s Hague was a vocal anticommunist, a strict enforcer of liquor laws in Jersey City, had made numerous public statements on the importance of family and the sanctity of womanhood, and had provided universal health care for his city's poor, all of which helped garner the support of the clergy. Finally, Hague's relationship with his own pastor at St. Aedan's Church, Monsignor McClary, was a factor. The mayor frequently put people from the congregation on the public payroll at McClary's request. Additionally, to solidify his standing in his home church Hague spent an estimated $50,000 (roughly $750,000 today) to import a magnificent marble altar from Italy and donated it to his home parish. The monsignor was also vicar general of the Newark diocese—basically, one of Walsh's key lieutenants—and met regularly with the archbishop. There are no notes from those meetings, but it's easy to believe that both men thought themselves indebted to Frank Hague for all his good deeds on behalf of the Church.

Following his meeting with Walsh, Governor Edge must have felt he had nothing to lose by going directly to Catholic voters. Edge and former governor Edison began making appearances before the Knights of Columbus, sacred societies, parish groups, and any Catholic audience willing to meet with them in the hopes of assuring Church members that "Church property would not be taxed, priests would not be forced to betray the secrets of the confessional, divorces would not be made easier, and that the new constitution would allow a greater chance for the bus issue to be resolved."[21]

Turse reported that "Walsh's files concerning this matter [the 1944 referendum] are conspicuously sparse; however, a major clue emerges in the

Vanderbilt-friendly *Newark News* of October 23, 1944. In an article entitled, 'Pamphlet Attacks Charter Revision,' an unidentified Nun from Montclair, in Essex County, attested to having received an anonymous twenty-eight-page pamphlet urging votes against the revised constitution."[22] Having received the booklet through the mail, the sister apparently decided that others besides members of the clergy should know about it. The pamphlet recites "the anti-revision arguments of Church taxation, easy divorce, and the Bus Bill."[23] What makes it so telling is that among Monsignor Glover's papers there is a memorandum that reads:

Confidential

Distribution of Manuals—1 to a House

    Discussion of Manual

        Sister to take Manual to her Convent and there read it and have it read and studied and mastered and used by all the Sisters of the given Convent.

        All Sisters registered to Vote should Vote NO on the Revised Constitution and should by presentation of the facts of the Manual induce lay women to Vote NO.

        Sisters should not make known except to Sisters the fact that this meeting was held. All Sisters should strive to obtain Voters NO and . . . to obtain voters No upon their own responsibility with the use of the Manual. Sisters should be prudent and diligent and should not discuss this question on the telephone and should not use the name of the Archbishop or any ecclesiastical authority publicly or privately.[24]

The marked-up file version of this confidential memo includes the monsignor's signature on the reverse side of the page. Several drafts of the pamphlet found in Glover's files provide evidence that clearly demonstrates Glover's and Walsh's involvement. "One handwritten partial copy, complete with 'cross-outs' in the handwriting of Glover, was also discovered in the files of the director of the Associated Catholic Charities, paper-clipped to the Confidential Memo."[25] Other copies, accompanied by revisions, are likewise included in Glover's private files. These drafts and notations indicate which words should be italicized and new language added; all these revisions appear in the final pamphlet.

    What motivated the nun to leak the contents of the pamphlet is unknown, but what is known is that despite giving the appearance of working toward a

consensus position of the Church on the new constitution, Glover had stealth-
ily ignored the advice of the Catholic lawyers serving on the CLC, none of
whom could find a reason for Catholics to oppose the new constitution. Nor
did any member of the CLC suggest opposition to the constitutional referendum as a tactic for countering the state Supreme Court's ruling on the Bus Bill.
What's more, the CLC's findings weren't part of the mix in the decision to issue
the memo to the nuns, nor were they considered prior to the circulation of the
anonymous letter the Sunday before Election Day. Regardless of the stated
task at the initial meeting of the CLC months earlier, namely to thoughtfully
determine "what stand we are going to take," there would be no formal/pub-
lic position of New Jersey's Roman Catholic Church from the CLC. Instead,
Catholics would be encouraged by anonymous sources to vote no.

The day following the "Nun Pamphlet" story, the *Jersey Journal* reported
that former governor Harry Moore had attacked the revised constitution on
the grounds of Church taxation. Moore stated that "the things left out of this
constitution are more important than the things they put into it."[26] Although
Attorney General Van Riper asserted that there were no plans to tax churches,
Moore argued that Van Riper couldn't guarantee Catholics that future legislatures would not approve a tax. Moore also attacked the revision by saying that,
since the state had already waited a hundred years, why couldn't it wait another
year or two until New Jersey's 50,000 men in the armed forces had returned
home? Moore remained a very popular figure with voters, and Hague-friendly
newspapers trumpeted his opposition.

With little more than two weeks remaining before Election Day, Frank
Hague ratcheted up his personal involvement, barnstorming around the state
to make antirevision speeches. He even traveled all the way to Cape May
County and other rural Republican counties to warn them that the new constitution would result in muffling their voices in the legislature. When he
appeared before Democratic audiences, the mayor attacked the new constitution as a vehicle to destroy "the party of the people," and as a Republican
document designed to bilk money from the pockets of Jerseyans into railroad
coffers. Depending upon the crowd, he never passed up the chance to stir the
pot on religion by muddying the waters on issues like divorce and bingo.

Hague took out full-page ads in all the state's newspapers having substantial circulation and rented space on billboards on the major highways blasting
the new constitution as a threat to the rights and livelihoods of farmers, veterans, public employees, women, and sportsmen. Working his contacts—by

means that could not have been lawful—he secured the confidential lists containing the names and addresses of all New Jersey residents serving in the armed forces and sent them literature distorting the changes proposed by the constitution and asking them to vote no.

Long before computerized mailing lists, Hague was able to deliver a personal letter to each and every committeeman and committeewoman in all 3,465 voting districts in New Jersey in which he warned that the revised constitution "will virtually result in wiping out the Democratic party in New Jersey" and urged committee people "to do everything possible to defeat this proposed constitution and to hold our party intact."[27] Accomplishing personal mailings in 1944 (long before photocopiers, not to mention computers) to both the soldiers and Democratic committee people—likely 50,000 to 60,000 letters in all—was an enormous undertaking requiring extraordinary cooperation, keen supervision, and significant resources.

Yet all those letters didn't equal the one read from the pulpits the Sunday before the election. As recounted by Turse, although inspection of the draft letter in Monsignor Ralph Glover's files demonstrates that Archbishop Walsh did not personally write it—it is not in his distinctively large and grandiose script—the handwriting appears to be that of Glover. This, added to the fact that the letter was found in Glover's personal files, points to the likelihood that once again Glover carried out the covert orders of the archbishop, as he had for the anonymous "Nun pamphlet."

Upon hearing that "Catholics were asked at church yesterday [November 5] for a blanket vote against the proposed constitution," Governor Edge was infuriated and issued a statement, followed by taking to the airwaves to express his "deepest regret." Edge went further to claim that Mayor Hague had "dupe[d] the Catholics into a blind vote on this non-partisan, nonreligious issue." He claimed once again that Hague had "done the state of New Jersey and its citizens the greatest disservice of his shabby political career by arousing unfounded fears among the clergy of the Catholic Church."[28] The governor also sent telegrams to leaders of the Church throughout the state, addressing the efforts urging Catholics to oppose the new constitution. Although he declined to state what exactly was in the telegrams, he did confirm he had sent a telegram to Walsh as well. As with Walsh's papers on the 1944 referendum, no such telegram can be found. Walter Edge and Vanderbilt had to know it was all over but for counting the votes. Hague and his friends in the Catholic Church had thrashed the WASPs yet again.

Newark's Warrior Lawyer was crushed; stress was beginning to take its toll. Too many times to count, Arthur Vanderbilt had to regroup; after each setback he had to rethink his strategy, revise the language for a new constitution, and return to allies for help. Adding to his misery was the knowledge that there would be no new constitution until someone negotiated a truce with Frank Hague.

Vanderbilt understood as well as anyone that politics is a transactional business in which all of the players having a stake in the outcome must be heard. And as his dominance of Essex County politics showed, he could play the game as well as anyone. Nonetheless, as his struggle for a new constitution wore on, he lost hold of a tenet embraced by every mature politician: for government to function—no matter how bitter the differences—compromise, or some semblance of the same, is indispensable.

Over the years, he had buttonholed hundreds of people on his odyssey; many were inspired, others found him overbearing, yet he had always found a way to stay on course. But after nearly twenty years, his quest had consumed him; his holy crusade didn't permit compromise. His ignoble adversary had to be vanquished, but Vanderbilt didn't have that kind of political muscle; no one did. The indispensable ingredient for restarting the reform effort was to broker a deal with the Celtic Chieftain, but the Warrior Lawyer couldn't bring himself to do it; he needed help.

CHAPTER 11

Haddonfield's Mensch

Almost twenty years into his quest, nine years following the theft of Lester Clee's election, and little more than eighteen months after being hammered by Hague and his pal the archbishop, Arthur Vanderbilt was exhausted. Yet there were no breathers on his schedule. His obligations to his law practice, fund-raising commitments made as dean of NYU's law school, duties as a trustee of Wesleyan University, traveling to meetings of ABA committees, and the endless details of presiding over the state's most powerful Republican organization were weighing heavily on the Warrior Lawyer.

Despite continued opposition to revising the constitution from lawyers, judges, and most elected officials, progressive Republicans sensed growing support for reform. Efforts by the League of Women Voters, the New Jersey Taxpayers Association, the NJCC, the New Jersey Parent-Teacher Association, and business leaders were making inroads; there was growing public awareness that New Jersey's government was broken and its courts were corrupt. Although the ruling elite felt no need for change, thoughtful citizens knew better.

Who succeeded Walter Edge as governor was critical. The wrong person could be fatal to reform. And so it was that Vanderbilt was called upon to woo a South Jersey Republican to run for governor in 1946. What's more, there was urgency to this assignment because the only other Republican with name recognition making noise about running was former governor Hoffman. Just the thought of Harold Hoffman returning as governor was unnerving to progressive Republicans. Regardless of his tarnished image, the prospect of a Hoffman candidacy was troublesome, especially if he managed to cut a deal with Hague.

Early in 1946, as he was beginning his final year in office, Walter Edge reached out to former senate majority leader Alfred Driscoll of Camden County in the hope of anointing him as his successor. Edge wasn't one to throw bouquets gratuitously; nearly thirty years Driscoll's senior, Edge had to have been impressed by this rising GOP star. At the time Edge approached him, Driscoll was serving as commissioner of alcoholic beverages; it was a challenging, albeit unglamorous job for several years following the repeal of Prohibition. Yet it was in that position that he demonstrated his independence by refusing to show favoritism to Republicans in issuing liquor licenses. His time as commissioner was also when Driscoll displayed a willingness to work sixteen-hour days, a trait that separated him from his predecessors as governor.[1]

As the new commissioner he carved out a bold presence in state government by asserting himself as an ethical overseer of an industry prone to scandal. In addition to his duties overseeing the alcohol industry, Driscoll "immersed himself in the movement for constitutional revision and administrative reorganization,"[2] having been appointed by Edge to serve on the Commission on State Administrative Reorganization. That position brought Driscoll into contact with the small but growing circle of academics and attorneys working for reform. Although at times it appeared that Vanderbilt was a lone voice, he wasn't—just the loudest and most persistent. Although defeat of the 1944 referendum was disappointing, the people committed to reform weren't discouraged. They knew that the opposition was mostly old guard politicos, none of whom would be around much longer. It was Driscoll's work with the commission that increased his knowledge of how state government functioned and acquainted him with the process and the players of the reform movement in a way that no other potential candidate could match.[3]

Political lore has it that when approached by Edge, Driscoll wasn't initially enthusiastic; now it was Vanderbilt's turn to try to convince him to run for governor. Unlike Edge, Vanderbilt had the clout to make it happen. After more than two decades as leader of Clean Government and as the most respected—and feared—voice in Essex County politics, Arthur Vanderbilt's role in the selection of Republican candidates for statewide office was equal to that of Frank Hague among Democrats; his endorsement was equivalent to the party's nomination.

It's unlikely Driscoll needed much persuading. The reluctance he reportedly expressed to Edge was belied by his willingness to travel from

Haddonfield to meet with Vanderbilt for lunch at the Down Town Club in Newark. Although Vanderbilt knew that Driscoll was the only horse left to ride, he wanted something in return for his endorsement: unflinching support for rewriting New Jersey's constitution. Driscoll bought into the vision of overhauling state government and was better equipped to handle the task than anyone knew; so much so that over time, his agility as a negotiator annoyed Vanderbilt, sending him into a rage.

"Education and opportunity should be available to everyone" was a central tenet and oft-repeated maxim of Alfred Eastlack Driscoll.[4] It was young Alfred's education that brought his family to Haddonfield in 1906. His father, Alfred Robie Driscoll, was a businessman from New York and his mother, Mattie Souders Eastlack, had her family roots in Elmer, Salem County, New Jersey. Mattie was active in the women's suffrage movement and was a bright, articulate, feisty little woman, standing just shy of five feet tall, who wanted the best for her son. After spending time in Pittsburgh, where Alfred was born in 1902, and Atlanta, Alfred's parents moved to Haddonfield, in large part because of the borough's school system.

Haddonfield is steeped in history. It was there at the Indian King Tavern where the rebellious Provincial Congress met in the winter of 1777 to formally declare New Jersey an independent state, divorcing itself from the British Empire. Originally settled by Quakers, Haddonfield has always been serious about educating its children (that continues to this day) and Mattie wanted her son to have a first-rate education. It was the right move. Graduating in 1921, Alfred was an exceptional student athlete, earned the Childrey Award (best all-around student) and lettering in football, track, and cross country, and was captain of the debating and track teams.

It was also in high school that Alfred met his future wife, Antoinette Ware Tatum, whose family's prominence in the borough dated back many generations: they were people of considerable means. The courtship was a long one and according to family members, a prerequisite to the Tatum family's blessing was for Alfred to attend Williams College.[5] So, it was off to Massachusetts, while the courtship continued through love letters. Williams was a pricey school even in those days and during the summer months Alfred earned money and sought adventure, working on merchant marine ships. While at Williams, Alfred displayed a commitment to excellence that he pursued throughout his career; he was one of only two students in his class to graduate as a four-year varsity letterman in three sports.

Early on, it was apparent that Alfred was brilliant, dynamic, and had the courage of his convictions. Yet he had something more: he had the ability to connect with people one to one. Throughout his career he never lost sight of his goals and was able to put content and substance over labels and personality; he was practical, reliable, and ethical. There is a term in Yiddish for someone like Driscoll: mensch. A mensch is a person of integrity. A mensch has a keen sense of right and wrong and always does the right thing. Alfred never let his ego get in the way of the public's business, nor did he permit himself to get bogged down by the hypersensitivities of small-minded politicians and their petty prejudices. He was able to see the big picture and doesn't appear to have had an agenda beyond making government effective. As political types go, Alfred Driscoll was a mensch.

Although there were significant differences in age and heritage, Driscoll and Vanderbilt had much in common; both attended an elite private college (Driscoll—Williams, class of 1925; Vanderbilt—Wesleyan, class of 1910) and went to an Ivy League law school (Driscoll—Harvard, class of 1928; Vanderbilt—Columbia, class of 1913). Of importance, they also shared a common view of government's role in people's lives. For them, the two core principles of the Republican Party were the protection of personal liberty through the rule of law and the inherent need for government to play a positive role by adapting to an ever-changing American society. Those principles had their origin in the single-minded determination of the abolitionists to eradicate slavery, the galvanizing issue that led to the founding of the Republican Party. Following the cataclysm of the Civil War, the Progressive Era was a natural outgrowth of the abolition movement.

Progressives were fiercely opposed to government being rigged in favor of the powerful and demanded fairness and efficiency from public officials. Republicans like Alfred Driscoll and Arthur Vanderbilt picked up where Theodore Roosevelt and Frank Sommer had left off. They believed government had a central role in keeping society a level playing field. Touching everything from social work, education, and women's suffrage, to journalism, government agencies, and workers' rights, in most instances it was the progressive Republicans who led the way in uplifting the condition of the working poor and immigrants who were being exploited in America's new industrial society.

One final item on the progressives' agenda was reform of the country's court systems. From having attended Harvard Law School, Driscoll was exposed to the teachings of Professor Roscoe Pound, one of the intellectuals in the law whom Vanderbilt admired greatly. Pound and the legal scholars of his generation pushed for fairness and efficiency in the administration of justice; they understood that the public's confidence in the judicial system was critical to the survival of America's experiment in freedom. They were pursuing nothing short of a renaissance in the nation's courthouses. Although Driscoll's ardor for reforming New Jersey's constitution never equaled Vanderbilt's, he quickly learned that the state's court system was in need of a shakeup if the public was to have any faith in it.

Despite the fact that both were "lawyer-politicians," the contrast in their approaches to their careers was stark. Having no family money, Vanderbilt needed to practice law to make a living and, as I have shown, exploited politics to do quite well for himself. Driscoll, once he married Antoinette Tatum, didn't need to have a career in the law yet pursued one knowing it could be an asset in public life. While Vanderbilt's involvement in politics always had the focus of reforming New Jersey's government, he was also a combative political animal with a take-no-prisoners intensity. And after two decades of slaying dragons in Essex County and doing battle in Trenton in pursuit of a new constitution, his passion for reform had ripened into what some viewed as fanaticism. On the issue of constitutional reform, Vanderbilt abhorred compromise.

Alfred Driscoll, on the other hand, wasn't a career politician, nor was he obsessed with anything: he was a citizen soldier looking to advance the public agenda by bringing New Jersey's government into the twentieth century, and he was not looking to establish a power base from which to influence events on an ongoing basis. For students of ancient Rome, Driscoll's career evokes the noble hero Cincinnatus, the Roman aristocrat who left his family during a time of trouble in the Roman Republic to serve in government—no longer than necessary to solve an urgent problem before returning home. Down through the millennia, Cincinnatus is remembered as a model of civic virtue who sought to serve the greater good without personal ambition.

For someone like Driscoll, Vanderbilt's Clean Government movement in Essex County had to be inspiring. By the mid-1930s, Clean Government was beginning to take its message statewide. Until 1934, Vanderbilt's organization was little more than a tight-knit group of white-collar types from suburban Newark, the emerging commuter voter, handpicked by Vanderbilt. They wanted to clean up Essex County's government, campaigning for office primarily on their reputations as successful professionals and businessmen.

Governor Harold Hoffman's relationship with Hague in 1934–1937 was so upsetting to Republicans throughout the state that it enabled Vanderbilt to build alliances in most of New Jersey's twenty-one counties. Bitterly betrayed by many of Hoffman's appointments of Hague Democrats to key positions that otherwise would have gone to GOP stalwarts, new groups of reform-minded Republicans emerged within county organizations around the state. Through a masterful use of public relations—everything from letters to the editor, political handbills, radio editorials, and talks before local Republican clubs—Vanderbilt tarred Hoffman with the Hague brush and married the two together as the source of every grievance these groups voiced, all the while preaching that constitutional reform was the remedy for political corruption.

After the 1934 election and in light of Hoffman's cozy relationship with Hague, Vanderbilt was determined to have a political machine of his own: a machine to ensure that only Republicans who shared his views on reform could win nomination for statewide office. As his power increased, Vanderbilt commanded loyalty akin to what Hague demanded in Hudson County. Why else would Newark lawyer Dominic Cavicchia go to Boston to ask Houghton Mifflin to alter its records?

Walter Edge—who up to that time was one of the more astute political operatives to sit in the governor's chair—had this to say when assessing Vanderbilt's mastery of Essex County politics:

> Although one of the outstanding lawyers of the country, past president of the American Bar Association, the dean of New York University Law School, Vanderbilt in a benevolent way, was as absolute a political boss in the Republican Party as Hague was in the Democratic organization. While the two men used their power to different ends . . . his [Vanderbilt's] control over the thirteen Essex legislators was just as absolute.[6]

Essex County was the most populated in the state, having a greater number of members in the state assembly than any other county—twelve, a potent 20 percent of the total. Vanderbilt's control over Essex County's votes both in a statewide Republican primary and on the floor of the legislature, together with bonds forged with other progressive Republicans throughout the state, made him the second most powerful person in New Jersey politics. Using the opportunity created by Hoffman's disloyalty to the Republican Party, Vanderbilt's organization had become a full-fledged statewide political powerhouse and Driscoll couldn't help but notice.

Yet when Driscoll returned to Haddonfield from Harvard Law School in 1928, Camden County's politics was much like the Republican machine of Jesse Salmon in Essex County. At the time, Camden County was dominated by the Baird family. David Baird Sr. had been a protégé of Senator William Sewell, a veteran of the American Civil War and a Congressional Medal of Honor winner. In the nineteenth century, as now, war heroes made popular candidates, and William Sewell, working from the bustling riverfront city of Camden, was for many years one of the stronger voices in southern New Jersey politics. When Colonel Sewell died in 1901, Baird became leader and in time—as had Sewell—went on to serve in the U.S. Senate.

Baird was successful in both real estate and banking, and he presided over his financial and political empire from his mansion on Cooper Street in Camden. Politics is often a hereditary business, and when David Baird Sr. died in 1927, David Jr. took the reins of power. Two years later, he too was named by the legislature to serve in the U.S. Senate. Typical of urban political organizations of the time, the Baird organization required people to "work the chairs," and when young Alfred Driscoll—then all of twenty-six—announced he was running for the Haddonfield Board of Education, it caused a stir among local Republicans. He was told he couldn't run because the local Republican Party had already selected a slate.[7]

Driscoll was having none of it; he ran as an independent and won, going on to serve for eight years. Serving on a local school board in New Jersey can be both thankless and gratifying. Because of the average person's indifference to the administration of public education, school board members receive little praise—mostly grumbling from taxpayers about costs— yet there are opportunities for improving children's lives. Driscoll valued greatly the education he had received and understood that a community that neglects to educate its children endangers its future. He had to work closely with other board members and school administrators to get anything done and, as one of nine board members needed to practice the sublime art of compromise. Importantly, he learned he didn't need the same majority on every issue to get things done. The Haddonfield School Board was an excellent incubator for his career in politics.

From school board it was on to the Haddonfield Borough Commission, where he served as finance director, focusing on fiscal management. This was a key issue among progressive Republicans who followed Democrat Woodrow Wilson's teachings that true reform of government began by making it more efficient and cost effective. Partisan politics in hiring, namely putting unqualified political hacks on the public payroll, was one practice that progressives attacked with zeal. Driscoll's growing reputation in Camden County was that of an independent thinker prepared to work with anyone interested in good government of any political stripe. He was patient, and when the opportunity came, he made his move.

In 1939, Driscoll decided to take on the Regular Republican's handpicked candidate for state senator in the primary election. The thirty-seven-year-old borough commissioner, well-educated, dapper, handsome, and articulate, was too much for the Baird organization. Haddonfield's mensch won the party's nomination, making his election a certainty in Republican-dominated Camden County. Once in the state senate, it was only natural that Driscoll allied himself with Vanderbilt's Clean Government senators. It was a perfect fit.

Although only a freshman senator, Driscoll's pedigree and charisma as the insurgent who had overcome the vaunted Baird organization catapulted him into the position of majority leader. During the brief time he served as leader of the Senate Republicans, he found himself wedged between Vanderbilt's allies looking to foil Hague at every turn and those Republicans who saw the benefit of going along with the Jersey City mayor. Confronted with this challenge, he later said, "My job was to get as much as I could and to yield as little as I would."[8]

Driscoll was eager to become more politically involved in all twenty-one counties, and in 1940 he managed Robert Hendrickson's campaign for governor. Hendrickson was a dynamic lawyer-politician from neighboring Gloucester County, and he and Driscoll bonded quickly. Despite suffering the disappointment of seeing Hendrickson lose to Republican-turned-Democrat Charles Edison, that campaign was Driscoll's first exposure to Frank Hague's role in statewide elections; as ever, Hudson County furnished the winning margin. It was an experience that proved valuable in the years ahead, as did his tenure as state senator.[9]

While in the state senate, Driscoll showed that he could work across party lines. One of the people he developed a close rapport with was Hudson County senator Edgar O'Mara, a key lieutenant in the Hague organization. O'Mara pursued the Hudson County agenda by raising objections to any efforts to revise the constitution, and Driscoll worked with Vanderbilt to support Governor Edison's tax bill, designed to give relief to the railroads, which were still struggling from the effects of the Great Depression. While they took conflicting positions on these and other issues, they each avoided any type of personal attack on the other. Driscoll and O'Mara's relationship was a model for how to get things done in Trenton.

Ed O'Mara wasn't a Hague puppet, but he still had had to climb the rungs of Hague's ladder to become a state senator. He had been born in Jersey City in 1897 and was a lifelong resident. Unlike some of the lawyers on Hague's team, O'Mara was the real deal; he was a legal scholar who had graduated as "the honor man of his class in 1922" from Fordham Law School. Additionally, he was a member of the faculty of his alma mater from 1924 to 1929. He paid his dues to Hague by first serving as legal counsel to the Hudson County Park Commission and later moved on to the city's corporate counsel's office. He also developed a private practice and served a term as president of the Hudson County Bar Association. O'Mara was elected to the senate for the first time in the November 1940 election and was reelected in 1943 and 1946. He was minority leader of the Senate in 1943 and 1945.

Not long after his meeting in Newark with Vanderbilt, Driscoll formally announced his candidacy for governor. Harold Hoffman immediately attacked him as the "crown prince." The former governor challenged Driscoll's legitimacy, framing his candidacy as the product of the strong-arm tactics of Walter Edge and Vanderbilt. Hoffman's strategy was aimed at striking a contrast between himself and Driscoll; he positioned himself as the unbossed outsider, free of control by bosses in Trenton whose agenda had nothing to do with the needs of ordinary people. By zeroing in on the support coming from Edge and Vanderbilt, Hoffman hoped to present Driscoll to the voters as just another reformer who would prattle on about revising the state constitution and neglect issues more important to the average person.

His efforts were for naught. Hoffman was seen as a retread, and his candidacy never gained traction with the new class of Republicans drawn to the party by the Clean Government movement. Nor was there tangible support among the old guard, many of whom resented his record of dispensing patronage to Hague supporters. Driscoll rolled over Hoffman in the primary, and from there it was on to the general election. And then things got curious.

Frank Hague never played to lose, but it's hard to understand how he thought Hudson County judge Lewis Hansen could pose a serious challenge to the likes of Alfred Driscoll; possibly he had other things on his mind. That year, knowing the futility of trying to overcome the Democratic Party votes in Hudson County, Charles Edison permitted supporters to file petitions for him to run as an independent, on the outside chance that Hoffman would gain the Republican nomination. When Driscoll won the nomination Edison withdrew, leaving the race between the mensch from Haddonfield and the judge from Jersey City.

After graduating from law school in 1913 Lewis Hansen wasn't admitted to the bar until 1916. In that era every lawyer was required to serve a clerkship with a senior member of the bar who acted as a preceptor; typically it was a twelve- to eighteen-month stint. After being admitted to practice law Hansen became active in the Hague organization and served a term as a Hague puppet in the assembly. From there he went to work in the Hudson County Prosecutor's Office and then in the Jersey City corporate counsel's office, where he remained until appointed to the bench by Harry Moore.

An interesting footnote to the campaign was Hansen's efforts to grab headlines. As we saw, an early move in 1944 by Walter Edge against Hague's organization was to assign the attorney general, Walter Van Riper, as acting prosecutor of Hudson County to investigate organized gambling in Jersey City. In the midst of the campaign, Hansen challenged Van Riper to justify the $51,000 invoice for his services, which the attorney general had demanded be paid by county government. When the county refused, the state finance commission withheld the money from Hudson County's share of the state highway funds. It's hard to imagine that was Hansen's intended result.

Driscoll won the election by more than 220,000 votes. Hansen played the game a while longer, until he snatched his brass ring, a sinecure: he was elected and reelected Hudson County surrogate, spending much of each year in Florida for the remainder of his life.

Despite the fact that constitutional reform wasn't a campaign issue, not long after the election the governor-elect quietly began laying the groundwork for revising the state constitution. Driscoll and his advisors had made a careful review of the constitutions prepared under Edison and Edge—in large part Vanderbilt's handiwork—and the reasons for their defeat; they secretly devised a strategy to transcend the past controversies. In his inaugural address of January 21, 1947, Driscoll framed the defeat of the 1944 document as a sign of voter rejection of the Edge proposal rather than a vote of confidence for the 1844 Constitution—which almost no one had ever read. "The people in 1944 did not vote in favor of our present constitution of 1844 as much as they voted against the document submitted to them as a whole to replace it."[10] This interpretation of events served as Driscoll's justification for reopening the issue with the voters and the legislature and igniting an all-out effort to create a new government for New Jersey.

As noted by historian Richard J. Connors, this was more than a novel interpretation of events; it was a game-changing blueprint for action. "Instead of the *good guys* writing a constitution and trying to defeat the *bad guys* in a referendum campaign, all major elements in the state's political life were to be brought into the drafting process itself. If things went well, the campaign to market a revised constitution would then become primarily a technical one—informing the voters as to the content of, and the need for the document."[11] From the outset it was apparent, though unspoken, that Driscoll wanted three new players at the negotiating table when the constitution was drafted: the lay reformers, the rural Republicans, and the Hague Democrats.

Alfred Driscoll's inaugural address is a window into the mind of a Cincinnatus-type public official. The new governor possessed the wisdom to appreciate the ebb and flow of electoral politics and cautioned his fellow Republicans on the need for restraint. "While we operate through the mechanics of majority rule, we must not indulge in majority excesses. Our philosophy of government recognizes that today's majorities may be nothing more than a coalition of yesterday's minorities." He also revealed a mature understanding of the limits of power and the need for government to adapt to a changing society. "Those of us who have served in the Legislature for any length of time have become particularly conscious of the fact that government is a dynamic thing, that problems do not stay solved, that legislative defeats will not remain quiescent under the pressure of constantly changing conditions in our society."[12]

In his first public speech as governor, Driscoll declared that he had decided to go the route of a constitutional convention and was willing to divorce the question of revising the Constitution from the call for legislative redistricting. Reapportionment was an issue that Edison, Edge, and Vanderbilt had all urged; abandoning it annoyed Vanderbilt. In detailing his thoughts about how the convention should be comprised, Driscoll stated unequivocally: "The convention shall be composed of 60 members elected from our counties, with each county to have the same number of delegates as it has members in the House of Assembly."[13] Arthur Vanderbilt was thrilled by this pledge, but the senator from Atlantic County was not and Driscoll knew who was more important to please if there was to be a convention.

Frank "Hap" Farley was an Irish American lawyer-politician who found his niche in New Jersey politics and then mastered it as few others have. Despite being admired by his local contemporaries as a "jock" for his athleticism—he played and coached sports for ten years after law school without developing much of a law practice—Farley was no hack politician. He was a graduate of the University of Pennsylvania and Georgetown Law School, where he formed a lifelong friendship with classmate John Sirica, who became the famed Watergate trial judge. After retiring from sports Farley got serious about politics—the only game worth playing in Atlantic City—and invested all his energy into becoming a leader in the local Republican organization, which had gained statewide clout under the reign of the notorious Enoch "Nucky" Johnson. When Nucky went to jail in 1941, Hap won out over several rivals to become the new boss.[14]

Despite doing his best to ignore his roots in Atlantic City, Walter Edge became Farley's benefactor. In no small part because he and Walter Edge hailed from the same county, in Edge's first year in office (1944) Hap was chosen senate majority leader; the following year he became senate president, making him a leader in his party's caucus. Riding on Edge's bandwagon, Farley was on his way; in terms of his influence in the New Jersey State Senate, Hap Farley never looked back.

While he could play both, Farley preferred statehouse politics to the local kind that involved daily meetings with party workers; he would rather cut deals in Trenton. Hap assigned day-to-day control of the organization to others, freeing him to be a full-time senator. He used his time well: traveling to Trenton when the legislature wasn't in session; schmoozing with career bureaucrats; and learning the nitty-gritty of state government—all vital to successful legislative efforts. After three terms in the assembly he was elected in 1940 to the senate, where he and Alfred Driscoll became acquainted.

While Driscoll was the citizen soldier and Vanderbilt the manic who juggled several careers, Farley had an almost monastic devotion to politics. His aims were few: to control the state senate and to snare revenue and pass legislation to aid and protect the Atlantic City tourist economy. He excelled. Over the next thirty years, Hap Farley established a record of accomplishment that made him a legend in Trenton. In time, he became the reality with whom every governor had to contend when creating an agenda. When Driscoll entered the governor's office, Hap had already become a force unto himself and no one to ignore.

Throughout much of the 1930s and 1940s the GOP maintained sizable majorities, consistently controlling thirteen to seventeen of the state's twenty-one counties. The seven southern counties were nearly always represented by Republican senators, and these were pretty much Farley's votes. While he cultivated a personal relationship with every member of the senate, remembering birthdays and wedding anniversaries and sending thank-you notes, Hap diligently looked after the interests of his six fellow senators from South Jersey. He mentored the younger ones and rounded up votes for those trying to make a name through passing bills important to their counties.

Even better, or worse, depending upon one's perspective, Farley had inherited from Nucky Johnson a pipeline to Hudson County's votes in the legislature. Dating back to Walter Edge's first election as governor in 1916, when Johnson and Hague aligned with one another to kill the candidacy of Hudson County Democrat Otto Wittpenn, the Republican boss of Atlantic County and the Democratic boss of Hudson County had a cordial relationship, and neither did anything to hurt the other. More than once during Farley's career, critical votes cast by Hudson County assemblymen saved legislation sponsored by Hap. From having served as a member of the Republican caucus and worked in state government full-time for several years, Driscoll saw Farley in action and knew he was much better to have as a friend than a foe.

When Senate President Barton of Passaic County introduced the bill urged by Driscoll calling for a constitutional convention of sixty delegates, it got Farley's attention. Like a strong-willed coach, Hap wasn't content unless he called some of the plays. Speaking for the rural senators, Farley countered with a proposal of his own: he suggested that there be an additional delegate for each of the twenty-one counties for a convention made up of eighty-one delegates, no tampering with one senator per county, and the requirement that everything approved by the convention must be returned to the legislature before going back to the voters at a referendum in November. Farley's intentions were clear: the rural Republicans wanted a veto over the work of the convention.

Although Driscoll was told he had the votes to push the Barton bill through both houses, Senator David Van Alstyne of Bergen County cautioned him that "jamming the bill through the Senate this way would leave a bitter aftertaste" with Farley and the rural Republicans that would come back to haunt him at the convention.[15] On February 10, the day the final vote was scheduled, the governor sent word through Van Alstyne to Farley that he would accept the eighty-one delegates and pledged not to tamper with one senator per county, but that the convention's work would not return to the legislature; it had to go directly to the voters. Driscoll and Farley had a deal.[16]

Driscoll was mature enough to accept the reality that the first step on the path to reform required capitulation. However, by yielding to Farley's demand on the number of delegates, Driscoll undercut Vanderbilt's ability to control the convention. Under the initial plan, Vanderbilt "owned" 20 percent of the delegates. With the compromise between Driscoll and Farley, Vanderbilt had only thirteen of eighty-one, or 16 percent. The effect was to increase the per capita representation of the smaller counties in comparison with the larger counties. For example, each citizen of a small county like Salem or Sussex would receive four times the representation of a citizen of a large county like Essex or Bergen. More problematic, of the twenty-one new delegates that Driscoll had permitted, Vanderbilt could count on no more than three or four being in his column.

Hours before the vote in the legislature, Driscoll had his staff deliver word to key legislators that he had accepted Farley's proposal expressly conditioned upon the bill authorizing a constitutional convention being passed unanimously in both the senate and the assembly. Driscoll insisted that Hague and Hudson County had to be on board. Farley handled that by working with Driscoll's pal Ed O'Mara, but that was only part of the bargaining with Frank Hague. There was more to come.

February 10, 1947, was a frantic day in the statehouse. Following an afternoon and evening of deliberations, arm-twisting and horse trading, a bill was passed unanimously by the senate at 10:00 p.m. and by the assembly at 1:00 a.m. early the next day. Because of Driscoll's decision to abandon the specifics of the delegate pledge made in his inaugural address—less than three weeks earlier—and his willingness to compromise with Farley, there was to be a constitutional convention in the summer of 1947, and every member of the legislature had voted in favor of it. Driscoll's negotiations had produced a valuable burst of momentum, but it came at the price of angering Vanderbilt.

Bad news has good legs, especially in politics.

Driscoll knew that Vanderbilt would be upset by the deal cut with Farley, and he wanted to deliver the bad news as swiftly and courteously as possible. He designated one of his key staff people to contact Vanderbilt directly as soon as the vote was final so that he could couple the good news of a constitutional convention with the bad news of the compromise. It was so late at night that his staff person decided to wait until early the next morning to make the call. But it wasn't too late for one of the Essex County assemblymen to call the boss at home in the wee hours.

Vanderbilt was enraged when the governor's staff person got him on the phone the next morning. With the increase in the number of delegates and with Driscoll's efforts to organize a bipartisan convention, which would require even more tête-à-têtes with the mayor, Vanderbilt was certain that the Hague delegates and rural Republicans would sabotage the convention. Vanderbilt believed Driscoll had blundered and that once more the chance of true reform had slipped from his grasp. During the conversation with the governor's staff person he stated that "the beaches strewn with the bleached bones of Republican politicians who had listened to the siren voice of Mayor Hague" would soon be joined by Driscoll's. The flustered staff person reportedly remarked, "Well, you will probably be in Maine this summer anyway," to which Vanderbilt replied, "That's exactly where I will be."[17]

What no one, including Vanderbilt, knew at the time was the reason he would be in Maine that summer.

CHAPTER 12

Things Get Curious

Irate doesn't quite describe Vanderbilt's state of mind. Following approval of legislation authorizing a constitutional convention, he began telling people that any hope of meaningful reform had been undermined and that Driscoll was "a damned double-crosser."[1]

Vanderbilt was always plotting: it's likely he had every vote counted in a sixty-delegate convention, but eighty-one? That was a disruption to his game plan and he didn't like the new arithmetic. In a mere twenty days Driscoll had done an about-face on what Vanderbilt viewed as a key element to ensure he would get his way at the convention. What other surprises did the new governor have in store?

Although Vanderbilt feared the worst, he urged his Clean Government troops to work toward a new constitution but not to let their guard down. A short time after adoption of the bill authorizing a public referendum on the June primary ballot, the governor and his staff got busy encouraging bipartisan slates of delegates from each county. He believed it was important for the voters to know who would be representing them from each county, not only to ensure the convention's political credibility but also to propel the process forward, strengthening his momentum. Political primaries are notorious for low turnouts, and Driscoll didn't want to run the risk of either party trying to sabotage things. What's more—assuming the referendum was successful—having an agreement about who would go to the convention from both parties would mean there was no need for a second election to choose delegates; they could get right to work. Yet at times your best allies can be your worst enemies.

While Driscoll was working to make the convention bipartisan—successfully persuading Hague to designate a minimum of three of Hudson County's ten delegates for Republicans—Vanderbilt wasn't playing ball: for weeks, he refused even to speak with the governor. According to longtime Vanderbilt ally, attorney Alan Lowenstein, "Unlike Vanderbilt, who distrusted compromise, Driscoll knew that if New Jersey was to have a new constitution, some compromises had to be made" and that the "opposition of Mayor Hague had to be dealt with, although Vanderbilt wanted no part of a bipartisan effort."[2]

Notwithstanding pressure from Driscoll's emissaries, members of the Essex County Bar Association, and the League of Women Voters, the Warrior Lawyer wanted no part of a truce with Frank Hague. The Essex County Republican chairman, George Becker, who had been handpicked by Vanderbilt, refused even to meet with the Essex Democrats, stating that it would be "nothing short of treason to our Republican constituents" to grant representation to people allied with Hague. "Vanderbilt himself labeled the whole concept of bipartisanship a fraud. The Republicans were in power in New Jersey, and like it or not, they would be assigned responsibility for success or failure of the convention."[3] Thumbing his nose at Driscoll, Vanderbilt defiantly selected a slate of thirteen Republicans from Essex County. To his credit, none of them were dim-witted, run-of-the-mill party hacks. They were all quality people, including the dean of the Newark College of Engineering, the outgoing president of the League of Women Voters, representatives of NJCCR, and the universally respected Frank Sommer, dean emeritus of NYU's School of Law.

Yet nothing could calm Vanderbilt. Still bristling with indignation at Driscoll's appeasement of Farley and the rural Republicans—not to mention making concessions to Hague—he stated, "I shall not deny that I have my misgivings as to the possibilities of the new Convention, but I personally intend to work for a new Constitution as insistently as I have in the past, reserving, however, my right as a citizen, as I hope the Delegates will, to oppose the new Constitution in November if it does not measure up to reasonable expectations."[4]

Although none of Vanderbilt's medical records from the spring of 1947 are available, it's probable he had some form of severe hypertension. Things were going poorly on several fronts. Vanderbilt's juggling act of performing his multiple responsibilities as a lawyer, political leader, law professor, dean and fund-raiser at NYU, and trustee at Wesleyan finally came tumbling down in the spring of 1947. Adding to the torment of what he feared was yet another dead end for reforming New Jersey's government and courts, there were problems brewing at both his alma mater and the law school, and things had gone awry in a lengthy jury trial.

Wesleyan University had a huge place in his heart, and he was always being pulled back to the school to help out. Beginning in the 1930s—prompted at first by difficulties with his college-days fraternity, Delta Kappa Epsilon— Vanderbilt began traveling to Connecticut ten to twenty times a year. He not only turned things around at the fraternity but also assisted in raising money and recruiting faculty. In typical Vanderbilt style, he got himself totally immersed in the business of running the college. In time he was asked to serve on the board of trustees and was later elected chairman. In the spring of 1947 he found himself—largely because of the personalities on the board— powerless to bring about changes in the school's curriculum that he believed were long overdue. It was one more frustration that had become a headache.

Worse still was the migraine at NYU, where he was now the dean of the law school. Frank Sommer, his mentor and the person who had introduced him to the law school in 1914, had retired in 1943. Vanderbilt's role in the school had grown to such an extent—and he had touched the lives and influenced the careers of so many alumni—that he was the logical choice to replace Sommer. Nonetheless, Vanderbilt had taken on a challenge that some saw as Homeric. The Great Depression and World War II had ravaged many schools of higher learning and despite Dean Sommer's best efforts, NYU's law school was limping along. There were thoughts within the university's administration of simply turning off the lights and closing the doors.

Located at Washington Square on the top two floors of an old and deteriorating twelve-story commercial building occupied principally by a textbook publisher, the learning environment was hardly ideal. The classrooms were shabby and the library was an embarrassment. Faculty and student amenities were nonexistent; further reducing confidence in the school were elevators that frequently jammed, leaving students stranded. It was little wonder that enrollment had dipped from 1,000 in 1938 to 175 in 1942. By the fall of 1943, enrollment barely reached 100. "It was at this time that Vanderbilt agreed . . . to attempt a salvaging operation" with the hope that things would improve when the war was over.[5]

Ever the visionary, Vanderbilt planned for a whole lot more than merely hanging on till things improved. Within months of becoming dean he was proposing dramatic changes. He had "a plan for developing the school into a leading law school of the nation, a plan to be realized both by strengthening it internally and by the establishment there of an institution that had long been germinating in his thoughts—a national law center." He believed it would attract students, professors, and money, and become "a force for the systematic and continuous revision of the law."[6]

Yet to realize his goal he had to become a "professional beggar,"[7] a role he detested, causing him more stress than he had bargained for. In time, Vanderbilt's vision of NYU as a leading national law school would be realized, but that spring was crunch time: more than $200,000 had to be raised within thirty days to satisfy a condition of a grant for the law school's building program. Much to his dismay, NYU's administration appeared to have dropped the ball in its support for the new Law Center; if the needed funds weren't forthcoming Dean Vanderbilt would be gravely embarrassed.

Finally, adding to his stress that spring was his daily commute to represent an important client in a lengthy jury trial in Trenton—before a judge in whom he had no confidence—where things had spun miserably out of control, resulting in a substantial verdict against his client. Vanderbilt didn't take it well. As he noted years later, "I sensed there was something very foul, and by some real sleuthing, we discovered that certain papers had been used by the jury in reaching their verdict which had never been offered in evidence and which were not submitted to them by the Clerk of the Court, nor returned to him by the jury—dirty work at the crossroads,"[8] which eventually resulted in a new trial but at the time caused much grief. The month of May 1947 had to be the worst of Arthur Vanderbilt's life.

On the evening of May 21, two weeks shy of the public referendum on the constitutional convention, Vanderbilt had to choose between an evening of his usual teaching class at NYU in New York City and speaking in support of the constitutional convention to a gathering of citizens in Montclair. Fortunately, he made the less burdensome trip to Montclair and drove home the ten miles when the event was over. The next morning—several weeks shy of his fifty-ninth birthday—the Warrior Lawyer was stricken. He awoke to find himself paralyzed on his left side: both his arm and leg were static. He had suffered a stroke, and it was more severe than the public ever learned. As he later related, "As I fell to sleep that night, I am afraid my will was not on guard. My old loathing of the raising of money must have asserted itself in my subconscious mind. At any rate, the next morning I was unable to carry on."[9] Not long after, Vanderbilt was off to Maine for several months of badly needed R and R.

Across Newark Bay, the end of the Celtic Chieftain's reign was beginning. That spring Frank Hague did something even more curious than supporting Lewis Hansen for governor; he resigned as mayor of Jersey City. On the same day, June 4, 1947, that New Jersey's primary voters approved going forward with the constitutional convention by a five-to-one margin, carrying Hudson County by a margin of 55,937, Frank Hague announced that he was retiring from City Hall after thirty years in office. He had proclaimed the selection of his nephew, Frank Hague Eggers, as his successor, and his fellow city commissioners dutifully complied with his selection. Eggers would also lead Hudson County's delegation to the constitutional convention, which was scheduled to begin the next week, on June 12. With guidance from Senator Edgar O'Mara and former chief justice Tom Brogan, who had resigned three months earlier, Eggers was prepared to do his uncle's bidding. As for Hague, when the action began at the convention, he would be on vacation in California.

Street politicians who make it to the top usually hang around too long. The ones who make too many enemies on their way up are often unceremoniously removed from power; those who are generous to their peers going up the ladder are customarily ushered gently into retirement and granted an honorarium. Those who step off the ladder themselves are atypical.

How/why/when people of enduring power decide of their own volition to throttle back on the ability to control events rarely lends itself to a simple explanation. Hague is no exception. Given his limited formal education and the absence of a diary, notes of a close friend, or personal correspondence taking history into his confidence, we are left to speculate. Yet what staggered the political world in 1947 appears somewhat clearer today. Despite being a sixth-grade dropout, Hague understood people and power the way few politicians in American history have. He had to have realized his personal power was waning, yet put his faith in his organization.

Like an army, political organizations need battles to stay in fighting trim; tranquility dulls the edge. More than thirty years had passed since Hague had become the unquestioned leader of Hudson County and New Jersey's Democrats in 1916, catapulting Harry Moore into the governor's chair the first of three times. In 1929 he went mano a mano with Senator Clarence Case and the entire Republican Party, staring down their arrest warrant and bludgeoning them in the courts. It had been ten years since the battles with Vanderbilt and the CIO, and although Hague had fared poorly, it had galvanized the troops. But that was also the time of the theft of Lester Clee's election as governor. In order to prevail in such an enormous fraud, Hague and the key players of his organization had to have nerves of steel and the discipline of academy-trained soldiers; no one could waiver, particularly Chief Justice Brogan. Also, while the defeat of the 1944 constitutional referendum had warmed the cockles of his heart, the municipal elections in 1941 and 1945 weren't anything to excite the faithful. Further adding to the stagnation of Hague's organization was his failure to reinvigorate the upper levels of the party. As aptly captured by Richard J. Connors, Hague "was too content with the leadership structure he had developed in the 1910s and the 1920s" and neglected to bring in new people to update the party to take account of the changing world in his own backyard.[10] The Celtic Chieftain was too loyal to his own kind, neglecting to share power in any meaningful way with the growing number of Polish and Italian voters who had become increasingly important to his dominance, and they were beginning to resent Irish politicians holding all the key positions in city and county government. Resentment squelches enthusiasm, which every political organization must have in order to prevail at election time. In the two decades preceding his decision to step down as mayor there had been very few changes among Jersey City's political ward leaders unless someone died, forcing Hague's hand.[11] The same was generally true for the people in City Hall, whether the city commissioners or upper-level staff people. The only exception was when he decided to give his nephew, Frank Hague Eggers, some hands-on training.

Compounding Hague's problems was the scarcity of jobs to dispense to the faithful. Then and now, every political organization depends upon on patronage of some sort. In the 1910s and 1920s, as Hague was establishing his power base, City Hall was flush with cash from the property tax on the railroads; services were expanding and positions were being created to implement new programs to provide constituent services. Then along came the Great Depression. Initially, Hague dealt with the shrinkage in revenue by padding the county's payroll, effectively using money from the neighboring communities in Hudson County to prop up his regime. He also tapped into the federal government's revitalization programs for every dollar, and job, that he could lay his hands on, the most tangible examples being the Medical Center and Roosevelt Stadium.

Yet it was state government from which his power was continually nourished. His control of the governor's patronage for nearly twenty years was the resource that made it possible for him to dispense political plums, large and small, powerful and nondescript: everything from janitors, clerks, and secretaries to schoolteachers, police, and firemen. Then there were the vendors, contractors and engineers who fed at the public trough on rigged bids and no-competition public contracts. Finally, there were the biggest prizes: scores of positions for lawyers at the city, county, state, and federal level, including the judiciary. The lawyers Hague had named to the bench were his last line of defense, and they never failed him. As others have chronicled, every position had its price, with a standard 3 percent of each salary and contract being kicked back to the organization. Loss of patronage meant loss of revenue for the organization.

Diminishing job opportunities within the organization not only limited upward mobility but also caused stagnation at the bottom. Precinct leader and ward leader were generally young men's job, but by the 1940s most such posts were held by old Irish men who had little connection with the city's newcomers. Some had remained in the same position for twenty to thirty years. One has to ask what it was that made Hague think that all these old men could still hold sway in neighborhoods where things had changed so much in the preceding thirty years.[12] From today's vantage point we can see that this stagnation meant that the opportunities for young politicians to get experience at handling power were in the hands of another generation. This didn't make for much of a future.

Through it all, Hague was becoming more and more disengaged from the day-to-day workings of the organization he had so carefully nurtured, leaving Deputy Mayor John Malone to run things. When he was in town and not on one of his extended trips to Florida, Europe, or other destinations, Hague still wasn't to be found in City Hall; he had built a grand private office in the Medical Center that had become his preoccupation. He was available to a handful of players in the organization by telephone, but appearances in public had become rare. By default, John Malone was perpetually the acting mayor. As Connors notes, "Malone, a dour little man with a rotund physique and a long, sharp nose [he was known as "Needle Nose"], was a faithful workhorse and attempted to keep Hague in touch with the local scene

via countless phone calls."[13] Having never run for office or fearlessly chased
down the likes of Frank Kenny's murderer Michael Rombolo, as Hague had
done early in his career, Malone had all the charisma of an Irish spud. He
worked tirelessly for the organization "ironing out the wrinkles and distributing the payoffs of a system in which decision-making was overly cluttered
at the top."[14] He may have been an able administrator, but he wasn't Hague; he
never understood the big picture or worked all the levers, nor could he lead
the organization's foot soldiers. Malone wasn't a chieftain.

Nonetheless, John Malone wasn't the problem; at the core of the stagnation was Frank Hague himself. He was the one who had to apply the personal
touch: going to wakes, throwing the first pitch of a Little League game, or
consoling a family burned out of its home; he had to play the heroic, pater-
nalistic role and be visible in the community. Instead, Hague looked more
like the absentee WASP landlord collecting land rents from his tireless but
impoverished subjects.[15] He had become an icon with all the warmth of one.
As his longtime friend and legal counsel, John Milton, said in an interview
with Connors: "By the 1940s, Hague felt he had built up an inexhaustible res-
ervoir of good will, because of past services and favors, that could be tapped
at his pleasure. So he didn't work as hard anymore, and this meant that his
organization didn't either."[16]

Hague and his lieutenants managed the withering of patronage and
papered over the troubles created by internal stagnation until 1941, Charles
Edison's first year in the governor's office. President Roosevelt had done
Hague no favor in persuading the inventor's son to switch party affiliation,
and the "deaf little S.O.B." was particularly hard of hearing when it came to
Hudson County. By the summer of Edison's first year as governor, the faucet
of state jobs was shut tight for anyone connected to His Honor the Mayor.
More than any other source of patronage, state government had placed the
best-paying and most prestigious jobs at his disposal: jobs to both reward
loyal troops and to encourage the up-and-comers necessary to keep rust
from setting in to his regime. Unsurprisingly, Walter Edge reinforced Edison's stance and, equally troublesome, state government had withheld millions of dollars of tax revenue paid by the railroad; by 1946 the cupboard was
bare of jobs.

That September, the *Newark Sunday Call*, consistently a Vanderbilt
backer, reported—almost gleefully—on the status of political jobs in Hudson County: "His type of political machine is built around jobs, and when

a choice spot is denied him at the patronage counter, he is bound to suffer. The great Trenton job drought is producing results. Six years without the key state bureau jobs, without the judgeships and most important, without the thousands of little jobs which keep a political machine functioning have hurt Hague and hurt him deeply."[17]

Also hurting Hague were the body blows he had taken over the years in the national media. While he had always been good copy for muckraking journalists, he seemed to enjoy his celebrity status. As for local fallout, he wasn't concerned; most of his supporters were faithful readers of a mainstay of the Hague cheering section, the *Jersey Journal,* where criticism of the mayor was hard to find. An investigation by the *New York Herald Tribune* had confirmed that editors at the *Journal* had been awarded well-paid political plums as receivers and administrators on matters in litigation by the Chancery Court—no matter that they were unqualified to play such roles in the legal system. The 1940s, particularly during World War II, were a time when thousands of people from Hudson County who had been taught to be proud of Jersey City, particularly young men who had joined the armed services, were beginning to see the mayor and his organization in a different light.

Barrels of ink had been used to print the stories—over and over—on three aspects of Hague's career that are retold to this day: stifling of dissent, political patronage, and rampant corruption. The most damaging stories began surfacing in the 1940s.

In an era when the prevalence and popularity of labor unions were increasing, the national publicity over the "CIO affair" and the manhandling and "deportation" of law-abiding citizens didn't play well with thinking people, specifically prominent national Democrats. When soldiers from Jersey City learned from their new acquaintances in the military that "civil liberty" wasn't "an ugly phrase, that freedom of speech was not a cloak to hide Communist subversion, they began to question the whole moral posture of Frank Hague."[18] And they brought those questions home after the war. Almost as embarrassing for thinking residents of Hudson County was Frank Jr.'s appointment to New Jersey's highest court, the Court of Errors and Appeals. His only qualification was his father. All of thirty-four years old, with eight years of higher education at three universities and not one degree, or any type of record of performance as a practicing attorney, it would have been comical had it not been such a sad spectacle. As for the third chapter, the story had no ending, rather a new beginning.

First, last, and always there were the stories of political corruption coming out of Jersey City, to which most of community was indifferent. Many
accepted the corruption because they, or someone close to them, benefited
from it. But in the 1940s the organization's corrupt ways had taken on a new
gloss in the telling of the tales of the Irish bullyboy through McKean's book.

The Boss wasn't a best seller, but thanks to the prestige of Houghton Mifflin
it was distributed nationally and was sold and read widely, especially by journalists and college professors. What most newspaper readers know instinctively without thinking about it is that substantial portions of many "news
stories" are a rehash of earlier articles, not unlike today's e-mail streams. With
the availability of McKean's book, journalists reporting on the evils flowing
from the corruption of big city politics and editorialists groping for examples
when pontificating about underhanded governmental practices now had a
handy reference manual penned by an Ivy League professor. Frank Hague's
organization had become the benchmark for assessing political corruption in
America. Arthur and David's book didn't earn a fortune for McKean or win
any elections for Clean Government, but it besmirched Hague's reputation for
all time and began to make him unwelcomed by the younger players in the
state and national Democratic Party.

The erosion of his image, the stagnation of his organization, and the
drought in jobs out of the statehouse had hurt Hague the politician, but
Frank Hague the man was doing well. At age seventy-one, outliving most
of his generation, which had a life expectancy of only forty-five, Hague was
tanned, trim, and fit; he looked nimble and tough enough, and he probably
was, to pummel most men half his age if the situation required. He still had
a swagger, so much so that that his "retirement" wasn't quite real.

Hague wanted to be free of "tiresome administrative chores and to end the
complaints that he had become an absentee mayor."[19] The game plan was for
his nephew to take over as the titular head of City Hall, with Hague quietly
calling the shots out of public view; Hague would remain in charge out of the
glare of media and would be freed of demands of the rank-and-file members
of the organization and the scrutiny of annoying Republicans like Vanderbilt. At the time the transition was moving forward, Hague remarked to a
reporter: "Don't worry, I'll be around for a long time."[20] Hague's confidence
was misplaced. As events unfolded, it became apparent that bestowing the
mayor's office to his nephew—as if he really were an Irish warlord in the Middle Ages—was a move that caused intense resentment: some people believed

he had gone too far in bypassing the organization, not to mention the voters; others, particularly John V. Kenny, younger brother of Frank Kenny, victim of Michael Rombolo, thought Hague hadn't gone far enough and that he should step aside entirely. Yet in the spring of 1947, the Celtic Chieftain was smugly content with his domain. It was wishful thinking.

While Frank Hague was fantasizing about the placid golden years that lay ahead as the distinguished elder statesman Alfred Driscoll was rethinking New Jersey's future and calculating how to avoid repeating mistakes of the past. As the experiences of the two governors prior to Driscoll revealed, rewriting the state's constitution was a rigorous undertaking. The task was a three-sided puzzle: first, deciding what the entire state's needs were and what sort of arrangement of the available instruments of government would meet those needs. New Jersey was straddled by two major cities with surging urban populations within its borders, and many small, rural areas wanting no part of change. The newcomers working and living in the New Jersey portions of the New York and Philadelphia metropolitan areas created issues for government that could be ignored no longer. The second part of the task was a technical one, involving the drafting of a written document in clear and simple terms once the analytical questions are answered. The third part of the task was the most troublesome: the political component.

As the failed efforts at reform of both Charles Edison and Walter Edge demonstrate, the political component was the key to adopting a new constitution. The political problems that Driscoll had to manage were basically ones of who, what, and how? *Who* sits at the table to hash out the provisions of the document and participate in *what* compromises are made regarding the distribution of power, and finally, *how* it was to be sold to the voters. The players involved in all three parts of the effort must be rowing in the same direction or the boat will sink.

What Driscoll understood, and had the moxie to act on, was that at this hour in New Jersey's history the principal political problem preventing reform was Vanderbilt, who believed, and had convinced both Edison and Edge, that Hague's corrupt ways made him "unworthy" of a seat at the table in drafting a new constitution. In truth, Vanderbilt didn't want to be part of a bipartisan effort, yet, as Driscoll understood, reform was going nowhere without Hudson County on board. The one true believer and keeper of the flame—despite his vision and brilliance—had become an obstacle to reform. Driscoll recognized this when no one else did and knew that nothing good could from Vanderbilt's sitting at the table.

Driscoll seems to have instinctively understood from the outset that he had to be out in front in managing the political process if he was to succeed where his predecessors had failed. Two private meetings, undisclosed to the public at the time, reveal his thinking on the need for bipartisanship and his determination to get the job done. Both meetings occurred prior to any legislation even being discussed.

Not long after Election Day, still in November of 1946, Driscoll invited several prominent leaders in the Republican Party to a meeting in Princeton where—after pledging them to secrecy—he laid out his strategy for creating the support needed to stage a constitutional convention. According to Connors, "Their first reaction was to be expected: 'Oh no, not that again!' But Driscoll made it plain that he was determined on this course of action, and presented his reasons for reviving the revision movement."[21] He countered by stating the obvious: the need to overhaul state government hadn't decreased since rejection of the 1944 referendum—the need was even greater. What's more, he argued that the voters hadn't rejected the need for a new form of government—the campaign of the opposition hadn't really defended the 1844 Constitution—but rather had refused to sign off on a blatantly partisan document drafted exclusively by the Republican legislature. Driscoll argued that a bipartisan convention would have the credibility needed to succeed and that was the course he intended to pursue.

The governor-elect's cohorts kept their pledge of secrecy and, when he used the grand stage of his inaugural address to unveil his plans, it had the intended effect, taking everyone by surprise. While one wouldn't call it a sudden groundswell, no one wanted to speak out in opposition so early in the new governor's tenure on an issue of such importance. Though tepid in many instances, all of the comments were positive; most important there were no negative comments from Hudson County, and that was where Driscoll was headed next.

Shortly after the inauguration, Driscoll arranged a meeting with the key Democratic leaders, including Senator O'Mara and former U.S. senator John Milton, who had been Hague's personal legal counsel for thirty years. Driscoll and Ed O'Mara went back to their days in the state senate together and had an excellent rapport. Milton was the level-headed adviser, and while he didn't speak for Hague, he could be counted on to report messages—both ways—reliably. Political legend has it that Driscoll opened the meeting by pulling at his cuffs to show that he had nothing up his sleeves. He then revealed the cornerstone of his plan, which was that the convention had to be a bipartisan event, pledging his cooperation and asking for theirs. He also reminded them that after the 1944 debacle, Hague had stated publicly that he could support a constitutional convention once "the boys are home." By all reports, the Hudson County pols were impressed by the sincerity of his pledge to work with them.

O'Mara and Milton were both savvy politicians and learned in the law; they knew that New Jersey's government, particularly the courts, was an embarrassment. Driscoll couldn't have chosen two better people to deliver his message to Hague. Not long after their meeting, word came to the governor that the Democrats of Hudson County would give him their support.[22] History doesn't record Hague's true motives in reversing himself—after all, Hudson County had fared quite well with the existing constitution—but he could spot a winner when he saw one and may have surmised that the fair-haired boy from Haddonfield would eventually get his prize. So, why not extract all the benefits he could from the new governor and get on board early, maximizing Hudson County's influence in a bipartisan convention? He was also satisfied that Driscoll wasn't going to continue the vendetta against Hudson County that Edison and Edge had encouraged. Finally, Hague is reported to have expressed to an ally that under any new constitution, the powers of the governor had to be increased and that the office would become the key to state government. The Republicans might win the office another time, but then the Democrats would have clear sailing. New Jersey was an urbanizing state and Roosevelt's impact on voter allegiance would ensure that the Democratic Party would have control of Trenton long into the future.[23]

Later that winter and early spring, prior to the June vote, Driscoll indicated he was willing to work toward revising the railroad laws to aid Jersey City in receiving additional revenue from railroad property within its borders. More important, he issued an executive order releasing $5 million in railroad tax money to Jersey City (equivalent to $60 million today) that had been frozen by Edge. Next, he agreed to call back Walter Van Riper and to discontinue any further investigation of illegal gambling in Hudson County. He also appointed Common Pleas judges in Hudson and Camden County supported by Hague Democrats and agreed to remove the Hudson County superintendent of elections who had been appointed by Edge. Finally, he orchestrated legislation modifying the state road aid formula to ensure that, for the first time, the larger cities were included. Haddonfield's mensch had won over the Celtic Chieftain, but his task wasn't complete; he still had to deal with the Warrior Lawyer. The constitutional convention in New Brunswick was in the offing and there was much to be done.

CHAPTER 13

Summer at Rutgers

North Harpswell, Maine, is mostly water, rock, and trees. Its beauty is austere and primal. This remote village on Casco Bay wasn't anyone's idea of a resort in the first half of the twentieth century, yet in the summer of 1947 it became a safe haven for the Warrior Lawyer.

Floss and Arthur lived in an era when teenage sweethearts married and remained faithful to one another until death. Floss was Arthur's refuge. At the end of the hunt, it was always Floss Arthur turned to, whether to regale her with the details of a victory, confide in her about troublesome matters, or seek comfort after a loss. Floss lived for Arthur. For nearly fifty years her steadfast love was the only constant in his helter-skelter world. Floss made his four careers possible by endlessly restoring tranquility to his frenetic life, something he needed now more than ever. May of 1947 had been the worst month of Arthur's life, and as soon as he was able to travel following his stroke Floss knew they had to leave for Maine.[1]

Not long after Vanderbilt had cleaned up the financial mess caused by his failed insurance company and while the nation was still in the depths of the Great Depression, an ad in the *Wall Street Journal* for a thirty-eight-acre estate in Maine caught his attention. Floss and Arthur had been looking for a summer home and decided to rent the place for the summer with an option to purchase. They fell in love with it and bought it for the sum of $25,000 (equivalent to $400,000-plus today). Floss and Arthur named their private sanctuary At Ease, and it was here that they would spend the months of July and August, with short stays in spring and fall, for the remainder of Arthur's life.[2]

Bowdoin College in Brunswick was the last outpost of "civilization" before heading southeast down the spire of Harpswell Neck, an eight-mile drive on a narrow road through pine forests, blueberry fields, and scrub oaks to At Ease. Upon reaching the "driveway," there was another three-quarters of a mile of majestic pines, maples, and birches before the woods opened to a clearing on which stood a large white, Georgian-style home with dark green shutters, with a row of ancient oaks in front and a lawn that rolled slowly down to the bay. Across the expanse of Casco Bay lay outcroppings of rock, tiny uninhabited islands, and sunsets behind Mount Washington in New Hampshire. With no other dwellings nearby, the only sounds were the wind in the trees and the chug of lobster boats in the bay.[3]

Arthur and Floss's home had five bedrooms, a large reception hall, a magnificent staircase, huge living and dining rooms, a fireplace capable of holding nine-foot logs, and a sun-room with floor-to-ceiling glass on three of the four walls, which Floss had converted into a study for Arthur. It wasn't long before a saltwater swimming pool was installed on the lawn, which sloped down to the bay; the pool gave Arthur the opportunity to swim, the only exercise regimen he enjoyed. It was here that Floss brought Arthur for the summer of '47; they did not return to New Jersey until the constitutional convention was over. The only link to the outside world was a single telephone, which Floss had installed in a walk-in closet at Arthur's request. Throughout the summer, Arthur received reports on the convention from Nathan Jacobs, Alfred Clapp, and Frank Sommer, all the while sitting in the closet. He could offer his thoughts on the events in New Brunswick without having to be in the thick of things. Floss was nursing him back to health.[4]

Frank Hague wasn't in the thick of things either. After retiring as mayor he left for an extended vacation in California around the same time Vanderbilt departed for Maine. Having anointed his nephew as his successor, and confident he could rely upon Ed O'Mara, John Milton, and Tom Brogan to look after Hudson County's interests, Hague had no desire to spend the summer in New Jersey; if needed, he was available by telephone.

Governor Driscoll left behind few personal reflections on these two gentlemen, but one has to believe he was relieved they were absent from the convention; they would have meddled with his plans.

Because there was no opposition to the June referendum, Driscoll began his planning early. In an effort to avoid the ever-watchful eyes of the statehouse news reporters, Driscoll held his strategy sessions on the front porch of Princeton's Nassau Inn less than fifteen miles away, yet far removed from the hubbub of Trenton. The two mainstays of these meetings were his advisors, Russell Watson and George Walton; the latter was legal counsel. Driscoll was the first governor to have his own lawyer, separate and apart from the attorney general. Others came and went, but Watson and Walton were always at these sessions. Driscoll, Watson, and Walton were not only concerned with an inclusive convention; more important, they wanted leadership positions held by people committed to bold reform.

Central to his game plan was avoidance of a convention that looked like the legislature. There was a feeling among assemblymen and senators that they were entitled to a seat at the convention. Driscoll was adamantly opposed to this approach and lobbied vigorously in every county to convince local party officials that the base of the convention had to be broadened beyond the political insiders. He succeeded. When the final list of delegates was prepared, only thirty-one of the eighty-one delegates were legislators or ex-legislators, including ten incumbent senators and two incumbent assemblymen.[5] At the end of the day, thirteen of the twenty-one counties submitted a bipartisan slate; it would have been more but several of the rural Republican leaders were unwilling to commit one of only two delegates to what was—in their county—a virtually nonexistent Democratic organization.

Remarkably, the governor convinced more than half of the state senators that they needn't be convention delegates. Nonetheless, two senators, Frank Farley and Ed O'Mara, were essential for success. He couldn't risk either one on the outside throwing in stones. Both were lawyers, and, not surprising, fifty of the eighty-one delegates were members of the legal profession—twenty-seven practicing attorneys together with ten judges and thirteen former judges. The remaining delegates were a fairly broad mix: nine businessmen, seven educators, seven female civic leaders, two publishers, two bankers, two farmers, two government employees, a union leader, and a medical doctor. Weeks in advance of the June referendum Driscoll was assured that the convention would be as bipartisan and as inclusive as could be hoped for in 1947. Next up, choosing the officers of the convention.

Prior to the convention, again working in private, Driscoll used his influence to secure convention officers acceptable to all sides; his first concern was the presiding officer of the convention. It couldn't be a prominent Republican. He needed someone above the fray of partisan politics and past reform

efforts, someone with no connection to any of the state's organized interests, and someone the delegates could trust to be fair. He chose someone
unknown to most the state's politicians: Robert Clothier, president of Rutgers
University.

Driscoll had wooed the Democratic Party leaders of Middlesex County to
run Clothier for a delegate slot and then had people begin floating his name
publicly as a possible chairman. The first opposition came from Hap Farley;
he wanted the position go to a legislator, suggesting Senate President Barton, a Driscoll ally who had sponsored the bill for the convention.[6] Driscoll
believed that appearances mattered greatly and made it clear that under no
circumstances would a leader of the Republican Party preside over the convention. What's more, the governor was counting on Clothier to make the
campus at Rutgers available for the proceedings. Again, as with his planning sessions, he didn't want the convention to take place in the contentious
atmosphere of the statehouse. His goal was to foster an atmosphere of "supra
partisanship." Because Rutgers had become the official state university two
years earlier, was centrally located in the state, and Middlesex County was
a stronghold of the Democratic Party, Clothier and Rutgers were a perfect
combination.

At Driscoll's insistence, one of the three remaining executive posts went to
a widely respected Democrat, Marie Katzenbach of Mercer County, a prominent leader in several civic and philanthropic organizations, a trustee of Rutgers, and a longtime member of the state board of education, appointed by
Democratic and Republican governors alike.

Once the officers were in place, the governor directed the state librarian
and bill-drafting commission to prepare procedural rules to govern convention procedures. Driscoll made every effort to prevent procedural bickering from sidetracking the work of the convention, and prior to circulating
the proposed rules for adoption, he sent them to Ed O'Mara for comment.
Driscoll saw to it that the rules of procedure and decorum—with no hidden
agenda or built-in bias—were known to everyone in advance and that those
rules would be enforced by a convention president who was not part of a
political clique. At the opening session, the rules were adopted with virtually
no comment.

In addition to the convention officers, the question of who would chair
the various committees was likewise critical to creating a bold document.
Nine standing committees were proposed in the draft rules, five to deal with

substantive parts of the constitution and four to handle technical and administrative matters. The standing committees were to have eleven members each, the others seven members, generally limiting the delegates to service on only one committee. Tentative lists of committee members were drawn up, with the final selection to be made by Rutgers resident Clothier. More important, efforts were made to balance the two parties and their interests, but still ensure that there were prominent voices strongly favoring reform serving on key committees. Thus, the proposed committee on the Judiciary was to have five laymen on it, and only one incumbent judge, plus five lawyers selected by Driscoll and Clothier. According to Alan Lowenstein, "To satisfy Vanderbilt, Driscoll made sure that the Judiciary Committee of the Convention would be dominated by Vanderbilt's choices. At his recommendation, Frank H. Sommer, at age seventy-five and despite his frail health, was named Chairman of the Judiciary Committee; Nathan L. Jacobs, a former associate of Vanderbilt [and Harvard Law School classmate of Driscoll], was named Vice Chairman to give major support to Sommer; and other committee members approved by Vanderbilt were named to assure that his goals for judicial reform would be honored and promoted."[7]

Yet Vanderbilt wasn't the only one entitled to a proxy in a major position. Despite general agreement that Senator Arthur Lewis of Burlington County could quite ably chair the Committee on the Legislature, Driscoll pushed for bipartisanship, urging that his former senate colleague and Hague emissary Ed O'Mara be named chairman of the Legislative Committee with Lewis as vice chairman. The convention record reveals that O'Mara had a high profile at the general meetings, playing an active leadership role from the outset. Before the opening session, everyone knew that the bosses of both Essex and Hudson Counties would have a seat at the table in drafting the constitution.

Driscoll was determined to set an understated tone that quietly said to the participants, "This affair should be something special." To that end, chairs from the state legislature were removed from Trenton and installed in the Rutgers gymnasium where the proceedings would take place. Stroking the delegates' egos, each of them was issued distinctive red-and-cream license plates for their cars, setting them apart then, and in the future, as people who had played a special role in state history. Additionally, a special reference library was set up for the delegates, along with staff from the New Jersey State Library and the governor's office, to assist delegates in finding answers on issues that might affect their vote.

Taking a huge step beyond helping delegates find answers were thirty-two research memos produced at Driscoll's request by the Governor's Committee on Preparatory Research. Headed by Sidney Goldman of the state library, this ad hoc committee composed of executive staff and volunteers was instrumental in connecting the dots and filling the gaps in Driscoll's blueprint for a new state government. To get things moving, Goldman "turned to some experts in the state administration, lawyer friends of Arthur Vanderbilt, etc., and gathered this group, along with available college professors, at Rutgers in early March."[8] At this meeting, Goldman detailed a list of topics and named the committee members to do the research and writing on the various issues. The memos were delivered to the delegates immediately following approval of the convention by the voters on June 3. "Reflecting the tone Driscoll was trying to set for the upcoming convention" and "due to Goldman's insistence that the articles be neutral and impartial," there was "no overall effort to present draft articles or to phrase alternative proposals in constitutional language. The research memoranda were essentially background reading: descriptive and explanatory rather than evaluative and hortatory."[9]

Yet truth be told, there was one topic on which it wasn't possible to be impartial: discussion of court reform. Not surprising, the first item among the memos on the Judiciary was a reprint of a speech by Roscoe Pound in which he argued for an "integrated court," the very theme Vanderbilt had raised throughout most of the past two decades, which had finally gained support. Over the years, the public's frustration with the courts had been eclipsed by a prevailing attitude of cynicism and resignation. Many people, when they had a serious legal problem, first sought out a politician either to intercede with the judge or, failing that, steer them to a politically connected lawyer. Although there was no guarantee of a new constitution, it was a safe bet that if there was one, the court system was in store for major changes.

Other aspects of the preparation for the convention were physical. Driscoll understood that the space in which business is conducted can affect how people behave. His goal was to create an atmosphere of sufficient solemnity and seriousness of purpose to encourage everyone to be on his or her best behavior and to leave petty partisan politics at home. They were there to work unselfishly, to create a modern government for dealing with the social changes New Jersey was experiencing. Additionally, arrangements were made for recording and printing transcripts of the proceedings—available within twenty-four hours—to answer questions as the meetings went along. Finally, plans were laid for elaborate opening day ceremonies—dignified pomp and circumstance—again, to encourage everyone to behave well and to promote a mood of high-minded dedication.

In addition to energizing scores of people to implement his game plan, Driscoll was barnstorming the state; the month of May was intense. While Vanderbilt was being overwhelmed with his professional and personal obligations, Driscoll was campaigning full-time, appearing before any group that would have him, particularly service clubs and civic groups. The talks he gave then became the basis for news articles and editorials in newspapers throughout the state. It was a low-budget, but very effective, educational campaign operation.

"Before these audiences, Driscoll went beyond delineating 'why' New Jersey needed a new Constitution, and gave his views on its nature and desired contents." His stump speech told voters that the work of the convention would be confined to "providing a basic skeleton for the State's government, focusing on New Jersey's need for a modern executive and judiciary."[10] Citing the 1944 debacle, Driscoll argued that the delegates should avoid controversial items and not put the voters in the position of dealing with an "all or nothing" document. If there were to be controversial issues, they could be dealt with later as separate amendments but for now, the focus should be on modernizing government.

Some think that in an attempt to soothe Vanderbilt, "Driscoll sketched out his position on the judicial article . . . going down the line for Vanderbilt's proposals for an integrated court of general jurisdiction, centralized administration of justice, and elimination of an independent Court of Chancery."[11] This drew a response from Walter Edge, who argued that "the State should go slow on Chancery now that Dayton Oliphant was shaping up that Court."[12] Edge had appointed Oliphant Chancellor the preceding fall, and for several days the newspapers tried to turn their exchange into a controversy, but neither of them took the bait. Within a short time, Edge stepped out of the limelight and permitted Driscoll to take the headlines in the campaign. By the time the convention began, Edge had left town for his fishing lodge in Canada.

Nine days after the referendum, things got under way in the gymnasium at Rutgers. Driscoll launched the convention with a speech of less than ten minutes that was a virtuoso performance. His address to the delegates was a thoughtful, eloquent, and bold call to action and showed a keen sense of history. His themes were the ones that he had been talking about since the inauguration, and now he had the audience he longed for: people with the power to make change. His message was resoundingly clear—there had to be a clean break with the past.

Speaking like a true progressive he explained how "the industrial revolution has brought aggregations of capital and labor, well described as 'private government,' in the form of business corporations and trade unions" and that in response to these changes, "Government has become so large that responsibility is difficult to identify."[13] At times he evoked the values and common sense of Lincoln, arguing that the constitution should be "a statement of basic fundamental principles" and that its provisions ought to be "restricted to the establishment of a sound structure, to the definition of official responsibility and authority, to the assurance of the fundamental rights and liberties of all the people."[14] The governor urged the delegates not to tackle issues better left to legislation by reminding them that "[o]ur Federal Constitution has the ageless virtue of simplicity. Its authors stated their fundamental concepts of government" and went no further than necessary to create three equal branches of government and articulate the rights and duties of citizens and their states. Expressing his frustration with the 1844 Constitution he decried the fact that "over a century ago your predecessors forged the handcuffs that today prevent your government from freely meeting the challenge of an industrialized society."[15]

Urging the virtue of brevity, he told the delegates, "The longer a constitution, the more quickly it fails to meet the requirements of a society that is never static. To quote one authority: 'The more precise and elaborate' the provisions of a constitution, 'the greater are the obstacles to the reform of abuses. Litigation thrives on constitutional verbosity.'"[16] Finally, when speaking of the judiciary, Driscoll echoed Vanderbilt: the cheerful Vanderbilt, the person who diligently climbed the ladder to success in four connected worlds, the Vanderbilt people knew before run-ins with Frank Hague, the gracious Vanderbilt before he became exasperated and distrustful.

When encouraging the delegates to completely overhaul the courts, Driscoll channeled the idealistic Vanderbilt from years earlier. "The highest trust in a constitutional government is imposed on the men who comprise the judiciary. It is in the judiciary that we find the balance-wheel of our whole constitutional system. Our unique institution of judicial review of the acts of the Legislature and Executive, giving power to courts to set aside laws and executive action where the judges determine that they violate the written constitution, has come to make the quality of our justice synonymous with the values of democracy held by the average citizen."[17] And, ultimately, there was classic Vanderbilt, with Driscoll reminding the delegates, "It is only in our courts that an individual of the lowliest estate can set himself up against his government by appealing to the kind of fundamental law which this Convention is about to formulate."[18]

Convention business recessed at 4 p.m. on June 12; when the delegates returned to work six days later, President Clothier formally announced his committee assignments. There were no surprises. From June 18 until August 4 the delegates met weekly to receive progress reports from committees and take action as needed. Throughout this period, Driscoll was kept informed by meeting with his counsel, George Walton, who was also a delegate, serving as chairman of the Rules Committee. In line with the governor's thoughts on smoothing out bumps in the deliberations, committee chairmen were encouraged to follow the tack of a skillful negotiator by agreeing to resolve the easy issues first. The controversial issues expected to become floor fights could wait. The least divisive issues would be heard first in order to build on the spirit of cooperation that Driscoll had fostered; the more yes votes recorded in the early days, the greater the positive momentum.

One early item that built on the momentum was the general consensus on the executive branch. It prompted little controversy. The question to be resolved was not whether the office should be strengthened, but by how much and in what manner? There was agreement from the outset that the governor should have power commensurate with his responsibilities. No one spoke against a four-year term, and only the delegates from the smallest counties objected to the expanded veto power through the authorization of conditional and line-item vetoes and increasing an override to a two-thirds vote. Eligibility to run for reelection was another story. A faction of rural delegates of both parties argued that lengthening the potential tenure could encourage future governors to build a political machine in their own image. Nonetheless, in a surprising show of unity, Vanderbilt and Hague delegates were willing to support unlimited tenure. After much debate, the convention decided on a two-term limitation.

In the end, there was to be a very different type of governor than any that came before Driscoll. New Jersey would have a strong governor, the lone state official elected statewide with a four-year term capable of succeeding himself, possessing a fearsome veto—including the power to kill particular items in appropriation bills; a streamlined executive branch limited to twenty departments all under the governor's control; the exclusive power to appoint judges and prosecutors subject to senate confirmation; authority to appoint members of state commissions and agencies; and the authority to investigate and discipline executive branch officials without involvement of the legislature.

Almost as harmonious as the work of the committee drafting language for the executive branch were the deliberations of the committee on the powers of the legislature. Again, there was an understanding from the outset: power flows, and if the governor's powers were to be expanded, that could only happen at the expense of the legislative branch. Chairman O'Mara and Vice Chairman Lewis were seasoned pros and decided to rely on the 1944 draft constitution as a reference. Consensus was achieved quickly on legislative terms, with terms in the assembly increased from one to two years and in the senate from two to four years. Also fostering cordiality among the committee was the fact that legislative reapportionment and "home rule" of the state's myriad municipal governments was off the table and local governments were granted the right to draft their own charters, as well as a provision instructing the courts to construe their powers liberally. "Legislative lightning" was an irksome issue, and it was agreed that the practice of ramrodding bills through the approval process on second and third readings without notice to the public or the minority party would be eliminated.

One subject upon which there was little harmony was gambling. The 1944 referendum was followed by renewed enforcement of the laws banning gambling (including bingo, which had previously been ignored by law enforcement in most places), except at racetracks that had been approved by means of a special referendum in 1939. The Catholic Church was not so lucky when supporters of bingo failed to gain support in the 1945 legislative term for a similar change in the law. The forces were lined up nose to nose and Senator O'Mara was right in the middle, pressured by Catholics in Hudson County and leaned on by Driscoll not to let bingo sidetrack the work of the convention. Protestant clergymen and most Republicans opposed gambling in all forms. The Catholic Church and veterans groups wanted bingo restored, legally. It was the one issue threatening to destroy all of Driscoll's efforts; Clothier and O'Mara exercised the greatest of patience and worked hard to keep the peace. After many heated debates at the committee's public hearings, what ultimately occurred was nothing—the status quo remained—with the acknowledgment that the issue would be addressed later. It was, and bingo is alive and well today in many churches and charitable organizations.

Another area of contention was taxation, particularly the taxing of railroad property, so crucial to Hudson County. Under the 1844 Constitution, everything was left to the whim of the legislature. For years, this was fine with Hague, but then along came Edison and Edge, both of whom refused to play along with Hudson County in using the railroads as cash cows. A major problem was a sentence added to the constitution in 1875 that ruled "Property shall be assessed for taxes under general laws and by uniform rules, according to its true value." Reformers wanted that language gone, believing that "the whole subject of taxation was too complex and changeable to be handled adequately in a constitution, and should be left to the Legislature."[19] Hudson County had other ideas.

Hague's personal lawyer, John Milton, was a delegate, and he wanted language preventing the legislature from permitting various types of property to bear different tax rates. His target was the earlier changes to the railroad tax law creating a 3 percent rate for second-class railroad properties. Upon first vote, the committee rejected Milton's language; this ignited a firestorm. Hague, still in California, delivered a threat: "I am fearful such action, if approved, will destroy every opportunity to obtain a new constitution. The people's attitude on this matter will never permit railroad influences to dominate the preparation of a new constitution."[20]

Milton refused to accept the committee's vote and moved to have the question debated before all the delegates. Clothier wisely permitted Milton to be heard by the full convention, but he also let the governor be heard. Driscoll couldn't let things get out of control, and he drove to New Brunswick to address the delegates. Although he was unhappy with the committee's decision, he could not support Milton's proposal. His "basic line of argument . . . was that New Jersey's tax system needed overhaul from top to bottom, that he and the Legislature hopefully would begin that job soon, and the constitution should not stand in the way."[21] Without mentioning Hudson County, he asked for language granting the legislature broad authority on taxation legislation. It was an unspoken pledge to modify the existing railroad tax laws. For several days in the third week of August, academics and lawyers worked to get to common ground. The product of their efforts was a general principle to guide future legislatures, which read: "Property shall be assessed for taxation under general laws and by uniform rules."[22] It took a phone call to the mayor's uncle in California together with a last-minute plea by President Clothier to secure the needed votes.

In one of the convention's more dramatic moments Clothier beseeched the delegates to "remember that New Jersey has 21 counties, not 20, and that we must have the best interest of the twenty-first county in mind as well as that of the other 20. It means that we must remember the twenty-first county. . . . It is not an island set apart by itself, but a part of the State."[23] Clothier was every bit the leader the governor had hoped for and prevented the convention from splintering apart at a crucial moment.

Alfred Driscoll faced challenges the way few politicians do: head on. That summer (sometime in late July or early August) he decided to meet with Arthur Vanderbilt. History doesn't record how their meeting in Maine came about, but it's likely that Nathan Jacobs had a hand in arranging things. Upon graduating from Harvard Law School in 1928 (with Driscoll as a classmate), Jacobs, a resident of Bayonne, sought employment with Vanderbilt in Newark. Jacobs was a brilliant legal scholar as well as a capable practicing attorney, making him every bit as elite a member of his profession as Vanderbilt. He practiced law with Vanderbilt for four years and left to start a firm of his own with two other attorneys, but Jacobs and Vanderbilt remained very close—jurisprudentially, they were of one mind. Throughout the twelve weeks of the committee's work, the two were in almost daily contact by telephone, and one of them probably concluded a meeting between the governor and the Warrior Lawyer was needed. Although there is no record of their conversation in Maine, hindsight enables us to infer at least one of the subjects they discussed.

Although Vanderbilt relied entirely upon Jacobs to make his views known; there was only one occasion when he communicated formally to the Judiciary Committee—a letter dated July 29, 1947. The letter addresses twelve specific provisions of the draft Judicial Article under consideration at the time. His letter speaks to everything from the procedures for handling appeals to his concerns that the creation of the position of presiding judges to supervise the three main divisions could "weaken the administrative authority of the Chief Justice."[24] Trying to navigate a minefield, he also touched upon the Supreme Court's rule-making authority. Ever so gingerly, he suggested that the state's high court alone should have the power to write the court rules. He asked the committee to delete the phrase "subject to law." In the months ahead it was to become a thorny issue. Jacobs saw to it that the letter was considered, and portions made their way into revisions to the Judicial Article; nonetheless, Vanderbilt's comments on the phrase "subject to law" were ignored.

As had been apparent from the outset, Frank Sommer wasn't physically up to the task of managing the committee's proceedings and Nathan Jacobs quickly became the de facto chairman. A review of the transcripts of the committee's hearings reveals that Jacobs "presided with grace, patience, and moderation."[25] He wrote the committee's report and crafted the language that became Article VI of the new constitution. A review of the many suggestions and draft language of provisions submitted to the Judiciary Committee reveals that the Judicial Article finally adopted "borrowed from many sources but copied none."[26]

Although Jacobs was a strong supporter of Vanderbilt's views of court reform, he was not an apostle doing the chosen one's bidding at the constitutional convention. Nathan Jacobs had a reputation for being a very independent thinker and one of the few people in Vanderbilt's inner circle that the Warrior Lawyer could not bend to his will.

From today's vantage it's clear that Driscoll—with Clothier's help—had stacked the deck to ensure there would be a total revamping of the state's court system. Much had been accomplished under Governors Wilson, Edison, and Edge—all of whom brought progressive ideas to the administration of state government—and, generally speaking, state government was adapting to a changing society. What drove the persistent demands for a new constitution was the sad state of affairs in the judiciary; the changes needed there couldn't come through legislation. The three primary goals of reformers were the same as had been expressed forty years earlier by Harvard dean Roscoe Pound: unification, flexibility, and concentration of judicial power and responsibility.

Because of public statements made by former governor Edge and supporters of Chancellor Dayton Oliphant, the Chancery Court was the only prickly issue for the Judiciary Committee. At Hap Farley's invitation, Oliphant had gone to Atlantic County to speak with the local bar association on the need to retain Chancery as a separate court. Oliphant had literally spent the months prior to the convention campaigning against a new constitution and had originally planned to run as a convention delegate from Mercer County until Driscoll convinced him otherwise. Opposition to ending the separation of law and equity came from both the chancellor and the chief justice of the Supreme Court, Clarence Case.

Oliphant and Case spoke for the entrenched politico-legal establishment, but they also spoke for themselves. Nearly seven decades after the fact, the extent of their self-interest is quite evident in the transcripts of the convention proceedings; reading their testimony before the Judiciary Committee reveals the seriousness with which the chancellor and the chief justice took themselves. As Shakespeare said, "Greatness knows itself."

Oliphant began his presentation to the committee by acknowledging, "I am profoundly conscious of the somewhat delicate position I am placed in by appearing before you in that some may attribute to it a selfish motive." Continuing, he stated, "I am firmly convinced that we have in this State the finest and best system of equity jurisprudence in this country, perhaps in the whole world, and I am not alone in this view. Why change it?"[27] He wasn't the least bit ruffled by the fact that all the other states, save Delaware, had merged their courts years earlier and that England had done so in 1873. In fact, Oliphant was so resistant to change that he argued that the English had made a mistake. Acknowledging that the dual system lent itself to gamesmanship, he had a solution of his own. "I have prepared a provision which, in my judgment, will properly take care of this situation so that litigants will not be unduly shuttled from one court to another."[28] There's no way of knowing if anyone on the committee was listening at this point, yet he proceeded to read into the record precise language that he said would cure everything. All the committee members had to do was follow his advice.

Chief Justice Case was every bit as emphatic. He made it clear, announcing, "I am authorized to speak for the members of the court, and in giving you my views I think I am giving you the views of all of the members of the Supreme Court." In essence, those views were that all was well with the State Constitution. "I have heard it said that the Constitution was designed for a rural State of small population and that, therefore, it is to be wiped out. Well, age in itself is not a flaw . . . merely having something that isn't perfect is hardly a reason why we should throw it out of the window."[29] Case then tried, by presenting a mind-numbing metaphor about the troubles a person can run into when building a new house, to make his point that there was no need to rewrite the constitution. From the chief justice's perch, things were just fine, and if changes were needed, they were best done by the legislature. Finally, the fall-back position of both Oliphant and Case was that if there were to be major change, then the new constitution should find a place for them. A provision should be included ensuring that current members of the

Chancery system and the Supreme Court would be able "to continue until their service is ended by death, resignation, or retirement."[30] In short, *change what you will, just don't put us out of a job.*

Fortunately, the Judiciary Committee also heard from the likes of Harvard Law School dean Roscoe Pound, federal judge Learned Hand, Rutgers Law School dean George Harris, Milton Conford, William J. Brennan Jr., and Judge Richard Hartshorne. Yet Chancery remained the rub; it had been Hague's refuge more than once. Although Tom Brogan and several of the other delegates were hesitant to merge Chancery into an integrated court system, when the time came to vote, everyone serious about reform had to concede that Chancery was a relic that must go. Every experienced lawyer had his own Sadie Urback story of being bounced back and forth between courts. When the vote on the final draft of the Judicial Article was called, Brogan, conceding that the new constitution was "overwhelmingly" superior to the old, informed everyone that he was prepared to live with the reorganization.

The only concession the delegates granted Brogan and Hudson County was the retention of the county courts, which would become the receptacle for several of the minor courts. In truth, it was a small concession to Hudson because both the superior courts and the county courts in each county would be administered by an assignment judge chosen by the new chief justice. At the end of the day, the Court of Common Pleas, the Circuit Court, the Orphans Court, the Surrogates Court, the Prerogative Court, the Court of Oyer & Terminer, the Court of Quarter Sessions, Court of Special Session, the Civil District Court, the Criminal Judicial District Court, the Police Recorder Court, the Justice of the Peace, the County Traffic Court, the Small Cause Court, along with the august E & A and others, would be consigned to the dustbin of history. Along with the jumble of courts, a countless number of "writs," which had evolved over the centuries, were also extinguished.

When all was said and done, Vanderbilt's vision for a new court system ruled the day. The proposed Judicial Article provided for a unified court structure, abolished the separation of law and equity, and created a central administrative responsibility in the chief justice, who made judicial assignments and appointed an administrator of the courts. The power to make rules governing the administration of all courts in the state also lay with the Supreme Court and, "subject to law," the state Supreme Court was empowered to promulgate rules governing the practice and procedures in all state courts. Judges were denied their former right to hold political office, or hold any other position for profit or politics. In a single stroke, the new constitution erased a hodge-podge of antiquated courts and replaced it with a modern structure, the envy of most states in America. It also granted mighty powers to the new chief justice and the members of the Supreme Court to mold the structure of the judiciary, enabling them to deal with a fast-changing society. "Never before had changes in court administration, organization, and procedure been initiated at one time in such a complete sweep of the judicial system."[31]

Driscoll's efforts to create a positive momentum carried over into the fall; hardly anyone of substance spoke publicly against the document prepared by the convention delegates that summer at Rutgers. The old guard political-legal establishment was forced to suffer in silence while the referendum to ratify the new constitution was approved by a huge majority: the yes votes were three and one-half times the noes—633,096 to 180,632—carrying Hudson County by a margin of 131,000 votes.

Arthur Vanderbilt's long-frustrated vision of a renaissance for New Jersey's courts was on its way to becoming a reality, yet the Warrior Lawyer's political battles were not over.

CHAPTER 14

The Chief

Education was central to Arthur Vanderbilt's life. Through his teaching evening classes to Newark factory workers while attending Columbia Law School, instructing law students two nights a week for thirty-four years, mentoring scores of young lawyers who had worked in his law firm throughout his career, and giving hundreds of speeches on law reform across the nation, many thousands of people had benefited from his knowledge of the law. On January 31, 1950, his years of service to the law and education had caught up with him. New York University honored him as it has few people.

On a cold and blustery afternoon at Washington Square in Manhattan, with Floss by his side, Arthur Vanderbilt laid the cornerstone for the vision he had expressed seven years earlier: construction on the NYU Law Center was under way. Despite his stroke in the spring of 1947, or possibly because of it, people from both within and without the university community were inspired to raise the revenue required to make Vanderbilt's dream a reality. Later that evening at the Cornerstone Celebration Dinner at the Waldorf Astoria Hotel, the chancellor of the university announced that "in recognition of his services to the University," the "lawyer, teacher, Dean, civic leader, exponent of law reform and Judge" was to become an everlasting part of the Law Center, for it would bear his name.[1] Twenty months later there would be a second day of ceremonies and celebration when construction of the Law Center was completed. For the next half century and beyond, thousands of lawyers in training would receive their education in Arthur T. Vanderbilt Hall.

Arthur and Floss were glowing. The joy of the celebration at the Waldorf Astoria would stay with them the remainder of their lives. Arthur's

commitment to education had been honored in a way neither of them could
have imagined when they were living in Roseville and he was teaching class
for four dollars a night at Newark's Central Evening High School nearly forty
years earlier. For the eighteen months preceding the NYU cornerstone ceremony, Vanderbilt had been holding classes in the law in a less formal setting
at the state capital in Trenton. His subject was the whys and wherefores of the
new state constitution. Not all his students appreciated his brilliance.

Not taught in civics class is the reality that the highest courts of every state,
and the U.S. Supreme Court, are "political" courts. They are "political" because
each represents one of the three branches of government through which power
flows. Arthur Vanderbilt understood that power is never static. If the authority
of government is to remain equally distributed by means of our unique system
of checks and balances within the tripartite arrangement that constitutes our
democratic republic, the leaders of each branch must be skilled in the fine art
of politics.

Our courts are obviously political when judges are elected to office (as
they are in more than half of the states) and when judicial appointments
become bargaining chips among politicians, as frequently occurs. These same
high courts are political in a somewhat more subtle sense when their rulings
impact public policy. A subtle exercise of political power by a court is an
instance in which a law that violates a provision of the constitution is voided
by the court; an overt exercise of political power by a court—guaranteed to
disturb one or both of the other two branches—is presented when the court
finds a violation of a fundamental right under the constitution and orders
public officials to perform the acts necessary to protect those rights. A striking example in New Jersey is the Mount Laurel litigation regarding affordable
housing. While many politicians pay lip service to an independent judiciary,
they frequently grow hostile when the court shows too much independence
for their liking. Thus, it is common for governors and presidents to select
people for the high court whom they believe will read the constitution the
way they want it read.

Critical to appreciating the position of the courts in pre-1947 New Jersey
is the awareness that after the American Revolution New Jersey's court system was a singular curiosity among the thirteen states. As James Madison
noted in the *Federalist Papers,* there weren't three branches of government
in New Jersey—only one, the all-powerful legislature. The governor was a
political eunuch and most judges were beholden to the politicians. Although

the governor's powers had been increased somewhat over the ensuing years, not much changed with the courts, and as of 1947, there still weren't three equal branches of government. Governor Driscoll understood this better than most people of his time and knew that the expanded powers of his office, as well as those of the new court system, would come at the expense of the legislature. He too would probably have wanted the new constitution to be read by friendly judges, but he was also a realist. And as much as he may have wanted to stack the bench with like-minded people, Driscoll knew that a lopsided court wouldn't foster respect for the judiciary. Just as he had compromised with Hap Farley, he was resigned to the fact that he would have to appoint people to the new Supreme Court who didn't necessarily share his views on reform; the two most obvious were Chancellor Oliphant and Chief Justice Case.

Driscoll was stuck with them despite their antediluvian, all-is-well resistance to change. It was taken for granted that Dayton Oliphant and Clarence Case would be two of the seven members of the new Supreme Court—such was their status in the Republican Party. In truth, many people believed that one of them would become chief justice, especially after Vanderbilt's temper tantrum when he learned that Driscoll was willing to compromise with Hague.

Looking every bit the part of a chief justice, with his white hair and mustache, Dayton Oliphant was thought of as a judge's judge. His grandfather was one of the early graduates of Harvard Law School and served as a general in the Union Army during the Civil War; Dayton's father (also a lawyer) served for many years as chief clerk to the Federal District Court of New Jersey. Oliphant was a graduate of Princeton and attended the University of Pennsylvania Law School; he was admitted to practice in 1911. Deeply involved in politics—both before and after becoming a judge—he had strong support among the party faithful. The Oliphants were as old guard Republican as it gets. Although the chancellor felt he was "entitled," he had to know that he would never be chief justice. History doesn't tell us if he was the second person Driscoll asked to serve on the new Supreme Court but it's likely either he or Clarence Case had that distinction.

The Case clan was one of the WASP families who had left Jersey City in the final years of the nineteenth century after the Irish won the "religious war." Case was a graduate of Rutgers and New York Law School in 1902. Trenton must have been like a second home; before going on the court, he served ten years as counsel to the New Jersey State Senate Judiciary Committee and then ten years as a state senator from Somerset County. It was during his final years as senator that he had his run-in with Frank Hague. While Case was still licking his wounds, Governor Morgan Larson appointed him to the Supreme Court in 1929, and seventeen years later, when Hague's pal Tom Brogan resigned from the court, he was named chief Justice by Governor Walter Edge. As with Oliphant, Case would have to be appointed to the new Supreme Court, but there was no way that the governor would appoint either as chief justice.

Driscoll had a keen sense of history and appreciated that this was a watershed moment, an opportunity for New Jersey to make huge strides in modernizing its court system. He wasn't going to forfeit the chance to signal a sea change in the appearance, function, and agenda of the new Supreme Court. The new chief justice had to be someone able to defend the independence of the third branch of government against assaults by politicians.

Driscoll's choice for chief justice would be a circuit court judge with no prior experience on the bench. A provision of the new constitution, no longer relevant today but critical at the time, was the mandatory carry-over of all sitting judges into the new court system and the requirement that the Supreme Court could be composed only of judges who had served on a higher court prior to adoption of the constitution. Throughout the fall of 1947 people in the know speculated that Driscoll would be forced to choose between Oliphant and Case. He had a surprise for them.

On October 30, 1947, six days before Election Day, the governor announced the appointment of Arthur Vanderbilt to the New Jersey Circuit Court, "in order that a man of his extraordinary experience as a lawyer, student of jurisprudence, judicial procedure, and judicial structure, may be available" to serve as chief justice upon approval of the upcoming referendum.[2] The day before the successful referendum, November 3, 1947, Frank Sommer administered the oath of office to Vanderbilt. It is hard to imagine a mentor being prouder of a protégé than Sommer was at that moment.

Within a month after the election, Driscoll formally nominated Vanderbilt to serve as the new chief justice, and seven days later, on December 15, 1947, the state senate confirmed the appointment. Also named to serve as justices were Oliphant, Case, Harry Heher (previously justice on the old Supreme Court and a former state Democratic Party chairman under Hague), William Wachenfeld (justice on the old court), Albert Burling (justice on the old court), and Circuit Court Judge Henry Ackerson, who had played a role in the 1944 efforts to revise the constitution. Driscoll had adroitly managed to retain four of the seven justices from the old court. All of these appointments were effective on September 15, 1948. It would be a hectic nine months for the new chief justice.

Most pressing for Vanderbilt was the need to draft new court rules. Prior court rules had been written many years earlier by the legislature. In most instances each court had its own rules of procedure and differently named orders and writs; adding to the confusion, legislators weren't always careful about consistency or economy of language. As Vanderbilt understood Article VI of the new constitution, the new Supreme Court had the freedom to scrap all the old rules and start over, without regard to the thoughts of the legislature. The new chief justice set about the task with his usual enthusiasm.

No longer was he pulled daily in a dozen different directions: his clients were now represented by others; Essex County politics was off limits; NYU's law school had to find a new dean; and Wesleyan University would have to do without his services as trustee. Now he had the freedom to focus all his legal knowledge, extraordinary energy, and savvy as a political operative on the task of organizing the new court system and asserting its presence as one of the three equal branches of state government.

With only nine months to prepare, the justices-designate quickly arrived at a consensus: there had to be a clean break with the past. A single set of rules governing procedures in each court was essential to the creation of an integrated court system. What Vanderbilt appreciated better than most of his colleagues was how traumatic that change would be for many of the state's lawyers. He had had a ringside seat to the uproar that ensued after adoption of the Practice Act of 1912, written by Frank Sommer; Vanderbilt feared that this time around things could be worse. He was right.

Having worked on numerous rule revision committees with both the American Bar Association and the U.S. attorney's office, Vanderbilt knew that the best way to begin the process was to solicit input from every judge, lawyer, and interested citizen. All were welcome to participate. He asked the state bar association and every county bar association to submit their suggestions for rules that they thought would be helpful. Assistance was sought from the Administrative Office of the United States Courts, National Conference of Judicial Councils, and American Judicature Society. Vanderbilt also contacted the chief justices of each of the other states to learn "what rules they had found essential in their own state and what they would do if they could reorganize their court system."[3] Throughout the process, all recommendations were shared with the other six justices; legal scholars and experienced trial lawyers were consulted; individuals were assigned to write specific rules that were then circulated to the others. It was a wide-open process. At the end of the day, the final court rules were shaped to closely follow the Rules of Civil Procedure and the Rules of Criminal Procedure used in the federal courts.

In addition to preparation of the court rules, Vanderbilt oversaw the work of a task force whose job it was to handle the logistics of the transition to the new court system. "Personnel to help administer court business were selected, modern office systems were planned, and the records of the existing courts were transferred to the new courts, all while the existing judicial system continued operating."[4] Of significant importance, an administrative office of the courts was also created by the legislature, modeled after the federal system, to manage the business end of the courts. It simply wasn't possible for "the Chief Justice alone to have handled the administrative affairs of the court system and still attend to his other judicial duties."[5] In creating this new office, New Jersey was the first state in the United States to do so, making it the envy of courts across the nation. By September 13, 1948, two days before the new system was launched, everything was in place.

Yet things weren't going to be that easy; the greater the number of entrenched interests affected by reform, the harder to get to the finish line. Whether it was because so few of them had been delegates to the constitutional convention and were miffed that they hadn't had a hand in the changes, or because they understood the magnitude of the changes and felt threatened by them—it wasn't Frank Hague making mischief—a majority of the legislature had decided to hurl an axe at the new Supreme Court. Whether it was resistance, push back, or counterrevolution, there were people of power scrutinizing the changes to the court system scheduled to go into effect in the fall of 1948, and they were angry. They began by mounting a broad-ranging counterattack on the proposed new court rules.

In the summer of 1948 four pieces of legislation were adopted by the legislature: Senate Bill No. 58—to Vanderbilt, a nauseating list of horribles, among other things challenging the Supreme Court's rule-making authority, attempting to supersede a rule banning court personnel from practicing law, restricting rules of pretrial discovery, and overturning a new rule restricting referrals by judges to lawyers; Senate Bill No. 48—providing for an inefficient duplication of criminal appeals from local courts to the county court and then to the appellate division; Senate Bill No. 349—proposing establishment of a judicial council with the power to suggest changes in the rules of practice and procedure, rivaling the Supreme Court; and Assembly Bill No. 53—eliminating a new rule requiring debtors to be provided with advance notice of an application for a garnishment of their wages. Each bill was an attempt to eliminate a proposed new court rule intended to raise the standards required of both judges and lawyers. While Vanderbilt fumed, Driscoll set about the task of drafting veto messages for each of the bills, in effect, telling the politicians "hands off!" Several weeks into the new court term, on October 30, 1948, the governor averted a constitutional crisis by vetoing all four bills. Days later, Vanderbilt wrote to him: "On behalf of my colleagues and for myself, I wish to very much thank you for your consistent cooperation and continued support of our efforts to build a great judicial system."[6]

By the time of Driscoll's vetoes, Vanderbilt and his fellow justices were working around the clock to get things up and running. The justices gave priority to the large number of cases that had been delayed for years—baggage from the past. In some of the courts, cases filed in the 1930s had yet to go to trial. Lengthy delays were, in part, attributable to a perverse sense of judicial independence. Much like the legislators holding all the power after 1776, no longer answerable to the royal governor, the judges under the old system had decided that they answered to no one—except the politico-legal establishment. Once on the bench, the only people they had to please were politically connected lawyers and the politicians to whom they owed their position; people having business with the court were a minor concern. Worse still were the judges who viewed their positions as a reward for past services to their political party: timely trials and the efficient administration of justice weren't high on their list but long lunches and a large number of vacation days were. That's not to say there were no capable judges—there were many; nonetheless, excellence wasn't the standard, and mediocrity was the norm. Combine undistinguished and indifferent judges with an archaic system and a just result in any given case was a hit-or-miss proposition.

Bold change was needed and Vanderbilt was just the person to bring it about; his mission was to dismantle the mishmash of courts afflicting the state and rejuvenate the judiciary. Early on he made it clear that a day in the life of a member of the New Jersey bench was going to get uncomfortable for mediocre judges. Procrastination was no longer acceptable.

Vanderbilt knew what every conscientious judge knows: the facts necessary to decide a case don't look better as they get older. The best time to make a decision is as promptly as possible following the hearing on a given matter. A judge must promptly make findings of facts, analyze them in light of the relevant law, and then issue a ruling. Consistent with that approach, a new rule of the court required that decisions on petitions heard by a trial court had to be ruled on by the following week and that all cases heard at a bench trial had to be decided by the judge within four weeks. In speaking of past delays, Vanderbilt made it clear that if indolent judges didn't pick up their pace, they would be publicly humiliated. "I am stating now for the record, that any such overdue decisions will be specified with the name of the judge and the name of the case in quarterly reports" that would be released to the news outlets.[7]

Vanderbilt's willingness to name names of dilatory judges was a nightmare come true for some of the old guard. In the past there was no administrative machinery to keep track of who was doing what. There was no supervision or maintenance of records beyond those kept by individual judges and their court clerks. The assignment of judges to various courts was made by the legislature and every judge was a little principality unto himself. Yet under Article VI of the new constitution, the chief justice was now in charge. He was not just the presiding justice of the Supreme Court, he was the head supervisor of the entire judiciary with the power to assign judges to a particular court and to look over their shoulders and inquire into their progress in handling their caseload.

One of the means by which the chief justice put pressure on laggards was the requirement of weekly reports of how judges used their time. The requirement that by the end of the week, every report listing "how many hours he had sat on the bench during the preceding five working days, how many cases he had presided over and their outcome, what motions he had heard and disposed of, and any other business attended to,"[8] caused great annoyance in court chambers across New Jersey. The weekly reports requested the number of cases pending on a judge's docket and the date(s) of any bench trial(s) heard but not yet ruled upon; they were then summarized by the administrative director into a digest of information, which was then delivered to the chief justice and the county assignment judges for each judge in the state. Finally, the reports were compiled into monthly and quarterly statements and delivered to every judge.

Weekly reports made it possible for every judge to see what his colleagues were doing and, if one was falling behind, his colleagues could remind him that he must pick up his pace. According to Vanderbilt, the effect on the dawdlers was "truly remarkable." While many of the dawdlers had tenure to age seventy and direct pressure was of little value, "it was found that when the weekly reports were circulated among the judges, the relatively few laggards began to mend their ways rather than incur the silent or occasionally vocal censure of their colleagues."[9] And if being rebuked by one's peers didn't do it, the chief justice had the ultimate weapon: the power to assign judges to various courts. Thus, a dilatory judge could find himself reporting to a different county—at great inconvenience—if Vanderbilt thought that was what was needed to motivate him. In a short time, his very name, Arthur T. Vanderbilt, became anathema to many of the old guard judges.

In his address to the public on the first day of the new court system, Vanderbilt stated, "It is our ambition to be known as an independent court, an efficient court, a just court, and I hope, a friendly court. We of the Supreme Court are determined to a man to give the State the finest judicial organization and administration within our power."[10] Moments after his initial public statement, Vanderbilt and his colleagues heard oral argument in the first case on their appeal list.

When it came to handling appeals, "Vanderbilt's goal for the Supreme Court was to have the maximum participation of each justice in each decision as contrasted with the practice of the old court system, where often one judge handled one decision by himself."[11] Although impossible to conceive of today, before 1947, the procedure in the E & A was for each case to be handled by a single judge. The rest were bystanders. That judge was responsible for writing the decision with virtually no input from the others. When lawyers appeared for oral argument they were able to determine which judge was assigned their appeal because, as their case was called for argument, a court attendant placed two large bundles tied in their original wrappings, containing the record and the briefs, before the judge who would write the opinion. "Practiced counsel learned to address the judge with the bundles."[12] Knowing of this custom, Vanderbilt had once quipped, "It is just as bad as letting one member of a jury hear all the evidence and bring in a decision while the eleven other members stay home."[13]

During Vanderbilt's first year as chief justice things changed dramatically. As the schedule of arguments was prepared, he required copies of all the pleadings of the litigants to be distributed to the seven justices two and a half weeks prior to hearing the appeal. Each justice was expected to write a memorandum concerning the issues raised and the questions that ought to be posed at oral argument. Each Thursday before the hearing on Monday, the seven justices gathered in Trenton to review the key legal issues. They did not discuss their thoughts on the merits of the case, nor did they share their memos with one another until after oral arguments, to ensure every litigant received a full and fair hearing by a panel of judges conversant in the law affecting their case and uninfluenced by their colleagues' thoughts until after they had the opportunity to hear from counsel. As well as anything can, Vanderbilt's restructuring of the process by which appeals were handled by New Jersey's high court illustrates his unflinching commitment to the rule of law.

After oral argument and before the end of the day, a vote was taken on two questions posed to the justices: should the decision below be affirmed, reversed, or modified; and considering the first answer, which point(s) of law raised in the legal briefs supported that position? If there were a consensus on the decision, one justice was assigned the task of writing an opinion and each of his colleagues provided him with a copy of his memorandum and notes on the case. No longer were there one-man decisions with the other justices mere observers.

Even bigger changes were coming to the trial court judges and the lawyers appearing before them. Taken for granted today, trials in America weren't always preceded by a thorough exchange of information between litigants in preparation for going to court. Among the many changes brought to the system by Vanderbilt, pretrial discovery and pretrial conferences may have been the most controversial among sitting judges and experienced attorneys. It annoyed many of them to no end.

Prior to the second half of the twentieth century, it had long been the practice in New Jersey, and most other states, that lawyers knew very little about the evidence their opponent would present at trial until they got to court. Frequently, it wasn't until the day of trial that lawyers learned the facts, witnesses, or documents the other side would present as the evidence in their case. Trials weren't a search for the truth but rather a type of sporting event based upon jarring revelations and unanticipated technicalities, hearkening back to a bygone era: combat among lawyers "with the victor and justice emerging together from the fray and the judge's decision [or jury verdict] awarded to the most skillful fighter."[14] It was a game of gotcha in which surprise was the norm.

Under the new court rules for pretrial discovery, namely, permitting each side to *discover* and learn about the facts of their opponent's case, lawyers were required to divulge the names of witnesses with a brief statement of their testimony, answer written questions concerning the facts of the case, and disclose to the other side those documents they intended to present at trial. Judges were required to conduct pretrial conferences where an order was entered reciting the legal issues in the case, the key facts in dispute, and the witnesses and documents upon which each side would rely. The intent was to chart the course the trial would take when the case was called for trial. Most of the longer-experienced judges viewed these changes as a nuisance. As for the lawyers, they resisted the requirement to disclose all their evidence, not wanting to reveal the strengths and weaknesses of their case prior to trial. "These discovery methods were contrary to their tradition of concealing facts until the last possible moment."[15] The early feedback from both bench and bar was hostile.

So convinced was Vanderbilt that pretrial conferences, following exchange of discovery, could upgrade the system by making both bench and jury trials a more orderly process focusing on the issues that he insisted upon making their use mandatory. Despite the whining and moaning, the chief justice believed that the new rules would help to dispose of weak cases, move the ones having merit to trial more quickly, and reduce the backlog of old cases. Pushing his agenda, the chief justice required each civil law judge to set aside one week each month for pretrial conferences of the cases on their docket where sufficient discovery had been exchanged. The lawyers involved in the case presented the judge with a memo listing the issues in dispute together with their factual and legal contentions. Rather than the judge learning about the case the morning of trial, he was required to read the lawyers' memos and their pleadings in preparation for the conference; the same was true of the adversaries. In the end, everyone had a better understanding of the case, and often the judge used the meeting as a basis for initiating settlement discussions. Over time, the cases that did go to trial were handled more efficiently and all cases were disposed of more quickly. Nonetheless, persuading judges to buy into the process "required salesmanship of the highest order, and throughout his years as chief justice it was a cause Vanderbilt could never neglect without losing ground."[16]

Another sector of New Jersey's court system in need of major reform but over which the chief justice had limited day-to-day control were the local courts in municipalities throughout the state. The delegates of the constitutional convention had wisely chosen to erase years of madness. When it came to the means by which to reward cronies, pacify constituents, cover up embarrassing situations, and quash criminal charges against the well connected, the legislature had created a plethora of courts. There was everything from justice of the peace courts, county traffic courts, recorder courts, and police courts to city district courts, criminal judicial district courts, and small cause courts, together with family courts, juvenile domestic relations courts, surrogate courts, and orphans courts. The first seven courts were merged into what ultimately became today's municipal courts; the last four were subsumed by the original county court and eventually by the superior court.

The justice of the peace, traffic, recorder, police, and city district courts were notorious as courts where politicians could—and usually did—dictate the outcome. Typically the charges ranged from speeding and drunken driving to shoplifting and street brawling. While some of the offenders may well have deserved the leniency granted by the local judge through the good graces of the ward leader—although many did not—the entire process tarnished the courts' image and bred disrespect for the rule of law. The chief justice understood something that the politicians did not. "It was in these courts of first instance that most citizens, particularly young people and the foreign born, received their first and perhaps only direct impression of American justice."[17] The percentage of the population appearing as litigants in the "upper courts" was a tiny fraction of those appearing in local courts for minor offenses, and the degree of respect for the law gained by people appearing before these courts—a respect Vanderbilt considered the cornerstone of a democratic society—"depended largely on their encounters with the municipal magistrates."[18]

Vanderbilt's solution caused an uproar. Again, he took aim squarely at the judges. Going forward, every newly appointed municipal court judge had to be a member of the New Jersey bar, making judges subject to the Canons of Judicial Ethics. The chief justice wanted the municipal court judges to be real judges, and, as with superior court and county court judges, political activities were forbidden. All judges were required to wear robes to encourage seriousness of purpose; fixed annual salaries replaced the system of judge's being paid based upon "court costs"; and a uniform schedule of fines and penalties was established. Finally, Vanderbilt invited the public to report to him on any rude or unprofessional behavior by any municipal court judge; he followed up on all complaints. By demanding competence and professionalism, Vanderbilt transformed the local courts. Less than five years into the changes, the legislature downgraded dozens of criminal charges to disorderly persons offenses, confident that they could now be handled competently at the municipal court level and relieving county grand juries from having to hear numerous offenses.

Yet it was the handling of traffic summonses that did more to improve the stature of municipal courts than anything else. Proof of widespread corruption in New Jersey's traffic courts required no more than a comparison of the number of summonses issued versus the number presented in court. Somehow, many of the charges disappeared or were dismissed without explanation. Vanderbilt had the cure: the "nonfixable" traffic ticket. Its simplicity was impossible to undo.

What few of the local judges likely knew was that Vanderbilt had been chairman of the National Committee on Traffic Law Enforcement since 1938. The chief justice was familiar with the problems of traffic courts and the available remedies. "The system of nonfixable tickets he introduced in New Jersey had been tried in several cities in Michigan and had proved simple and effective."[19] The new traffic ticket, which became mandatory statewide on January 1, 1949, was printed in quadruplicate: the original was filed with the local court clerk; one was issued to the driver; and the remaining two copies were retained by the police department, one filed with the local chief of police and the other maintained in the work file of the police officer who issued the summons to the driver. Each ticket was numbered in sequence, and each one had to be accounted for; the penalty for destroying a ticket was criminal contempt—for which the chief justice himself would decide the penalty. No longer could tickets get "lost." In order to "fix" a traffic violation, as local politicians and police departments had being doing for years, three public officials—the court clerk, the chief of police, and the police officer—would have to violate their oath of office.

Old ways die hard and the reaction to this new system of traffic tickets from local officials bordered on hysteria The mantra invoked by local politicians was "you're taking away home rule." As the chief justice related to another lawyer interested in reform, he had to spend several days "keeping the hands and feet of some of my colleagues from becoming too chilled." The head of the New Jersey Police Chiefs Association expressed his view in two words: "It stinks." The politicians fed the clamor by implying that the new system was a scheme for a power grab and that "a gigantic fraud was about to be perpetrated upon an unsuspecting public." When the furor failed to subside, Vanderbilt invited the police chiefs to a conference with the full Supreme Court "so that they might air their grievances and explain to us the defects, if any, of the new ticket."[20]

As he described it, nearly four hundred men in uniform "with lowered brows and tight-set lips were there to greet us." Their hostile questions made it clear that they wanted no parts of the new traffic ticket. One even went so far as to request continuance of a widespread practice of police officers being able to collect fines from motorists who wished to plead guilty at the time of being stopped for a violation. When Vanderbilt made it clear that wouldn't happen, the police chief bawled, "But I am a Republican." As the evening wore on, Vanderbilt refused to budge; the new system was going forward. Finally, as the meeting was nearing an end, the executive secretary of the New Jersey Patrolman's Benevolent Association asked to be heard. To Vanderbilt's pleasant surprise, he characterized the nonfixable traffic ticket as "an Emancipation Proclamation for the ordinary policeman, who resented the fact that his chief had all too often kicked the traffic tickets he had issued."[21]

Results after only three months supported Vanderbilt's change. During the first quarter of 1949, the City of Newark experienced a sharp drop in "no shows" for hearings on traffic tickets. For the same period in 1948, there had been 14,529 tickets that were not answered in court. For the months of January, February, and March of 1949, the number was 607, most of them nonresident drivers passing through the state. Revenue from traffic fines increased significantly in every municipality and the public gained new respect for the law. With the implementation of the no-fix system, New Jersey virtually overnight became the only state in which fixing a traffic ticket became impossible, weakening the influence of many old guard politicians.

While more battles lay ahead, the chief justice was in control of his world and the judiciary was on its way to being an equal branch of New Jersey's government. Across Newark Bay, the same could not be said for the former mayor of Jersey City. He was at the end of the road.

Maybe it was hubris, or paranoia, or possibly it was the weariness that comes with age and a life of waging political war: Frank Hague's resignation as mayor was a mistake he couldn't undo. He had miscalculated his strength and that of Second Ward leader John V. Kenny within the city's political power structure. As the realization of what had occurred—that is, the brazen transfer of power to his nephew—sank in to the psyche of the community, it didn't sit well. It wasn't about Eggers; it was about being taken for granted. As Jersey City historian Owen Grundy observed, "Democracies do not cotton to dynasties. Rebellion was in the air."[22]

In politics and in life, what you are catches up with you. Despite his many past deeds to help the working poor, to launch the careers of scores of politicians, and to enrich many of his cronies by spreading the wealth that came with power, Frank Hague had grown much too detached from the street. Even though he had resigned and was spending more time than ever out of the city, he insisted on controlling the organization and hadn't let go of the reins of power. Conspicuously, he had not resigned as chairman of the Hudson County or New Jersey Democratic committees. While Hague's nephew, Mayor Frank Hague Eggers, was an able and even-handed administrator, he wasn't Hague. More important to control of the organization, Eggers's political problem-solving skills were limited; he didn't connect well with the average citizen. Power is never static and if it isn't exercised by one person it will be by another. As Hague grew more remote from ordinary people and as it became difficult for even ward leaders and precinct captains to meet with him, another savvy pol filled the void created by his absence.

Like Hague, John V. Kenny was a child of the Horseshoe. As a bartender's son, he had moves and ways with people that made him a natural for politics. Nearly thirty years earlier Hague had seen his potential and had tapped him as the leader of the Second Ward. Kenny worked tirelessly to keep the Horseshoe the most politically potent ward in the city, registering everyone to vote and oftentimes getting nearly unanimous turnout for the Democratic ticket. Kenny never missed a wake and made time to visit city residents in the hospital nearly every day. His nominal day job was as an employee with the Hudson County Freeholder Board, and he was associated with the dock workers union, Terminal Workers Local 1730, which was believed to be a significant source of revenue for both him and Hague, yet his full-time job was street politics.[23] He had worked as a loyal, high-ranking lieutenant of the Hague organization for two decades and had intimate knowledge of the organization's strengths and weaknesses. At age fifty-six, he knew who to see—every bit as well as Hague did—to get things done in the city.

Many people had long viewed Johnny Kenny as the number 2 person in the Jersey City political power structure. Over time, with Hague disengaged from the streets, Kenny became the go-to guy when people needed a favor. He was a pillar of St. Michael's Church and a daily visitor at St. Francis Hospital. "He was unobtrusive, a man easily lost in a crowd or even in a small gathering."[24] Kenny was so approachable that very few addressed him as "mister." If your own precinct captain of ward leader couldn't get it done, the refrain became "go see Johnny." Frequently the favor was granted, and as the years went by Kenny built a personal following that reached far beyond the boundaries of the Second Ward. By the time Hague had decided to transfer power to his nephew, Johnny Kenny was the best-known, most popular, resourceful, and effective politician in the city, embraced by every ethnic group and social tier. His was the type of power that could go unnoticed until it was too late.

It isn't known what ultimately inspired Hague to move against Kenny—arrogance, suspicion, or crankiness at age seventy-one; nonetheless, he miscalculated badly. In May of 1948, nearly two years into Eggers's reign as mayor, Warden Joseph Buckley of the Hudson County Penitentiary was indicted. Everyone knew the entire prison system was corrupt, and when Paul Hanly of the Secaucus Penitentiary *wasn't* indicted this aroused suspicion among Hague's people. News stories were reporting that an "unnamed prominent Democrat had been the finger man."[25] Paul Hanly was married to Johnny Kenny's daughter, and rumors quickly spread that Kenny was the informant. This was the cue for which Hague had apparently been waiting, and he moved swiftly to oust the Second Ward leader; little more than two weeks after the Buckley indictment a meeting of the Jersey City ward leaders was convened. Johnny Kenny wasn't invited. The meeting at which Kenny was stripped of his position was presided over by former judge William McGovern, who later told a newsman, "We're glad to get rid of a stool pigeon."[26] Kenny was later fired from his county position despite the fact that he never testified concerning the Buckley indictment and there is nothing to support the theory that he was an informant.

Within days of his ouster people were encouraging Kenny to put together a slate of his own to challenge Eggers and the incumbent Hague-controlled city commissioners in the municipal election of May 1949. While Kenny pondered the idea of leading a rebellion, he cautioned his supporters to tread lightly, and with good reason: fear. Fear of Hague's raw power, fear of the Zepps bringing sham criminal charges, fear of reprisals by the ward leaders, fear of being fired from a position in City Hall or the county, even fear of being scolded by the parish priest were all part of the Celtic Chieftain's arsenal. In the summer of 1948 Kenny began working a clever strategy of silence and secrecy. As chronicled by news reporter Marin Gately,

> From September through the end of the year, a strange political war raged throughout the city. It had aspects of an underground war, a resistance. Kenny signs began appearing all over Jersey City. Hundreds wore "Kenny in '49" buttons behind their suit lapels. The lapel was quickly turned forward, exposing the Kenny button, whenever Kenny supporters met. Pro-Kenny chalk messages were scrawled on sidewalks all over the city. Some of this necessarily had to be done at night. The Kenny stickers appeared on city streets, buildings, telephone poles. Tiny one-inch stickers eventually were placed on mouth pieces of public telephones in every high mobility area of the city.[27]

By the spring of 1949, battle lines had formed. The incumbent slate would be led by Mayor Eggers, running with three Irish Catholic Democrats and a token Protestant, all products of Hague's organization. That winter, Ed O'Mara had traveled to Florida to plead with Hague, asking him to reconsider modifying the slate. Hague reportedly told O'Mara, "If I put an Italian candidate and a Polish candidate on the ticket now, they'll boss me, and there will be no point in my being leader. If I put them on after the election, I'll boss them."[28]

Kenny was determined to lead a "fusion ticket" made up of a multiethnic slate of candidates and a well-known and respected Protestant Republican; he knew there were significant numbers of Republicans who sat out every municipal election, believing that their participation was futile. When the March filing date arrived, Kenny's slate was like nothing Jersey City had ever seen: Kenny and another Irishman, an Italian, a Pole, and a WASP. The Protestant was Donald Spence, an insurance executive in Newark, and more importantly the son of Dr. Henry Spence, a kind and generous physician who was loved by the working-class Irish of Jersey City. As stated by one news reporter, "Elderly Irish people mention his name with a reverence and respect usually accorded a beloved bishop."[29] The catalyst of Donald Spence's candidacy was Governor Alfred Driscoll; he and Spence had been fraternity brothers at Williams College. Kenny's slate ran under the banner "The Freedom Ticket" and was swept into office by an overwhelming majority, with Kenny being named mayor by his running mates.

Hindsight of nearly seventy years makes clear Hague's miscues: the transfer of the mayor's office to his nephew—his namesake no less; his refusal to let go of the reins of power; and making Johnny Kenny a martyr by viciously ejecting him from the organization. All worked to crystallize resentment against the Celtic Chieftain. Frank Hague had become an aged, out-of-touch autocrat, and after May 1949, his political clout eroded to nothing. He made one more effort that fall, but his support of Elmer Winne in the gubernatorial election didn't make a dent. Hague was done.

Hague's fall from power likely made Vanderbilt smile, yet final word on their decades-long clash and the role Vanderbilt saw for the courts hadn't been written. That would come later, and the chief justice would tackle both through authoring two high-handed Supreme Court decisions, each controversial for its own reasons.

CHAPTER 15

The Chief Supreme

Commuting to work by train was a routine for Arthur Vanderbilt dating back to his years attending Columbia Law School. Most days began with a quick drive to the Short Hills railroad station, where he parked his car and boarded a train to Newark or, depending upon his schedule, continued on to Trenton, New York, or Washington. Not long after Vanderbilt was appointed chief justice, one of his neighbors mentioned to the station ticket agent how special it was to have the state's most important judge living in their community. The agent, who had seen Vanderbilt come and go for years, remarked, "It can't be much of a job; I see he still takes the 7:23 every morning."[1]

Yet it wasn't just a job: Roseville's prodigy was living his dream. He had reorganized New Jersey's court system and rewritten its rules; he had stirred apathetic judges out of their stupor and some into retirement; he had made tremendous strides in restoring the public's faith in the courts as a place where they would be treated fairly. In little more than eighteen months he had revitalized what had long been the stunted, rotten branch of state government, transforming it into a force equal to the other two. Still, the chief justice remained the Warrior Lawyer.

It's easy to believe that from the moment he was sworn into office Vanderbilt was scanning the legal landscape, on the lookout for an appeal to the state's highest court that would give him the chance to make a bold statement declaring his court's independence and parity. For certain, after the four bills vetoed by Governor Driscoll in the fall of 1948, he had to have been looking for the right moment to strike back at the counterrevolutionaries. The opportunity came in the spring of 1950 on an appeal involving a dispute that on its face didn't appear to warrant such a brazen ruling.

In February of 1949, John Winberry, a New Brunswick lawyer, filed suit in the superior court seeking a court order to expunge a Presentment of the Middlesex County Grand Jury, the findings of which, he believed, defamed him. The nominal defendant in the lawsuit was Burton Salisbury, the foreman of the grand jury. The events leading up to the presentment are as follows. In April of 1947, Winberry was appointed to serve as a deputy attorney general specially assigned to Middlesex County to prosecute gambling operators on twenty indictments returned by a prior grand jury. During the twenty months he served, Winberry took five of the indictments to trial—all resulting in acquittals—and petitioned the court to dismiss the remaining fifteen; the petition was granted.[2] On November 17, 1948, Attorney General Walter Van Riper terminated Winberry's appointment. His termination was preceded by inflammatory exchanges between Winberry and Van Riper in the newspapers, each accusing the other of bad faith, with Winberry having started the volley.

Shortly after the filing of Winberry's complaint, the Attorney General's Office moved to dismiss. In an affidavit filed with the state's motion pleadings, Van Riper charged Winberry with "inefficiency, incompetency, insubordination, and dereliction of duty."[3] While the basis of Van Riper's accusations can't be known with certainty, the grand jury's presentment chided Winberry for multiple failures in the exercise of his duties and concluded that his explanation for his conduct "does not measure up with the facts."[4] The trial judge granted a dismissal of Winberry's complaint on May 25, 1949. Winberry's notice of appeal was served on July 26, seventeen days beyond the forty-five-day appeal period provided by the new court rules adopted by the state Supreme Court in September 1948. In his appeal, Winberry relied upon a statute from years earlier, which permitted one year in which to file an appeal and asserted that, as stated in the Judicial Article of the new constitution, all court rules were "subject to law." He argued that if there was conflict between the court rules and the statute, the one-year statutory appeal period controlled, and his appeal must therefore be heard by the court, notwithstanding his failure to file it within the time period provided by the court rules.

On appeal, the Appellate Division upheld the dismissal based on the late filing. It agreed that "subject to law" meant that "the Legislature is given final word in matters of procedure [and that] it may . . . nullify a procedural rule

[of] the Supreme Court,"⁵ but because the legislature had taken no action to void the court's rules, the forty-five-day appeal period controlled.

Vanderbilt couldn't abide an opinion that questioned his court's power to promulgate the court rules, free of legislative control. Seeing this as an occasion to stake out the Supreme Court's territory, he carefully crafted a bold opinion for five of the seven justices, asserting the court's exclusive authority to control its domain and making it clear that the state's high court had the final say on interpreting the constitution. His ruling was a shot across the bow of the legislature, letting its members know that he intended to interpret the new constitution as he believed necessary in order to preserve an independent judiciary. If the old guard politico-legal establishment wanted to create a constitutional crisis through its belligerent interference with reform of the judiciary approved by the voters, so be it. He was ready to do battle with the politicians in the court of public opinion.

Eloquent as ever, the chief justice launched into a lesson in law, history, and semantics, proclaiming "that the rule-making power of the Supreme Court is not subject to overriding legislation" and declaring that "[w]hatever confusion there may be as to the nature of the rule-making power stems from an oversimplification of the doctrine of the separation of powers."⁶ Masterfully obscuring the issue and blurring recent history of public discussions on the phrase "subject to law," he stated that the phrase did not mean "subject to statutory law or legislation," because "[i]f this is what the Constitutional Convention intended, it would have been easy for it to say so."⁷ Demonstrating his knowledge of seventeenth-century British history, he traced the roots of the dispute to the doctrine of parliamentary supremacy and the Glorious Revolution of 1689, which had resulted in the English Parliament's overthrow of King James II, equating that with the "legislative hegemony" existing in the United States prior to the American Civil War. The chief justice was telling the legislators they were no longer "supreme."

Driven by his need to express what he conceived of as the judiciary's proper relationship with the other two branches of government, Vanderbilt's opinion beclouded the pivotal phrase by subjecting it to a lexicographical analysis. According to the law school professor of thirty years, "The phrase 'subject to law' is not only ambiguous but elliptical. No word in the law has more varied meanings than the term 'law' itself. Nor is the phrase 'subject to' crystal clear, for the phrase implies a limitation rather than a grant or power." As he saw it, the only acceptable definition of "subject to law" was *his*, namely, one that "will not defeat the objective of the people to establish an integrated judicial system . . . is to construe it [law] as the equivalent of substantive law as distinguished from pleading and practice. The distinction between substantive law, which defines our rights and duties, and the law of pleading and practice, through which such rights and duties are enforced in the courts, is a fundamental one that is part of the daily thinking of judges and lawyers."[8]

Expanding the reach of his opinion to address the events of the summer of 1947 at Rutgers, the chief justice pronounced that the formal Report of the Judiciary Committee of the Constitutional Convention wasn't pertinent to his analysis. The committee's report included language stating that the new Supreme Court's "power to make rules" was "subject to the overriding power of the Legislature with respect to practice and procedure." Nonetheless, according to Vanderbilt, the report couldn't be relied upon to interpret the phrase because "though dated August 26, 1947, [the report] was not handed to the members of the Convention until August 28th . . . two days after the Judicial Article had been adopted by the Convention on August 26th. . . . [T]he report of the Judiciary Committee therefore cannot be deemed a part of the parliamentary history of the Constitutional Convention."[9] It's an audacious statement, especially in view of the fact that the final draft of the new constitution was approved on September 10. To arrive at his conclusion, the chief justice not only overlooked the discussions of the convention but, more brazenly, he ignored his own letter to the Judiciary Committee of July 29, 1947. In his letter, Vanderbilt acknowledged the meaning of the language used in the draft of the Judicial Article and very pointedly addressed the phrase "subject to law," advising that the "trend" in America was to "confide rule-making with the highest court" and "suggest[ed] the deletion of the phrase."

In a "concurring" opinion that agreed with the ruling of the Appellate Division but rejected Vanderbilt's reasoning in its entirety, Justice Clarence Case took the chief justice to task with far more civility than might have been expected.[10] Although he didn't discuss Vanderbilt's letter in his opinion, Case did trace the history of the constitutional reform movement in New Jersey; he cited the several drafts, in all of which Vanderbilt had played a role, and showed how the use and application of the phrase "subject to law" had evolved, granting unfettered freedom to the Supreme Court only as to rule-making regarding administration of the courts. He chastised Vanderbilt, stating, "It is quite out of character that a group of legal experts, intent upon drawing the most notable document of their lives, would use the same word [law] in a whole series of related paragraphs and intend in one of those instances, in the midst of all the others, to give a very special and limited meaning without adding some adjectival distinction."[11]

Justice Chase reminded the chief justice that the "widely praised Federal Rules of Civil Procedure, used as the basis for framing our own rules, were promulgated by the U.S. Supreme Court, not by inherent authority or by constitutional enactment, but pursuant to an Act of Congress." Finally, he addressed Vanderbilt's thoughts on the separation of powers. "Our American conception of constitutional government is one of checks and balances. If the governor exceeds his limitations, if the legislature goes beyond its powers, the courts are available to enforce the constitutional restraints. But if our Supreme Court exceeds its powers, who shall impose the check? Therein lies the danger when the court undertakes, not to construe law, but to *make* it."[12]

Yet the danger of a hostile legislature turning back the clock to impose its antiquated views of how the courts should function was quite real. The politicians weren't backing off; they were determined to continue meddling with the courts to their own selfish ends. The old guard judges, gray-haired trial lawyers, angry chiefs of police, and lay municipal judges now forced to work under a new set of standards beyond their manipulation had powerful friends in Trenton, and the only person preventing serious harm to the new Supreme Court was Governor Driscoll. His four gubernatorial vetoes in October 1948 were essential to preventing serious damage to the stature of the newly created court system.

Notwithstanding Driscoll's popularity with the voters, in 1950, within months of the Supreme Court's decision in *Winberry v. Salisbury*, the politicians again flexed their muscles by approving four more bills, each one undermining some aspect of the new court system as had been crafted by the Supreme Court: Senate Bill 237 provided for restoration of lawyers' fees in instances limited by the new court rules; Senate Bill 273 attempted to make a backdoor revival of the chancery court as a court of separate jurisdiction; Assembly Bill 87 granted municipal court litigants a right of direct appeal to the Appellate Division; and Assembly Bill 256 authorized the county courts to appoint guardians for an incompetent without notice to relatives. Again, it was necessary for Governor Driscoll to veto each of these warlike bills in order to preserve the Supreme Court's independence and avert yet another constitutional crisis.[13]

So, in crafting his opinion in *Winberry v. Salisbury*, did Vanderbilt over-react by poking his pen in the eye of the legislature? That's a tough call. Often the lens of history and the context it affords us brings thing more clearly into focus, but not so here. More than sixty years after the fact, nothing can be read to gauge the true depth of the rancor of the old guard judges so fixed in their ways, or the resentment of a sizable portion of the trial bar accustomed to easy fees flowing from the cozy relationship between bench and bar, together with the ire of the politicians who saw their control of the courts slipping away to a man they detested. Nor can the zeal of Arthur Vanderbilt and the animosity he created among his adversaries be accurately measured. The man was a lightning rod. He had bent the ear of so many people so many times that many people found him insufferable. He had been pushing reform of the courts for so long that one of the consequences was that the reform movement was too closely identified with him, virtually guaranteeing that his enemies would oppose constitutional reform. Yet without Vanderbilt's persistence it's unlikely there would have been a reform movement at all, much less one with such a stunning record of success.

And again, there's the role of the "mensch," Alfred Driscoll. It's diffi-cult to imagine how the new court system would have fared without him to defend it. It is one of the more serendipitous sets of circumstances in New Jersey history that Driscoll was a former law student of Roscoe Pound. Driscoll understood the need for true "checks and balances" among the three branches of the state's government, not "checks" that permitted poli-ticians to write court rules at their whim to satisfy their cronies. More-over, he had the personal maturity and strength to see past Vanderbilt's overbearing ways and the wisdom to realize that if the corrupt, antiquated mess in New Jersey's courts was to be brought into the twentieth century he had to appoint this brilliant "son-of-a-bitch" chief justice. Finally, Driscoll understood that entrenched politicians don't go away without a fight, and he was there to smack their hands every time they grabbed for power.

Was Vanderbilt's opinion in *Winberry v. Salisbury* "sound law"? At the time probably not, but Vanderbilt had keen political instincts and knew that some-times the best defense is a good offense. He knew that until the voters said otherwise at a public referendum on an amendment to the state constitution, "subject to law" meant what the state Supreme Court said it did. The student of Machiavelli and savvy political infighter had opted to publicly scold his enemies for daring to violate a concept so central to the American experience as the separation of powers, something every citizen has a feel for, even if they don't fully understand it.

Vanderbilt knew something else that the politicians did not: his reforms had reached the people. The nonfixable traffic ticket, removing politics from the courtroom, and moving litigation through the courts more fairly and efficiently had all been very well received by the public. The turnaround in the state court system was undeniable. During the first year of the new integrated court system, the Law Division disposed of 98 percent more cases and the county courts 77 percent more cases than their predecessor courts; likewise, the Chancery Division disposed of 126 percent more cases per judge than had the chancery court in the previous year.[14] This remarkable progress can be explained by the reforms forced upon the court system by the chief justice: pretrial discovery, pretrial conferences, and the judges' weekly reports.

Yet many legislators were unimpressed. For them, it was about power. To their thinking they had ceded far more control over the courts through the new constitution than they ever would have had all of them been delegates to the constitutional convention; they wanted the old system back. The court's decision in *Winberry v. Salisbury* was issued on June 27, 1950. When the legislators met again—several weeks later—they obsessed over Vanderbilt's ruling. "They pushed aside all other business at hand to examine it."[15] They even considered the introduction of a constitutional amendment to restore to the legislature the power it had lost as a result of Vanderbilt's decision. But alas, there wasn't enough time under the amendment provisions of the new constitution to place the question on the November ballot.

As the showdown ensued, the state's major newspapers all backed Vanderbilt, publishing glowing editorials and news articles supporting the enlightened reforms he had brought to New Jersey's court system. Despite their hatred for him, the legislators knew that an impeachment effort would be political suicide. As for yet more legislation tampering with the courts, Governor Driscoll had been reelected in 1949 to a new four-year term; he made it clear that he was prepared to veto any attacks on the courts that came across his desk. The politicians howled, but in the end, Vanderbilt prevailed and New Jersey benefited from a vastly improved court system. What was then perceived as the chief justice's brash snatch of power from the legislature is now the norm; each September since the *Winberry* decision, the New Jersey Supreme Court issues the annually updated Rules Governing the Courts without any assistance from the legislature.

Within a year of the governor's veto of the second set of bills aimed at the judiciary's powers, Alfred Driscoll bestowed another benefit on New Jersey's high court. With the retirement of Justice Clarence Case, he appointed someone to work with the chief justice in continuing court reform, someone both Driscoll and Vanderbilt hoped would one day become chief justice.

William J. Brennan Jr. hailed from Newark and was the second of eight children born to Irish immigrants. A graduate of the University of Pennsylvania and Harvard Law School, Brennan's thirty-four years on the U.S. Supreme Court (thought by many to be the most influential tenure of the twentieth century) greatly overshadow his five years on New Jersey's high court. Though nearly twenty years separated them in age, Vanderbilt admired Brennan as a scholar of the law; each shared the other's progressive outlook on jurisprudence and the need for the courts to adapt to the challenges created by an ever-changing American society. Yet, Brennan wasn't meant to play the heavy in pushing the progressive agenda. That role was left to Vanderbilt. Years later, Brennan said that Vanderbilt had once told him, "I now recognize that one has to be a complete son-of-a-bitch to get this job done. One man in this set-up has to be the son-of-a-bitch and I'm it."[16]

Vanderbilt's commitment to the progressive legal agenda is demonstrated not only through his dogged and sometimes pugnacious pursuit of constitutional reform and his willingness to do battle with the legislature, but through the 211 decisions he wrote as chief justice. A common thread runs through these decisions, seeking to make the courts responsive to the needs of society. As Vanderbilt's grandson noted in his authoritative chronicle of his career, his guiding principle was to "make the substantive law of New Jersey suitable to the contemporary conditions by pushing aside procedural or technical intricacies and discarding legal doctrines, no matter how ancient or revered, that were no longer compatible with a modern court system or with the economic and social realities of the age."[17]

Arthur Vanderbilt continued to advance the progressive agenda. "He did not feel bound by history and tradition when it could be shown that a legal principle was not only outworn but deleterious."[18] Vanderbilt believed that the courts were under as great an obligation to revise an outmoded principle of the common law as the legislatures were to update an antiquated statute. His decisions as chief justice are a model in clarity and precision and embody progressive thinking about the status of the law in America; they continue to be quoted by judges across the country.

Yet one decision still stands apart. It was an appeal that he was eager to hear; so much so that the Supreme Court granted certification on its own motion, cutting the Appellate Division out of the process. Unimaginably, it was a case in which compliance with judicial ethics would have obligated the chief to disqualify himself from any participation. That's because Canon 4 of 1950, "A judge's official conduct should be free from impropriety and the appearance of impropriety," clearly barred his involvement. It was a case on which Vanderbilt wrote the opinion for the state Supreme Court on a 4–3 vote: worse still, it was an appeal in which Frank Hague was a party.

Politics in most of New Jersey's counties is hardball; in Hudson County it's a blood sport. Following his campaign efforts on behalf of the losing Democratic candidate in the gubernatorial election of 1949 and Driscoll's reelection, Hague and his family decamped to a Park Avenue apartment in Manhattan. The Celtic Chieftain was completely retired from politics, his allies were all aged, and the only time he returned to Jersey City was for their funerals. Yet the new people in City Hall wanted a pound of flesh, or more precisely, they wanted $15 million (about $300 million today) from him, a nice round number for which there was little factual or legal basis. The complaint filed with the court included a stanza endlessly repeated:—"theft, defrauds, and extortions"—to describe a portion of Hague's modus operandi in exercising the powers of the mayor's office. Hague nemesis John V. Kenny had a hand in seeking revenge, but by the time the city's lawsuit reached the New Jersey Supreme Court in 1955, Kenny, who was under intense scrutiny of federal investigators, had already resigned from office.

In addition to humiliating the Celtic Chieftain, the stated purpose of the lawsuit was to return to the public treasury all of the funds of which the city was purportedly defrauded through the 3 percent payroll kickback scheme, or "rice pudding day," that Hague's organization had perfected over the years to the point that most City Hall employees viewed the payment of a portion of their salary as akin to union dues. Nonetheless, Mayor Bernard Berry and the city commissioners demanded that the money be returned to the city, so a lawsuit was filed against Hague, Deputy Mayor John Malone, and Hague's nephew Frank Hague Eggers.

Recognizing political revenge when he saw it, the trial court judge dismissed the city's lawsuit, terming the allegations of the complaint "contradictory, ambiguous, and confusing."[19] In the opinion of the trial judge, "The complaint appears to me to be completely stultified by its incongruities."[20] The city appealed to the

Appellate Division. Not content to permit the appeal process to run its normal course, at Vanderbilt's urging the Supreme Court short-circuited the process by granting certification without being asked to do so by either party. It's inconceivable that anyone else on the court knew of the chief justice's ties to David Dayton McKean.

Vanderbilt's ruling was shamelessly pontifical. Quoting one of his own opinions on political corruption from several years earlier, he wagged his finger at Hague and his codefendants, stating, "As fiduciaries and trustees of the public weal they are under an inescapable obligation to serve the public with the highest fidelity."[21] The city's lawyer characterized the "rice pudding" money as having been "extorted" from City Hall employees by Hague. Yet the city's complaint was fuzzy on whether the city was entitled to the $15 million or if it should be returned to the employees. The fatal inconsistencies of the city's pleading are revealed by language trying to have it both ways: "All such money ["rice pudding"] extorted by the defendants from City employees under defendants' three percent extortion scheme were and are subject to be forfeited to the City for its own use and benefit, or as trustee for the use and benefit of the defrauded employees."[22]

The contradiction of the relief sought was obvious. Most of Jersey City's employees were willing participants in the scheme, especially the ones with no-show jobs. So why couldn't the money simply be returned to the city's treasury without equivocation? What was the need for the city to serve as "trustee" of the supposedly defrauded employees who had participated in the scheme? Plaintiffs probably envisioned a shakedown of Hague with the money paid into to "trust" for city employees aligned with the current administration, and their lawsuit was the only means to accomplish that. Yet another problem with the city's pleadings, which the trial court noted at the time of dismissing the complaint, was the general allegations of fraud. For centuries, courts have required facts supporting fraud to be stated with a fair amount of detail so a defendant knows exactly with what he's been charged.

Neither the discrepancy in the relief sought nor lack of detail of the fraud claim troubled the chief justice. For him, "The substantial question before us is whether they [Hague and company] can be permitted in law to do this [orchestrate the 3 percent scheme]."[23] Obviously, the law doesn't condone "rice pudding," but as noted by the trial court and the three dissenting justices, Heher, Oliphant, and Wachenfeld (the first a Democrat the other two Republicans), that's not the issue. On a motion to dismiss a complaint, the inquiry is whether or not the pleadings state a coherent cause of action for which relief can be granted under the law.

Justice Heher pointed out to the chief justice that, in his rush to remand the city's lawsuit back to the trial court, he had overlooked one of his own rulings in which he had opined years earlier, "While a party may claim inconsistent claims or defenses and may be heard to argue inconsistent principles of law, he cannot be heard here to contend for two diametrically opposed set of facts."[24] In taking one last swipe at the Celtic Chieftain, the Warrior Lawyer was willing to ignore that it wasn't legally, or factually, sustainable for any money obtained from a judgment against Hague to be payable to both the city and to Hague's coconspirators in the 3 percent extortion scheme.

Vanderbilt's ruling sent the city's lawsuit back to the trial court, but nothing became of it. The history of any further court proceedings is a mystery; no records survive. What isn't a mystery, though, is that Frank Hague never paid a single dollar to Jersey City. In truth, it's unlikely that Hague was the least bit concerned about Vanderbilt's legal opinion. Within six months of the ruling in *City of Jersey City v. Frank Hague, et al.,* Frank Hague was dead. Following a lengthy stay for an unrevealed condition at Columbia Presbyterian Medical Center, where he had been undergoing treatment since early October with no statements granted to the press by his family or the hospital, he was quietly discharged in late December. All the newspapers could squeeze out of anyone was that he was suffering from "bronchitis and arthritis."

His Honor the Mayor was home in time for Christmas with his family and friends and several more days with them before departing this world on New Year's Day, 1956. It's reported that his last words, spoken to his two closest friends, John Milton and John Malone, both at his bedside, were: "I never thought you two bastards would outlive Frank Hague."[25] Sixteen days shy of his eightieth birthday, the sixth-grade dropout from the Horseshoe died in a home in one of Manhattan's most exclusive residential properties. To this day, one can only guess at the size of the fortune he amassed. The only clue to leak out was during probate of his wife's estate seven years later: there was a dispute among the heirs, which required the sale of a portion of her assets, $5 million in blue chip stocks, comparable to $35 million today.

Vanderbilt's archives at Wesleyan University contain nothing recording his thoughts on Hague's demise, but we do know that 1956 was a special year for the chief justice. It was the year his colleague, and hoped-for successor, William Brennan, was appointed to the U.S. Supreme Court. Brennan had come to the attention of the Eisenhower administration when he delivered a speech, substituting for Vanderbilt, at a conference where Attorney General Herbert Brownell was in attendance.

Eisenhower was preparing for reelection and was impressed with Brennan's résumé: that of an Irish Catholic state court judge from the Northeast. Even better, Brennan was a Democrat, and Eisenhower was concerned about the need for a bipartisan Supreme Court, his two prior appointments both being Republicans: John Marshall Harlan II, a U.S. Court of Appeals judge for the Second Circuit in New York, and Earl Warren, an extraordinarily successful lawyer-politician who had been elected governor of California three times—once with no opposition.

Vanderbilt was delighted for Brennan and personally wrote to the president informing Eisenhower that, in more than forty years in the legal profession, Brennan was "the finest judicial mind" that he had ever encountered.[26] Vanderbilt's own name had been mentioned several times: first, in connection with Thomas Dewey, unsuccessful candidate for president in 1944 and 1948, then again upon the deaths of Chief Justice Fred Vinson in 1953, Justice Robert Jackson in 1954, and Justice Sherman Minton in 1956. However, because of "his age and rapidly failing stamina,"[27] combined with his belief that he could do more to advance reform as chief justice of New Jersey than starting over as an associate U.S. Supreme Court justice, he asked that his name not be considered.

More revealing was a confidential letter in 1954 to his friend Alexander Holtzoff, a federal judge who had encouraged him to permit his name to be considered by Eisenhower's staff when Justice Robert Jackson passed away. According to the letter, Newark's Warrior Lawyer wasn't prepared to play second fiddle to anyone. He explained to Holtzoff that for thirty-four years he had run his own law practice, sans partners, and for twenty-five of those years had served as Essex County counsel, receiving assistance exclusively from associates in his law firm, refusing to permit the appointment of an "assistant" county counsel "because I knew he would be sure to get in the way." He also recounted his roles with Clean Government and NYU's law school, explaining that while he had "plenty of advice . . . the ultimate decisions [were] my own." Going to Washington and being one of nine instead of first among seven wasn't something he relished. "It was very hard for me to learn to work in harness, but I think that all of my colleagues will grant that I have practiced the art of cooperation without deviation. I should doubt very much, however, my capacity to do so elsewhere."[28]

With Brennan off to Washington, and his heir apparent gone, with little more than two years remaining until his mandatory retirement at age seventy, Vanderbilt's seven-day-per-week schedule of reading legal briefs, writing opinions, and overseeing the administration of the courts was taking its toll on his health. He wasn't good at delegating tasks to others. The job was working him; he wasn't working the job. What's more, his personality didn't allow him to turn down invitations to speak at law school symposiums, judicial conferences, and bar association meetings, most requiring extensive travel. The correspondence relating to his many speaking engagements for court reform after becoming chief justice is much like reviewing his client list from 1935 on those crinkly carbon-paper pages; it's a marvel that he could do it all, but there's no doubt it took a toll on his health.

Vanderbilt didn't have much use for doctors and kept his own counsel when it came to his health. Even after his stroke in 1947, there was little that Floss or family members could do to slow him down. Despite his promise to work only "eight hours four days, four hours two days, and nothing on the seventh,"[29] that was not to be. He pushed himself beyond reason. He neither drank nor smoked nor had a weight problem, but he got little physical exercise and maintained a regimen that would have fatigued men half his age. By his own admission, he refused to "cut down on my outside activities . . . for fear of drying up."[30]

A national figure for more than two decades, Vanderbilt feared becoming irrelevant and "drying up" so much that he exerted himself to the point of damaging his health. People close to Vanderbilt saw his decline and worried; one of them wrote to him from Washington. The occasion was one of the few for which he suggested to the dean of a law school that U.S. Supreme Court Justice William J. Brennan would make an able substitute graduation speaker. Writing to Vanderbilt to acknowledge that he would be his replacement at the commencement ceremony Brennan said:

My Dear Chief:

Of course I understand; and I really wish you would make it a standard practice not to succumb to the temptation of accepting any of these invitations. You have so many important things to do that you must think of preserving your strength for them and not dissipating it on such other occasions.

Sincerely,

Bill[31]

Within ninety days of receiving the letter from Brennan, Vanderbilt's strength was dissipated beyond restoration. The tank of endless energy that seemed to never empty finally had. On the evening of Thursday, June 13, 1957, the chief justice spoke at a testimonial dinner for Judge Frank Cleary of Union County—one of the few judges from the old system who had vocally supported constitutional reform. Vanderbilt's voice was so weak that dinner guests had difficulty hearing him. He was too tired to drive himself, and Justice Nathan Jacobs and Judge Alfred Clapp, his friends and allies of many years, drove him home at the end of the evening. The next morning, as ever, he drove to the Short Hills railroad station to catch the 7:23 train. As he drove into the parking lot he was stricken. Keeping his wits about him, he pulled the emergency brake and pressed the horn, coming to a stop as he slumped over the steering wheel. Other commuters called for help, and within minutes he was rushed to the Overlook Hospital in nearby Summit.

Over the next sixty-six hours he was mostly comatose, lying on a hospital bed in an oxygen tent, receiving nourishment through an intravenous tube. On Saturday morning he rallied long enough to ask for his secretary, to whom he dictated a legal opinion on which he had been working; moments later he fell briefly back into a coma, then revived and faltered several times until the end came in the early morning hours of Sunday, June 16, three weeks shy of his sixty-ninth birthday. His accomplishments could fill the biographies of several people. Days later, when he was laid to rest, numerous dignitaries, judges, politicians, fraternity brothers, clients, business associates, longtime adversaries, and friends from across the nation were on hand. But for his heartbroken wife, Floss, and their children, the saddest person in attendance at Christ Church in Short Hills had to be the frail eighty-five-year-old Frank Sommer, who had lived long enough to see his star pupil leave the world before him.

Among the nation's many state supreme court justices over the past two centuries, Chief Justice Arthur T. Vanderbilt of New Jersey stands alone. He consciously set about to alter the status quo by charting a new course for America's courts and had remarkable success. Throughout his career, he had a deep appreciation for the impact of judges' decisions upon the workings of society. Vanderbilt saw the mission of America's courts as being one of protecting and expanding individual liberties. He understood that America is an experiment in freedom and believed that in a dynamic society such as ours the legal system has a never-ending responsibility to adapt to an ever-changing social landscape. For Vanderbilt, there were no final answers for the workings of our courts and their role in American society, nor were there any immutable truths. He believed that the law must grow and evolve with the human condition to ensure that the people who come before the courts are treated fairly. Arthur Vanderbilt knew that at the end of day, the rule of law is the one indispensable cornerstone of a free, civilized society.

Frank Hague had a more primal notion of justice: there had to be retribution for the war waged upon his tribe. For him, the rule of law was about revenge. Once Hague had control of New Jersey's politics he exploited that control for all it was worth, easing the path of immigrants into American society and humiliating the WASPs each election day. The scale on which he both accumulated a financial fortune and garnered political power made him one of the most accomplished sixth-grade dropouts ever.

Shadows cast by large figures in history change shape over time depending on the angle of light cast over them. Vanderbilt and Hague—and the battles they waged—illustrate this metaphor well. Only now can we see the extent to which they breathed and bled for their visions of the world, remaining steadfast in their aims and tireless in their pursuits. In their own inimitable ways, Vanderbilt and Hague fulfilled their destinies and left large footprints in our nation's history. Nonetheless, two generations after their passing, both are all but forgotten by mainstream America. Hague is fictionalized in a bit part in a television series and Vanderbilt, when mentioned, is frequently mistaken for an heir of the railroad tycoon. Yet both men's greatness continues to be felt, in ways large and small.

Thanks to *The Boss*, Hague's name is synonymous with political corruption; in turn, for many people, political corruption is synonymous with New Jersey. Yet other portions of Hague's legacy include tens of thousands of babies born on clean sheets in a first-rate hospital and a generous hand lent to a generation of newcomers, helping them and their families to make their way in a strange land. Frank Hague was a complicated and flawed person, yet few people have wielded power as skillfully as he did. Given his start in the Horseshoe, he has no peer in American history.

And while Vanderbilt's uncompromising nature and his hatred for Frank Hague reveal an equally complicated and flawed person, that's hardly the measure of the man. More than half a century after his passing, the NYU Law Center he established has flourished and expanded its mission in ways that do Vanderbilt proud. His legacy from his years on the bench is that the New

Jersey judiciary remains one of the most highly regarded state court systems in America. In terms of its decisions being followed by other state courts, it is one of the more influential in our nation. To this day, judges and scholars travel from foreign countries to study how New Jersey's court system operates. If there were a hall of fame for judges, Vanderbilt would be a member.

Sports fans frequently debate which of the great athletes of the past could compete in today's world. Often there are players whose accomplishments put them in a league of their own, likely to excel regardless of when they played. So it is for Arthur Vanderbilt and Frank Hague: their brilliance, tenacity, and personal confidence would have enabled them to triumph in today's world. They would assess the situation, determine whence power flowed, and promptly plot a path for taking control. Vanderbilt and Hague were giants for their time and any time, two of America's last great power brokers. Their like won't be seen again anytime soon.

NOTES

PROLOGUE

1. The 1937 gubernatorial election generated two report decisions, both written by New Jersey Supreme Court Justice Thomas Brogan. Those cases are *Lester H. Clee, Contestant v. A. Harry Moore, Incumbent* 119 N.J.L. 215 (1937) and *In The Matter of the Petition of Lester H. Clee, to Contest the Election of A. Harry Moore, as Governor* 119 N.J.L.310 (1938).

2. Alan V. Lowenstein, "The Legacy of Arthur T. Vanderbilt to the New Jersey Bar," 51 *Rutgers Law Review* 1319 at 1321 (1999).

CHAPTER 1 — SADIE'S SAGA

1. The case law on Sadie Urback's claim is epic. See the decisions in *Metropolitan Life Ins. Co. v. Urback* at 127 N.J. Eq. 253 (E&A, 1940) 127 N.J.L. 585 (E&A, 1942), 130 N.J.L. 210 (E&A, 1943) 138 N.J. Eq. (E&A, 1946).

2. Ibid.

3. Ibid.

4. See "Politics and the Colonial Courts: 1704–1716," an essay by Edwin T. Tanner (1908), one of a collection of essays contained in *Jersey Justice: Three Hundred Years of the New Jersey Judiciary*, ed. Carla Vivian Bello and Arthur T. Vanderbilt II (Newark: New Jersey Institute for Continuing Legal Education, 1978).

5. There are many excellent biographies and accounts of Franklin's career. The two I found helpful in my research because of their discussion of the relationship between Benjamin and William are the biographies by Edmund S. Morgan and Walter Isaacson: Morgan, *Benjamin Franklin* (New Haven, CT: Yale University Press, 2002), and Isaacson, *Benjamin Franklin: An American Life* (New York: Simon & Schuster, 2003).

6. Thomas Fleming, *New Jersey: A History* (New York: W. W. Norton, 1977), 54. Fleming is a New Jersey treasure. A native of Frank Hague's Jersey City, he is nationally renowned for his many fine historical works. This concise history provides valuable perspective on modern New Jersey.

7. Ibid., 55.

8. Isaacson, *Benjamin Franklin*, 322.

9. Kermit W. Smith, "The Politics of Judicial Reform in New Jersey" (Ph.D. diss., Princeton University, 1964), 13, quoting John Bebout, "Introduction," *Proceedings of the New Jersey State Constitutional Convention of 1844*, xvii.

10. James Madison, *The Federalist Papers*, no. 47.

11. There is an excellent discussion of the 1844 Constitution in Frederick Herrmann, "The Constitution of 1844 and Political Change in Antebellum New Jersey," *New Jersey History* 101, nos. 1–2 (Spring/Summer 1983): 30.

12. Arthur T. Vanderbilt II, *Order in the Courts: A Biography of Arthur T. Vanderbilt* (New Brunswick: New Jersey Institute for Continuing Legal Education, 1997), 81. Art Vanderbilt is a wealth of information on his grandfather and New Jersey history.

13. Herrmann, "The Constitution of 1844," 35.

14. Vanderbilt II, *Order in the Courts*, 80.

15. Ibid.

16. Ibid.

17. Wilson's time as New Jersey governor is handled well in Barbara Salmore and Stephen Salmore, *New Jersey Politics: The Suburbs Come of Age* (New Brunswick, NJ: Rutgers University Press, 2008).

CHAPTER 2 — ROSEVILLE'S PRODIGY

1. Interview with Arthur T. Vanderbilt II.

2. Frank J. Urquhart, *A History of the City of Newark, New Jersey: Embracing Practically Two and a Half Centuries, 1666–1913* (New York: Lewis Historical Publishing, 1913). This work was very helpful in "grounding" me in the founding and development of early Newark. The narrative and quotes concerning "old Newark" included in chapters 2 and 3 of this book are found on pages 30–43, 64–69, and 75–80.

3. Ibid.

4. John T. Cunningham, *Newark* (Newark: New Jersey Historical Society, 1966; revised and expanded by author in 1988), 240.

5. Interview with Vanderbilt II.

6. Ibid.

7. Jennie B. Johnson, author's mother.

8. Arthur T. Vanderbilt to Mrs. R. N. Crane, February 8, 1952, as shared by Mrs. Crane with ATV II.

9. Arthur T. Vanderbilt's scrapbook, box 1, Arthur T. Vanderbilt Papers, Olin Library, Wesleyan University, Middletown, Connecticut. Hereafter Vanderbilt Papers.

10. ATV to Wayland Stearn, April 10, 1913, box 4, Vanderbilt Papers.

11. http://www.wesleyan.edu/president/pastpresidents/fisk.html.

12. Vanderbilt to Samuel H. Brockunier, February 12, 1945, box 14, Vanderbilt Papers.

13. Arthur T. Vanderbilt, "The Primary Responsibility of College Today," *Association of American Colleges* 32 (October 1946): 370.

14. *Seventy-Five Years of Gamma Phi* [at Wesleyan University], ed. James E. Stiles (1942), 227.

15. A brief sketch of Sommer is contained in Eugene C. Gerhart, *Arthur T. Vanderbilt: The Compleat Counsellor* (Albany, NY: Q Corporation, 1980), 18. Gerhart was a Vanderbilt acolyte and his self-published work contains many gems on ATV's career.

16. http://www.law.nyu.edu/students/studentawards.

17. Sommer's role with Woodrow Wilson is discussed in Arthur T. Vanderbilt II, *Order in the Courts: A Biography of Arthur T. Vanderbilt* (New Brunswick: New Jersey Institute for Continuing Legal Education, 1997), 12.

18. Ibid.

19. Interview with Vanderbilt II.

20. Vanderbilt II, *Order in the Courts*, 14.

21. Ibid., 14-15.

22. Ibid., 15.

23. Ibid.

24. Vanderbilt speech at the presentation of Sommer's portrait at NYU Law School, April 24, 1950, box 263, Vanderbilt Papers.

25. Gerhart, *Arthur T. Vanderbilt*, 43.

26. 208 U.S. 412 (1908).

27. 277 U.S. 438 (1928).

28. 304 U.S. 64 (1938).

29. Vanderbilt speech at NYU Law Alumni Dinner, February 10, 1948, box 279, Vanderbilt Papers.

30. Gerhart, *Arthur T. Vanderbilt*, 22.

31. Vanderbilt, "From Where I Sit," *Bar Examiner* 25 (1956): 3, box 267, Vanderbilt Papers.

CHAPTER 3 — THE LAWYER AS PUBLIC PERSON

1. *Selected Writings of Arthur T. Vanderbilt*, ed. F. J. Klein and J. S. Lee (Dobbs Ferry, NY: Oceana Publications, 1965), 19-21.

2. Ibid.

3. Ibid.

4. Eugene C. Gerhart, *Arthur T. Vanderbilt: The Compleat Counsellor* (Albany, NY: Q Corporation, 1980), 58.

5. *Newark Evening News*, December 13-29, 1917; T. H. Reed, *Twenty Years of Government in Essex County, N.J.* (New York: D. Appleton-Century, 1938), 47.

6. James K. Shields to Arthur T. Vanderbilt, February 18, 1919, box 81, Vanderbilt Papers.

7. Reed, *Twenty Years of Government*, 59.

8. Gerhart, *Arthur T. Vanderbilt*, 62.

9. Vanderbilt speech, November 3, 1947, upon retiring as Essex County Counsel, box 281, Vanderbilt Papers.

10. Gerhart, *Arthur T. Vanderbilt*, 66.

11. *Newark Evening News*, May 10, 1920.

12. Ibid.

13. Gerhart, *Arthur T. Vanderbilt*, 62.

14. Ibid., 64.

15. Vanderbilt to Judge A. Holtzoff, October 18, 1954, box 194, Vanderbilt Papers.

16. Reed, *Twenty Years of Government*, 62-63.

17. Vanderbilt II, *Order in the Courts*, 40.

18. Ibid., 41.

19. Vanderbilt, "From Where I Sit."

CHAPTER 4 — A FORCE IN FOUR WORLDS

1. Roger Baldwin's involvement in Paterson is discussed by Samuel Walker, *In Defense of American Liberties: A History of the ACLU* (New York: Oxford University Press, 1990), 77–79.

2. Thomas Fleming, *New Jersey: A History* (New York: W. W. Norton, 1977), 161, 162.

3. See *New Jersey v. Butterworth* 104 N.J.L. 43 (1927).

4. Ibid.

5. Ibid.

6. Walker, *In Defense of American Liberties*, 78.

7. Ibid.

8. Arthur T. Vanderbilt II, *Order in the Courts: A Biography of Arthur T. Vanderbilt* (New Brunswick: New Jersey Institute for Continuing Legal Education, 1977), 52.

9. Ibid.

10. 104 N.J.L. 43.

11. Eugene C. Gerhart, *Arthur T. Vanderbilt: The Compleat Counsellor* (Albany, NY: Q Corporation, 1980), 37.

12. Ibid., 30.

13. Vanderbilt II, *Order in the Courts*, 23.

14. Client list, box 26, Vanderbilt Papers.

15. Ibid.

16. Robert H. McCarter's book, *Memories of a Half Century at the New Jersey Bar*, was published by the New Jersey Bar Association in 1937. His slight of Vanderbilt is commented upon by Gerhart, *Arthur T. Vanderbilt*, 42.

17. http://www.law.harvard.edu/about/history.html.

18. Vanderbilt, county counsel retirement speech, box 281, Vanderbilt Papers.

19. Vanderbilt II, *Order in the Courts*, 24.

20. Ibid.

21. Vanderbilt, county counsel retirement speech.

22. Richard J. Connors, *The Process of Constitutional Revision in New Jersey: 1940–47* (New York: National Municipal League, 1970), 10.

23. Vanderbilt II, *Order in the Courts*, 43.

24. Interview with Vanderbilt II.

25. Ibid.

26. Vanderbilt II, *Order in the Courts*, 44.

27. John Parker, "The Federal Judiciary," *Tulane Law Review* 22 (1948): 575.

28. Vanderbilt II, *Order in the Courts*, 118.

29. Richard Hofstadter, *The Age of Reform* (New York: Vintage Books, 1955), 9.

30. Gerhart, *Arthur T. Vanderbilt*, 50.

31. Nucky Thompson in *Boardwalk Empire*, season one, episode one (HBO), September 2010

32. Vanderbilt II, *Order in the Courts*, 57.

33. Ibid.

34. Arthur T. Vanderbilt to Hendon Chubb, December 26, 1934, box 85, Vanderbilt Papers.

35. Interview with Vanderbilt II

36. Vanderbilt II, *Order in the Courts*, 61.

37. Gerhart, *Arthur T. Vanderbilt*, 71.

38. T. H. Reed, *Twenty Years of Government in Essex County, N.J.* (New York: D. Appleton-Century, 1938), 56.

CHAPTER 5 — UP FROM THE HORSESHOE

1. Douglas V. Shaw, "The Making of an Immigrant City: Ethnic and Cultural Conflict in Jersey City, New Jersey" (Ph.D. diss., University of Rochester, 1972), 11.

2. *New York Times,* August 21, 1870.

3. Shaw, "The Making of an Immigrant City," 52.

4. Ibid., 57.

5. Ibid., 61.

6. Ibid., 169.

7. Ibid.

8. Ibid., 205.

9. Quoted in ibid., 219.

10. Ibid.

11. Quoted in ibid., 238.

12. Quoted in ibid., 241.

13. Steven Hart, *The Last Three Miles: Politics, Murder, and the Construction of America's First Superhighway* (New York: The New Press, 2007), 37.

14. Ibid., 39.

15. David Dayton McKean, *The Boss: The Hague Machine in Action* (Boston: Houghton Mifflin, 1940), 8.

16. Interview with Richard Jackson, former mayor of Atlantic City, one of the "Atlantic City Seven" and longtime member of the Nucky Johnson–Hap Farley political ward organization that ruled Atlantic City for seventy-five years.

17. McKean, *The Boss*, 35.

18. Hart, *The Last Three Miles*, 45.

19. Ibid.

20. Ibid.

21. Bob Leach, *How Frank Hague Became a Hero: A Tale of Derring-Do* (Jersey City: Jersey City Public Library, 1995), is an excellent historical study of the Rombolo murder of Frank Kenny written by a local Jersey City historian.

22. Ibid., 24.

23. Ibid., 28.

24. Ibid., 32.

25. Ibid., 31.

26. The Edge–Colgate primary and Nucky Johnson's role in maneuvering Hague to support Edge is discussed in Nelson Johnson, *Boardwalk Empire: The Birth, High Times and Corruption of Atlantic City* (Medford, NJ: Plexus Publishing, 2002), chapter 6.

27. Alfred Steinberg, *The Bosses* (New York: Macmillan, 1972), 40.

28. Ibid.

29. Ibid., 41.

30. Clayton W. Gilbert, *Newark Evening News,* October 21, 1925. Hague's determination to squeeze the railroads is also discussed in McKean, *The Boss*, and Steinberg, *The Bosses*.

CHAPTER 6 — THE CELTIC CHIEFTAIN

1. Thomas Fleming, *Mysteries of My Father: An Irish-American Memoir* (New York: John Wiley & Sons, 2005), 213.

2. Frank Hague and Nucky Johnson's role in the 1928 election is discussed in chapter 5 of Nelson Johnson, *Boardwalk Empire: The Birth, High Times, and Corruption of Atlantic City* (Medford, NJ: Plexus Publishing, 2002).

3. Ibid.

4. Leonard F. Vernon, *The Life & Times of Jersey City Mayor Frank Hague: "I Am the Law"* (Charleston, SC: History Press, 2011). A copy of the letter is reproduced in that book's appendix, 136.

5. David Dayton McKean, *The Boss: The Hague Machine in Action* (Boston: Houghton Mifflin, 1940), 107–116.

6. Ibid.

7. Ibid.

8. See *In Re: Frank Hague,* 103 N.J. Eq. 505 (1928).

9. Ibid.

10. Ibid.

11. Ibid.

12. 381 U.S. 479 (1965).

13. James T. Fisher, *On the Irish Waterfront: The Crusader, the Movie, and the Soul of the Port of New York* (Ithaca, NY: Cornell University Press, 2009), 38.

14. Ibid.

15. Ibid., 39.

16. Clayton Gilbert, *New York Evening Post,* October 23, 1925.

17. Fisher, *On the Irish Waterfront,* 36.

18. Gilbert, *New York Evening Post,* October 23, 1925.

19. Walter Evans Edge, *A Jerseyman's Journal* (Princeton, NJ: Princeton University Press, 1947), 257.

20. McKean, *The Boss,* 97.

21. Steven Hart, *The Last Three Miles: Politics, Murder, and the Construction of America's First Superhighway.* (New York: The New Press, 2007), 93.

22. Vernon, *The Life & Times of Jersey City Mayor Frank Hague,* 93.

23. Hart, *The Last Three Miles,* 93.

24. Eugene C. Gerhart, *Arthur T. Vanderbilt: The Compleat Counsellor* (Albany, NY: Q Corporation, 1980), 149.

25. Paul A. Stellhorn, biographical profile of Harold G. Hoffman, contained in a collection of profiles of the governors in the New Jersey State Library Bureau of Archives and History, Trenton, 2005.

26. Alfred A. Steinberg, *The Bosses* (New York: Collier Macmillan, 1972) 59.

CHAPTER 7 — CLEAN GOVERNMENT VERSUS HAGUEISM

1. Vanderbilt's archives in box 96 at the Olin Library at Wesleyan University reveal that Clee was an ally and member of Clean Government from the early years.

2. Arthur T. Vanderbilt II, *Order in the Courts: A Biography of Arthur T. Vanderbilt* (New Brunswick: New Jersey Institute for Continuing Legal Education, 1977), 72–73.

3. *Newark Evening News,* November 5, 1937, 1.

4. David Dayton McKean, *The Boss: The Hague Machine in Action* (Boston: Houghton Mifflin Company, 1940), 84–88, and Richard J. Connors, *A Cycle of Power: The Career of Jersey City Mayor Frank Hague* (Metuchen, NJ: Scarecrow Press, 1971), 115–117.

5. McKean, *The Boss,* 84–88.

6. *Lester H. Clee, Contestant v. A. Harry Moore, Incumbent,* 119 NJL 215, 218 (1937).

7. *In The Matter of the Petition of Lester H. Clee, to Contest the Election of A. Harry Moore, as Governor,* 119 NJL 310, 322 (1938).

8. Ibid., 325.

9. Ibid., 326.

10. Ibid., 330.

11. Steven Hart, *The Last Three Miles: Politics, Murder, and the Construction of America's First Superhighway* (New York: The New Press, 2007, 94).

12. *Newark Evening News,* November 23, 1937, 1.

13. *Hague, et al. v. The CIO,* 101 F. 2d 774, 778 (1939).

14. *The CIO, et al. v. Hague, Mayor, et al.,* 25 F. Supp. 127 (1938).

15. *Hague, et al. v. The CIO,* 307 U.S. 496, 505 (1939).

16. Ibid.

17. Ibid., 513.

18. Ibid., 516.

19. 125 NJL 185, 192 (1938).

20. *Norman Thomas v. Daniel Casey,* 123 NJL 447 (1939).

CHAPTER 8 — BOX 96: ARTHUR AND DAVID

1. David Dayton McKean, *The Boss: The Hague Machine in Action* (Boston: Houghton Mifflin Company, 1940).

2. Arthur Vanderbilt to Ralph Bischoff, December 10, 1940, box 96, Vanderbilt Papers.

3. Box 96 of the Vanderbilt Papers at Olin Library confirms that Arthur Vanderbilt was a major contributor to the preparation of the book, worthy of being called a coauthor.

4. Interview with Judge Clapp by Eugene C. Gerhart as recounted on page 63 of Gerhart, *Arthur T. Vanderbilt: The Compleat Counsellor* (Albany, NY: Q Corporation, 1980).

5. Vanderbilt to David McKean, March 7, 1940, box 96, Vanderbilt Papers.

6. Vanderbilt to McKean, March 14, 1940, box 96, Vanderbilt Papers.

7. Ibid.

8. Vanderbilt to McKean, February 21, 1940, box 96, Vanderbilt Papers.

9. McKean to Vanderbilt, April 6, 1940, box 96, Vanderbilt Papers.

10. Vanderbilt to McKean, April 13, 1940, box 96, Vanderbilt Papers.

11. McKean to Vanderbilt, March 11, 1940, box 96, Vanderbilt Papers.

12. McKean, *The Boss,* 166.

13. Ibid.

14. Ibid., 63.

15. Ibid., 109.

16. The five decisions comprising the litigation are: *Ex Parte Hague,* 103 NJ Eq.

505(Ch.1928); 104 NJ Eq. 31(Ch.1929); 104 NJ Eq. 369 (E&A 1930); 105 NJ Eq. 134 (Ch. 1929); and 123 NJ Eq. 475 (E&A 1930).

17. 123 NJ Eq. 475, 479 (E&A 1930).

18. McKean to Vanderbilt, August 24, 1940, box 96, Vanderbilt Papers.

19. Memorandum, Dominic A. Cavicchia to Vanderbilt [undated], box 96, Vanderbilt Papers.

20. Ibid.

21. "Acknowledgement of Order," from Burelle's Press Clipping Bureau, Inc., October 5, 1940, box 96, Vanderbilt Papers.

22. *Trenton Times,* October 3, 1940.

CHAPTER 9 — THE INVENTOR'S SON

1. John D. Venable, *Out of the Shadow: The Story of Charles Edison* (Dorrance & Company, 1978), 116.

2. Ibid.

3. John T. Cunningham, *Newark* (Newark: New Jersey Historical Society, 1966), 177.

4. John D. Venable, *Out of the Shadow: The Story of Charles Edison* (Philadelphia: Dorrance, 1978), 25.

5. Ibid., 45.

6. Ibid., 46.

7. Ibid., 55.

8. Edna St. Vincent Millay, *A Few Figs from Thistles* (New York: Harper, 1920).

9. Venable, *Out of the Shadow,* 57.

10. Ibid., 165–166.

11. Ibid., 164.

12. Ibid., 166.

13. Ibid.

14. Ibid., 169.

15. Ibid., viii.

16. Ibid.

17. Charles Edison, address to New Brunswick Regional League of Women Voters, September 30, 1943.

18. Ibid., quoting from the Gilbert and Sullivan comic opera, *Iolanthe,* or *The Peer and the Peri* (1882).

19. Ibid.

20. *New Jersey Law Journal* 64, July 3, 1941, 332.

21. Arthur T. Vanderbilt II, *Order in the Courts: A Biography of Arthur T. Vanderbilt* (New Brunswick: New Jersey Institute for Continuing Legal Education, 1977), 123.

22. Quoted in ibid., 124.

23. William Evans, *New Jersey Law Journal* 64, March 20, 1941, 132.

24. Robert Carey, *New Jersey Law Journal* 64, July 31, 1941, 368.

25. Vanderbilt II, *Order in the Courts,* 126.

26. Arthur T. Vanderbilt to Robert Vanderbilt [his son], November 24, 1943, box 378, Vanderbilt Papers.

27. *In Re: Borg,* 131 N.J.L. 104 (Sup. Ct. 1944).

CHAPTER 10 — THE ARCHBISHOP SHOWS HIS GRATITUDE

1. Nicholas Turse, "Vote No: Archbishop Walsh, the Catholic Church, and the New Jersey Constitution," *Journal of the Rutgers University Libraries* 59 (2000): 25–52. The note read as follows: "We would ask you to read the enclosed important announcement, Sunday, November 5, without comment or explanation. Should you be asked the reason or source of the announcement your answer should be: 'No comment.' This letter is personal and confidential to you. T.J.W."

2. Ibid., 51.

3. Ibid., 38.

4. Ibid., 39.

5. Ibid.

6. Ibid., 38.

7. Ibid.

8. Ibid., 39.

9. Ibid., 40.

10. Richard J. Connors, *The Process of Constitutional Revision in New Jersey* (New York: National Municipal League, 1970), 98.

11. Ibid., 99.

12. Ibid.

13. *Everson v. B.O.E. of Ewing Township,* 132 N.J.L. 98 (1944) decision reversed by U.S. Supreme Court at 330 U.S. 1 (1947).

14. Turse, "Vote No," 41.

15. Ibid.

16. Walter E. Edge, *A Jerseyman's Journal* (Princeton, NJ: Princeton University Press, 1948), 283.

17. Ibid.

18. Turse, "Vote No," 51.

19. Ibid., 52.

20. Thomas Fleming, "The Political Machine: A Case History, "I Am the Law," *American Heritage* 20, no. 4 (June 1969).

21. Turse, "Vote No," 42.

22. Ibid.

23. Ibid.

24. Ibid., 43

25. Ibid.

26. Connors, *Process of Constitutional Revision,* 103.

27. Ibid., 105.

28. Turse, "Vote No," 49.

CHAPTER 11 — HADDONFIELD'S MENSCH

1. Alvin Felzenberg, "The Impact of Style on Policy Outcome: An In Depth Study of Three New Jersey Governors" (Ph.D. diss., Princeton University, 1978), 129.

2. Ibid.

3. Ibid.

4. Interview with Toni Vieleher, granddaughter of Alfred Driscoll, autumn 2013.

5. Ibid.

6. Walter E. Edge, *A Jerseyman's Journal* (Princeton, NJ: Princeton University Press, 1948), 295.

7. Felzenberg, "The Impact of Style on Policy Outcome," 126.

8. Ibid., 155.

9. Ibid., 126.

10. Governor Driscoll's inaugural address, Trenton, January 21, 1947.

11. Richard J. Connors, *The Process of Constitutional Revision in New Jersey* (New York: National Municipal League, 1970), 119.

12. Driscoll's inaugural address.

13. Ibid.

14. The transfer of power from Johnson to Farley is discussed in Nelson Johnson, *Boardwalk Empire: The Birth, High Times, and Corruption of Atlantic City* (Medford, MA: Plexus Publishing, 2002), chapter 7.

15. Connors, *Process of Constitutional Revision*, p.

16. Ibid., 125.

17. Interview with Arthur T. Vanderbilt II.

CHAPTER 12 — THINGS GET CURIOUS

1. Alan V. Lowenstein, "The Legacy of Arthur T. Vanderbilt to the New Jersey Bar," 51 *Rutgers Law Review* 1335 (1999).

2. Ibid.

3. Richard J. Connors, *The Process of Constitutional Revision in New Jersey* (New York: National Municipal League, 1970), 127.

4. Ibid., 128.

5. Arthur T. Vanderbilt II, *Order in the Courts: A Biography of Arthur T. Vanderbilt* (New Brunswick: New Jersey Institute for Continuing Legal Education, 1977), 132.

6. Ibid., 137.

7. Arthur T. Vanderbilt to Evelyn Seufert, May 11, 1946, box 38, Vanderbilt Papers.

8. Vanderbilt to Herbert Sims, July 7, 1947, box 18, Vanderbilt Papers.

9. Ibid.

10. Richard J. Connors, *A Cycle of Power: The Career of Jersey City Mayor Frank Hague* (Metuchen, NJ: Scarecrow Press, 1971), 158.

11. Ibid., 159.

12. Ibid., 161.

13. Ibid., 162.

14. Ibid.

15. Ibid., 163.

16. Ibid.

17. *Newark Sunday Call*, September 22, 1946, 4.

18. Connors, *Cycle of Power*, 164.

19. Ibid., 169.

20. Ibid.

21. Connors, *Process of Constitutional Revision*, 122.

22. Ibid., 123.

23. Ibid.

CHAPTER 13 — SUMMER AT RUTGERS

1. Interview with Arthur T. Vanderbilt II.

2. Ibid.

3. Ibid.

4. Ibid.

5. The transcripts of the proceedings of the 1947 Constitutional Convention at Rutgers in July through September can be accessed by the public at the New Jersey State Library's website: njstatelib.org/new_jersey_information/digital_collections/new_jersey_constitution. Hereafter cited as CC Transcripts.

6. Richard J. Connors, *The Process of Constitutional Revision in New Jersey* (New York: National Municipal League, 1970), 131.

7. Alan V. Lowenstein, "The Legacy of Arthur T. Vanderbilt to the New Jersey Bar," 51 *Rutgers Law Review* 1321, 1336 (1999).

8. Connors, *Process of Constitutional Revision*, 133.

9. Ibid., 134.

10. Ibid., 135.

11. Ibid.

12. Quoted in ibid.

13. CC Transcripts, 1:6.

14. Ibid.

15. Ibid., 1:7.

16. Ibid.

17. Ibid.

18. Ibid.

19. Connors, *Process of Constitutional Revision*, 162–166.

20. *Jersey Journal*, July 25, 1947, 1.

21. Connors, *Process of Constitutional Revision*, 166.

22. Ibid.

23. CC Transcripts, 1:766.

24. CC Transcripts, 4:729.

25. Leo Yanoff, "Justice Nathan L. Jacobs: Prelude to a Judicial Career," 28 *Rutgers Law Review* 213, 244 (1974–1975).

26. Ibid.

27. CC Transcripts, 4:396.

28. Ibid.

29. Ibid.

30. Ibid.

31. Lowenstein, "Legacy of Arthur T. Vanderbilt," 1337.

CHAPTER 14 — THE CHIEF

1. Address by Dr. Harry W. Chase at the NYU Law Center Cornerstone Celebration, January 31, 1950.

2. "Arthur T. Vanderbilt: Chief Justice of the New Jersey Supreme Court," *ABA Journal* 35 (1949): 791.

3. Arthur T. Vanderbilt II, *Order in the Courts: A Biography of Arthur T. Vanderbilt* (New Brunswick: New Jersey Institute for Continuing Legal Education, 1977), 166.

4. Ibid.

5. Ibid., 178.

6. Arthur T. Vanderbilt thank-you note to Driscoll, along with a discussion of the four bills vetoed, discussed in Voorhees E. Dunn Jr., "Chief Justice Arthur T. Vanderbilt and the Judicial Revolution in New Jersey (Ph.D. diss., Rutgers University, 1987), 176–182.

7. Vanderbilt II, *Order in the Courts*, 177.

8. Ibid., 176.

9. Ibid., 177.

10. Vanderbilt, "New Rules of the Supreme Court on the Argument and Deciding of Appeals," *New Jersey Law Journal* 71 (March 18, 1948): 2, 4.

11. Vanderbilt II, *Order in the Courts*, 170.

12. Ibid.

13. Vanderbilt, "Some Principles of Judicial Administration," speech delivered to California State Bar Association, October 5, 1950.

14. Vanderbilt II, *Order in the Courts*, 183.

15. Ibid.

16. Ibid., 181.

17. Ibid., 192.

18. Ibid.

19. Ibid., 194.

20. Vanderbilt to Anthony P. Savarese, January 19, 1949, box 195, Vanderbilt Papers.

21. Ibid.

22. Owen Grundy, foreword to William Lemmy, "The Kenny Era," Jersey City Free Public Library (1977): N974-9J.

23. James T. Fisher, *On the Irish Waterfront: The Crusader, the Movie, and the Soul of the Port of New York* (Ithaca, NY: Cornell University Press, 2009), 38.

24. *Jersey Journal*, April 14, 1969. There is an excellent series of articles discussing the transition from Hague to Kenny (a twenty-year retrospective) by Marin Gately of the *Jersey Journal*.

25. *Jersey Journal*, April 15, 1969.

26. Ibid.

27. *Jersey Journal*, April 17, 1969.

28. *Jersey Journal*, April 29, 1969.

29. Ibid.

CHAPTER 15 — THE CHIEF SUPREME

1. Arthur T. Vanderbilt II, *Order in the Courts: A Biography of Arthur T. Vanderbilt* (New Brunswick: New Jersey Institute for Continuing Legal Education, 1977), 169.

2. The discussion of John Winberry's service as a D.A.G. is based upon the archival records of his litigation against the Middlesex County Grand Jury found Docket No. L-3797-48, Bate Stamp #s 5235 thru 5312.

3. Affidavit of Walter D. Van Riper, April 30, 1948.

4. Presentment of the Middlesex County Grand Jury, March 4, 1949.

5. 5 N.J. Super 30 (App. Div. 1949).

6. 5 N.J. 240 (1950)., 251.

7. Ibid., 244.

8. Ibid., 243

9. Ibid., 248.

10. Ibid., 256.

11. Ibid., 260.

12. Ibid., 265.

13. Vorhees E. Dunn Jr., "Chief Justice Arthur T. Vanderbilt and the Judicial Revolution in New Jersey" (Ph.D. diss., Rutgers University, 1987), 187–189.

14. Arthur T. Vanderbilt, "Our New Judicial Establishment: The Record of the First Year," 4 *Rutgers Law Review* 353, 363 (1950).

15. Vanderbilt II, *Order in the Courts*, 208.

16. Interview with Justice William J. Brennan Jr. by Arthur T. Vanderbilt II, Washington, D.C., January 28, 1972.

17. Vanderbilt II, *Order in the Courts*, 198.

18. Ibid., 199.

19. Vanderbilt quoting trial judge, *City of Jersey City v. Frank Hague, et al.*, 18 NJ 584, 600 (1955).

20. Ibid., 601.

21. Ibid., 590, quoting *Driscoll v. Burlington-Bristol Bridge Co.*, 8 NJ 433, 474.

22. Vanderbilt quoting the Plaintiff's Complaint, ibid., 589.

23. Ibid.

24. *Flint Frozen Foods, Inc. v. Firemen's Insurance Co. of N.J.*, 8 NJ 606, 611 (1952).

25. Thomas F. X. Smith, *The Powertricians* (Secaucus, NJ: Lyle Stuart, 1982), 180.

26. Vanderbilt II, *Order in the Courts*, 215.

27. Ibid.

28. Ibid.

29. Vanderbilt to W. Gordon Murphy, August 8, 1947, box 18, Vanderbilt Papers.

30. Vanderbilt memo, December 31, 1954, box 267, Vanderbilt Papers.

31. William J. Brennan Jr. to Vanderbilt March 20, 1957, box 199, Vanderbilt Papers.

BIBLIOGRAPHY

Connors, Richard J. *A Cycle of Power: The Career of Jersey City Mayor Frank Hague.* Metuchen, NJ: Scarecrow Press, 1971.

———. *The Process of Constitutional Revision in New Jersey.* New York: National Municipal League, 1970.

Cunningham, John T. *Newark.* Newark: New Jersey Historical Society, 1966.

Dunn, Vorhees E. Jr. "Chief Justice Arthur T. Vanderbilt and the Judicial Revolution in New Jersey." Ph.D. diss., Rutgers University, 1987.

Edge, Walter E. *A Jerseyman's Journal.* Princeton, NJ: Princeton University Press, 1948.

Felzenberg, Alvin. "The Impact of Style on Policy Outcome: An In Depth Study of Three New Jersey Governors." Ph.D. diss., Princeton University, 1978.

Fisher, James T. *On the Irish Waterfront: The Crusader, the Movie, and the Soul of the Port of New York.* Ithaca, NY: Cornell University Press, 2009.

Fleming, Thomas. *Mysteries of My Father: An Irish-American Memoir.* New York: John Wiley & Sons, 2005.

———. *New Jersey: A History.* New York: W. W. Norton, 1977.

———. The Political Machine: A Case History, "I Am the Law." *American Heritage Magazine,* June 1969.

Gerhart, Eugene C. *Arthur T. Vanderbilt: The Compleat Counsellor.* Albany, NY: Q Corporation, 1980.

Hart, Steven. *The Last Three Miles: Politics, Murder, and the Construction of America's First Superhighway.* New York: The New Press, 2007.

Hofstadter, Richard. *The Age of Reform.* New York: Vintage Books, 1955.

Isaacson, Walter. *Benjamin Franklin, An American Life.* New York: Simon & Schuster, 2003.

Johnson, Nelson. *Boardwalk Empire: The Birth, High Times, and Corruption of Atlantic City.* Medford, NJ: Plexus Publishing, 2002.

Leach, Bob. *How Frank Hague Became a Hero: A Tale of Derring-Do.* Jersey City: Jersey City Public Library, 1955.

Lowenstein, Alan V. "The Legacy of Arthur T. Vanderbilt to the New Jersey Bar." 51 *Rutgers Law* 1319 (1999).

McKean, David Dayton. *The Boss: The Hague Machine in Action.* Boston: Houghton Mifflin, 1940.

Morgan, Edmund S. *Benjamin Franklin.* New Haven, CT: Yale University Press, 2002.

Parker, John. "The Federal Judiciary." 22 *Tulane Law Review* 569–584 (1948).

Reed, T. H. *Twenty Years of Government in Essex County, N.J.* New York: D. Appleton-Century, 1938.

Salmore, Barbara, and Stephen Salmore. *New Jersey Politics: The Suburbs Come of Age.* New Brunswick, NJ: Rutgers University Press, 2008.

Shaw, Douglas V. "The Making of an Immigrant City: Ethnic and Cultural Conflict in Jersey City, New Jersey." Ph.D. diss., University of Rochester, 1972.

Smith, Kermit W. "The Politics of Judicial Reform in New Jersey." Ph.D. diss., Princeton University, 1964.

Steffens, Lincoln, *The Shame of the Cities.* New York: Hill and Wang, 1957. Originally published in 1904 BY McClure, Phillips and Company.

Steinberg, Alfred A., *The Bosses.* New York: Collier and Macmillan, 1972

Turse, Nicholas. "Vote No: Archbishop Walsh, the Catholic Church, and the new Jersey Constitution." *Journal of the Rutgers University Libraries* 59 (2000): 25–52.

Urquhart, Frank J. *A History of the City of Newark, New Jersey: Embracing Practically Two and A Half Centuries, 1666–1913.* New York: Lewis Historical Publishing Company, 1913.

Vanderbilt, Arthur T. II. *Order in the Courts: A Biography of Arthur T. Vanderbilt.* New Brunswick: New Jersey Institute for Continuing Legal Education, 1977.

VanDevander, Charles. *The Big Bosses.* New York: Howell and Soskin, 1944.

Venable, John D. *Out of the Shadow: The Story of Charles Edison.* Philadelphia: Dorrance, 1978.

Vernon, Leonard F. *The Life & Times of Jersey City Mayor Frank Hague: "I Am the Law."* Charleston, SC: History Press, 2011.

Walker, Samuel. *In Defense of American Liberties: A History of the ACLU.* New York: Oxford University Press, 1990.

Yanoff, Leo. "Justice Nathan L. Jacobs: Prelude to a Judicial Career." 28 *Rutgers Law Review* 213–225 (1974–1975).

INDEX

In Re: Borg, 140
In re Hague, 117–119
insurance law, 53
Irish, Jersey City, 66, 68–71; as Hague voting bloc, 85–86
Ironworkers Local 45, 105
Italian War Veterans, 108

Jackson, Andrew, 13
Jackson, Richard, 239n.16
Jacobs, Nathan L., 32, 52, 185, 188, 195–196, 231
Jamieson, Crawford, 136
Jayne, Wilfred, 134
Jersey City, 3, 37, 67; charter, 71–73, 79; Hague's City Hall New Year's ritual, 85; and the Roman Catholic Church, 80; tax assessments, 82 (*see also* railroads: property taxes)
Jersey City Charity Hospital, 96, 116–117
Jersey City Medical Center, 102, 105, 176
Jersey City Mission and Tract Society, 70
Jersey Journal, 77, 148, 178
A Jerseyman's Journal (Edge), 148
Johnson, Enoch "Nucky," 78, 86, 118, 120, 139, 167
judges: administrative accountability of, 207–208, 209; chancellor of equity, 13; of E & A, 13; justices of the peace, 13, 14–15, 198, 211; lay, 13, 15; professionalism of, 211–212; of state Supreme Court, 13
Judicial Council, 135
judicial reform, 158–159; and constitutional convention of 1947, 189, 195–199; legislative, of 1944, 140
Justice of the Peace courts, 16
Justices Court, 10
Juvenile and Domestic Relations Court, 16

Katzenbach, Marie, 187
Kean, Hamilton, 86
Kearney, James, Jr., 136
Kenny, Frank, 76–77, 177
Kenny, John V., 92, 180, 213–217
Kenny, Ned, 75, 77
Kerbaugh, H. S., 88–89
kickbacks, 91–92, 226–228. *See also* "rice pudding"
Knights of Columbus, 147
Know-Nothing Party, 70, 71

labor movement, 104–105. *See also individual labor organizations*
Ladies of the Grand Army of the Republic, 108

land: Hague's transactions in, 88–89; railroad, and taxation (*see* railroads: property taxes)
Lane, Merritt, 54, 90, 119
Langdell, Christopher Columbus, 53–54
Larson, Morgan, 86, 118, 203
lay judges, 15
Leach, Bob, 76
League of Women Voters, 143, 146, 147, 155, 171
legislative redistricting, 165
legislature: challenges state Supreme Court reform, 205–206; and divorce, 14; mastery over courts, 13, 15, 16; powers of, and the 1947 constitutional convention, 193
Lewis, Arthur, 188
Lindbergh kidnapping trial, 102, 134
Lions Club, 108
litigation: Mount Laurel affordable housing, 201; obsessional nature of, 9; railroad crossing safety, Sommer's, 27
Llewellyn Park, West Orange, 127
lord chancellor, 17
Lowenstein, Alan, 2, 171, 188

Madison, James, 12, 201
magistrate courts, 16
Malone, John "Needle Nose," 78, 85, 176–177; codefendant in "rice pudding" suit, 226
Margaret Hague Maternity Hospital, Jersey City, 94, 96–97, 105
Mariano, Gene, 145
Mathis, Tom, 134
mayors' courts, 16
McCarter, Robert H., 53–54, 101, 103
McClary, John C., 150
McGovern, William, 215
McKean, David Dayton, 112–123, 133, 179
Methodist Church: ethos of, 23; Roseville's, 22
Metropolitan Life Insurance Co., 8–10, 17
Millay, Edna St. Vincent, 131
Miller, Lewis, 129
Miller, Mina, 129
Milton, John, 75, 85, 88, 177; appointed U.S. senator by Moore, 104; and the constitutional convention, 181–182, 194; as Hudson County prosecutor, 87, 90
Minton, Sherman, 229
Moore, A. Harry, 75, 85, 86, 103; and 1937 governor's race, 2, 104; declines to run and retires from politics, 138, 139; elected governor, 83, 92; elected to U.S. Senate, 97; judicial appointments, 101, 108–109,

ABOUT THE AUTHOR

Historian Nelson Johnson is best known for his award-winning *New York Times* best seller, *Boardwalk Empire: The Birth, High Times, and Corruption of Atlantic City*, which inspired the HBO series of the same name. He is also the author of another award-winning book, *The Northside: African-Americans and the Creation of Atlantic City*.